C000172077

WILTSHIRE

Ralph Whitlock

WILTSHIRE

B. T. Batsford Ltd
London

First published 1976
Reprinted 1983

© Ralph Whitlock 1976

Typeset by
Input Typesetting Ltd, London
Printed in Great Britain by
The Pitman Press, Bath, Avon
for the Publishers, B. T. Batsford Ltd
4 Fitzhardinge Street, London W1H 0AH

ISBN 0 7134 3117 2

Contents

		page
	Acknowledgments	6
	List of Illustrations	7
1.	Introduction to Wiltshire	9
2.	The Grey Plain	29
3.	Salisbury	44
4.	The Valley of the Salisbury Avon	58
5.	The Wylye Valley	78
6.	The Nadder, the Ebble and Cranborne Chase	97
7.	The Bourne Valley and the South-East	115
8.	Savernake, Chute and the Pewsey Vale	127
9.	Marlborough and the Northern Downs	137
10.	Swindon and the Thames Valley	151
11.	The Populous Valley of the Bristol Avon	162
12.	Animals, Plants and Humans	192
	Index	203

Acknowledgments

The Author and Publishers would like to thank the following for permission to reproduce the photographs in this book:

J. Allan Cash Ltd, no. 6; Noel Habgood, no. 24; Hydatum Picture Library, nos. 3, 10; A. F. Kersting, nos. 7, 8, 9, 11, 14, 16, 17, 18, 19, 20, 21, 23; Kenneth Scowen, nos. 1, 2, 4, 12, 13, 15, 22.

The map is by Patrick Leeson

Illustrations

		page
1.	Salisbury Cathedral	17
2.	College of Matrons, Salisbury	18
3.	Cathedral Close, Salisbury	18
4.	Durnford	35
5.	The Porch House, Potterne	35
6.	Stonehenge	36
7.	Longleat House	53
8.	Wilton House	53
9.	Tithe Barn, Bradford-on-Avon	54
10.	Old Wardour	71
11.	Castle Combe	71
12.	The River Avon near Amesbury	72
13.	Stourhead Park	89
14.	Longford Castle	89
15.	Lacock	90
16.	Avebury Stone Circle	107
17.	The White Horse at Cherhill	107
18.	Malmesbury Abbey Nave	108
19.	Mompesson Monument, Lydiard Tregoze	141
20.	St John Effigies, Lydiard Tregoze	141
21.	St John's Church Nave, Devizes	141
22.	Marlborough	142
23.	Philipps House, Dinton	159
24.	Savernake Forest	160

WILTSHIRE

◇W White Horse site   ═══ Roman road

0   5   10 mi
5   10   15 km

GLOS.

OXON.

Inglesham
Thames
Latton
Ashton Keynes
Castle Eaton
Highworth
Crudwell
Oaksey
Cricklade
Broad Blunsdon
Minety
Stanton Fitzwarren
Brokenborough
Charlton
Braydon Pond
Purton
Stratton St. Margaret
Malmesbury
Braydon
SWINDON
Easton Grey
Lydiard Millicent
Lt Hinton
Sherston
Corston
Brinkworth
Lydiard Tregoze
Wanborough
Bishopstone
Gt. Somerford
Wootton Bassett
Coate Resr
Liddington
Hullavington
Seagry
Wroughton
Baydon
Lyneham
Chiseldon
Liddington Castle
Stanton St. Quintin
Bradenstoke cum Clack
Broad Town
◇W Broad Hinton
Ridge Way
Kington St. Michael
Sutton Benger
Cliffe Pypard
◇W Barbury Castle
W. Kington
Castle Combe
Langley Burrell
Hilmarton
Winterbourne Bassett
Ogbourne St. George
Aldbourne
N. Wraxall
Bremhill
Hackpen Hill
MARLBOROUGH
Ramsbury
Chilton Folia
Biddestone
Compton Bassett
Berwick Bassett
DOWNS
Colerne
Chippenham
Calne
Cherhill
Yatesbury
Mildenhall
Littlecote House
Corsham
Lackham House
Bowood House
◇W
Avebury
Marlborough
Box
Lacock
Sandy Lane
Beckhampton
Kennet
Froxfie
Atworth
Bromham
Wansdyke
Silbury Hill
W. Kennett ◇W
Savernake Forest
S. Wraxall
Broughton Gifford
Roundway Hill
long barrow
St. Anns Hill
Wootton Rivers
Gt. Bedwyn
Bradford on Avon
Holt
Melksham
Bishops Cannings
Allington
Milk Hill
Kennet and Avon Canal
Shalbourn
Freshford
Rowde
Devizes
Alton Priors
Pewsey
Burbage
Seend
All Cannings
◇W
Woodborough
Trowbridge
Poulshot
VALE
Wexcombe
Potterne
Urchfont
Chirton
OF PEWSEY
◇W
Southwick
Steeple Ashton
Charlton
Upavon
Collingbourne Ducis
Chute
N. Bradley
Edington
Ridge Way
Everley
Ludgershall
Cheverell
W. Lavington
Enford
Sidbury Hill ▲
Bratton
Imber
Netheravon
N. Tidworth
Westbury ◇W
Tilshead
Figheldean
Chapmanslade
Upton Scudamore
S A L I S B U R Y
Corsley
Cley Hill ▲
Warminster
Battlesbury Hill ▲
Chitterne
Shrewton
Durrington
Bulford
Bulford Camp
Longleat House
Bishopstrow
Heytesbury
P L A I N
Stonehenge □
Cholderton
Horningsham
Sutton Veny
Codford St. Mary
Winterbourne Stoke
Amesbury
Newton Tony
Longbridge Deverill
□Yarnbury Castle
Berwick St. James
Boscombe
Idmiston
Maiden Bradley
Brixton Deverill
Stockton
Stapleford
Durnford
Kingston Deverill
Wylye
Netton
Woodford
Winterbourne Earls
Winterslow
Stourhead
Chicklade
Gt. Wishford
S. Newton
Stourton
Fonthill Bishop
Grovely Wood
Quidhampton
Old Sarum ◇
Clarendon
Pitton
Zeals
Mere
Hindon
Chilmark
Teffont Magna
Wilton
Farley
East Knoyle
Tisbury
Dinton
Barford St. Martin
Harnham
SALISBURY
Alderbury
Nadder
Fovant
Coombe Bissett
Odstock
Grimstead
W. Dean
Semley
Ansty
Swallowcliffe
Bishopstone
Ebble
Wardour Castle
Broad Chalke
Clearbury Ring ▲
Trafalgar House
Donhead St. Mary
Alvediston
Ebbesborne Wake
Whiteparish
Berwick St. John
Bower Chalke
Downton
◇W Winklebury Camp
Win Green
Landford
DORSET
CRANBORNE CHASE
Tollard Royal
No Mans Land

AVON
Fosse Way
Avon

SOM.

HANTS.
Portway
Bourne
Wylye
Avon

ONE

Introduction to Wiltshire

That the saying 'as different as chalk from cheese' originated in Wiltshire is not widely known. It refers to the division of the county into two distinct but unequal parts. Approximately two-thirds, in the south and east, are chalk country, characterized by rolling downs that undulate like an ocean in a heavy swell. Here are long vistas of open country, broken only by occasional hill-top clumps of beeches. The valleys, with their meadows, farmsteads, willows and churches, are hidden in folds of the downland. Only a few decades ago nearly all of this high country was unploughed and unfenced, clothed only in rabbit-cropped, springy turf, the home of innumerable sheep. Now most is cultivated. The downs have become a granary for wheat and barley.

The lowlands of the north-west are, by contrast, cosy, sheltered country, where the villages crouch and drowse among meadows lined by elms. Here the plough was traditionally as little active as on the high downs. It was meadow land, dairy land, a land of milk and of cheese. It was as different from the chalk downs as chalk is from cheese.

Wiltshiremen added a further phrase. 'And chalk is church, while cheese is chapel.' The chalk country in high farming days, and when wool provided the wealth of England, was a rich land of large estate-owners and big farmers. The parish livings were well endowed, and the farmers could, in general, be relied upon to support the establishment. The cheese country, on the other hand, was largely occupied by small farmers. It was a region of family farms, and the farmers were the 'teat-pullers' despised by their haughty brethren on the chalk. Absentee landlords and parsons tended to be the rule rather than the exception. Nonconformity naturally flourished, encouraged by the growth of wool towns, which were populated by workers of an independent turn of thought.

Devizes, which marks the approximate centre of the county, is supposed to owe its name to the Latin term '*ad divisas*'. It is said that the Normans built a castle here, at the point where the boundaries of the parishes of All Cannings and Potterne met. It is more than that. It marks effectively the frontier between the chalk and the cheese.

The two sections of Wiltshire are not so much hostile as indifferent to each other. The most extensive chalkland territory, Salisbury Plain, is tilted to the south-east, and that is the direction in which its inhabitants look. They go to Salisbury for shopping and market days. Beyond that, they are aware of Winchester, Southampton, Blandford and Bournemouth; these are all places which they expect to visit from time to time. But Swindon and Chippenham, Melksham and Malmesbury, are foreign places to them; they might as well be in Arabia. People of the cheese country, on the other hand, naturally go downstream, along what is appropriately known as the Bristol Avon, to Bath and Bristol for shopping and recreation. It is easier for them to make an excursion to see Westminster Abbey than to Salisbury Cathedral. Sports addicts in the cheese country support Gloucestershire or Somerset in the cricket season and Swindon in the F.A. Cup. South Wiltshiremen regard Hampshire as their home cricket team and are staunch supporters of Southampton football club.

It is a matter of regret and disapproval among Salisbury people that the, to them, obscure and remote little town of Trowbridge has been selected as the county town. Salisbury, the cathedral city, they consider ought to have that honour and status. Who ever would want to go to Trowbridge of his own free will?

There are other anomalies all around the border fringe. Tollard Royal in the far south belongs geographically to Dorset. Limpley Stoke to Somerset. Ramsbury and Aldbourne turn naturally towards Newbury. Landford and Plaitford are, in character, New Forest villages. And who, without a map, could hope to define where the boundary between north Wiltshire and Gloucestershire runs?

Wiltshire is thus by no means a homogeneous county. Most of its boundaries are about as unnatural as those of the new countries of Africa. Strangely, however, they are more ancient than those of most English counties. A plausible explanation for each section of them can be found by digging back deep into history or prehistory.

To the ignorant and uninitiated, Wiltshire is a county to be hurried through on the way elsewhere. An old friend of mine who farms some of that magnificent, spectacular downland in the south-west of the county once commented:

'Every Friday evening and Saturday morning in summer I stand in my fields and watch the interminable procession of cars, coaches, caravans and motor-bikes, piloted by serious, harassed drivers who glare straight ahead, surging along the A 303 on their way westwards, and I breathe a prayer, "Thank God they aren't stopping here!"'

A selfish but understandable sentiment. Like St John, we can manage better without the sea.

In the far distant past, however, in which the roots of most Wiltshire matters lie, Wiltshire was a destination rather than a channel for through traffic. A map of primeval Britain, before Man took over, provides a clear explanation. Most of the country lay buried beneath a dense carpet of trees, intersected by bog-marginned rivers. The exception was the chalk downland, which extends diagonally across England from Dorset to Lincolnshire and south Yorkshire, and which was perhaps always, since the first men trod the green ways, virtually treeless. The chalk measures reach their broadest extent in Wiltshire, Hampshire and Berkshire, with Salisbury Plain as the nexus. From this centre they throw out eastward-groping arms to encompass the Weald and to reach the sea at Dover and Beachey Head. The North and South Downs form natural corridors by which newcomers from Europe were led on to Salisbury Plain, there to meet others who had landed in Weymouth Bay and found a similar turfy highway to take them north-eastwards.

We are not disappointed when we look for traces of these early travellers and colonists on the chalk downs of Wiltshire. The countryside is littered with them. There are probably more legacies of prehistoric man, in the form of barrows, megaliths and assorted earthworks, than in any comparable area in Britain.

Best known, of course, are the imposing stone circles of Avebury and Stonehenge, the first antedating the second by perhaps two hundred years in the second millenium B.C. Some of the downland long barrows are even older, and most of the round barrows and bell barrows belong to approximately the Stonehenge period. Silbury, which clearly has associations with Avebury, is said to have the distinction of being the largest man-made mound in Europe, though just what that signifies is difficult to explain. Of the fate of another stone circle, which may have approached the dimensions of Avebury, we read on page 140.

Of the people responsible for these mighty monuments we still know little, but our respect for them increases with the accumulation of each new piece of information. They brought some of the stones of Stonehenge all the way from the Prescelly Hills in Pembrokeshire, if not, as some say, from Ireland. They had relations with ancient Greece, as the carvings of a Mycenean-type dagger and axe found on one of Stonehenge's standing stones in the 1960s, testify. The revelation by Professor Gerald Hawkins that Stonehenge could be used as a computer for predicting the dates of eclipses and other lunar events, which seems to me as conclusive as anything we are likely to get, stamp the builders as men of remarkable intelligence and sophistication.

We know little of the social life of the Wiltshire people of those centuries, of what they wore and ate or where they lived (though in a later chapter I suggest an explanation for the dearth of relics of dwelling-houses). Some of the earliest domestic sites that have been excavated, such as that of Little Woodbury near Britford, which dates from the early Iron Age, reveal simple and somewhat rambling farmsteads, without at first any fortifications. They were built in an era of peace, though there is evidence to suggest that war may have threatened later.

War seems to have become endemic in southern Britain with the arrival, probably from about 500 B.C. onwards, of gangs of pugnacious Celts, who landed in Kent and made their marauding way westwards and northwards. By the time the Romans appeared and imposed a veneer of civilization on the reluctant Britons, the Celts had got as far as west Wiltshire, but not much farther. No doubt the tangled Forest of Selwood blocked their advance.

They seem to have set themselves up as an aristocracy, lording it over the natives. There was no dominating Celtic kingdom of Britain, though Cassivellaunus was creating a sizeable state in Hertfordshire when the Romans intervened. The Celts were tribal. They loved feasting and song, they loved bright clothes and glittering ornaments, but more than anything they loved fighting. They were continually at it, tribe against tribe. So they built those hill-top fortresses, the encircling earthworks of which are still such prominent features of the chalk escarpments. One can imagine the gay young hotheads riding out in their chariots from Battlesbury and Scratchbury, on the hills above Warminster, to do battle with each other on the plain beneath. And afterwards retiring to brag of their exploits or listen to minstrels singing of them around the evening camp-fires.

The Romans naturally came to Wiltshire early on in their campaign of subjugation. Unlike the Regnenses of Sussex, the Belgae of our county did not submit easily to the conquerors. Of the twenty or so *oppida* recorded as being taken by Vespasian in his two years of campaigning in the West Country some, perhaps Battlesbury and Scratchbury among them, were in Wiltshire.

Thereafter the inhabitants settled down to three or four hundred years of Roman peace – a militarily-imposed peace incidentally, which gave full scope to the tax collector. Although Wiltshire occupies the centre of southern Britain, no Roman towns of any size developed within its area. Perhaps the most important settlement was that of Sorbiodunum (Old Sarum) though even that was so obscure that no-one has yet been able to find any certain trace of it. Roman roads ruled their precise lines across our territory. At least four radiated from Sorbiodunum, one striking east to Winchester, another north-westwards in the direction of the mines of Mendip, a third, the Port Way, northeastwards to Silchester, and a fourth south-westwards to Durnovaria (Dorchester). A local road running approximately due north linked Sorbiodunum with Cunetio (Mildenhall) but, as Mrs M. E. Cunnington comments in her *Introduction to the Archaeology of Wiltshire,* 'then as now the Plain divided the county into two distinct areas; there was no direct communication between the north and south . . .'

In the north the town of Cirencester, just outside the present Wiltshire boundary, was the chief focus of the Roman road system. Of the two major roads striking south from Cirencester (Corinium) the great Fosse Way, which cuts across England from north-east to south-west, forms in part the county boundary. It is ruled more or less directly across country from Cirencester to Bath. The south-eastern road, Ermine Street, forked just south of Wanborough, one branch leading to Silchester and the other to Winchester (Venta Belgarum). This last passed through Cunetio, where it crossed another major road, from London to Bath.

These were all through roads, designed for use by the military and administration rather than for the convenience of local residents. No doubt there were many minor roads leading from them. Sections of some of them have been traced.

The western section (in Wiltshire) of the road from London to Bath is incorporated in that mighty and enigmatic earthwork, the Wansdyke. This mysterious ditch and bank, in places climbing steeply twenty or thirty feet from the bottom of the ditch to the top of the parapet, stretches across the entire width of Wiltshire from Inkpen to Bathford and beyond, to reach the sea near Portishead. Its total length is more than sixty miles. Constructing it must have been a tremendous undertaking, and, in its probable historical context, we are at a loss to understand why it was made. For archaeological evidence, and the way in which it makes use of the Roman road, show that it belongs to the post-Roman era, probably the sixth century.

This was the age of the half-legendary hero, Arthur, who briefly halted the advance of the invading Saxons and gave the old Roman civilization a few years of sunset glory. But in that period one would have expected central Wiltshire to be the heartland of Romano-British influence, not a frontier zone. The rampart of the Wansdyke is on the south side of the ditch and is unmistakeably intended as a defence against an enemy from the north. Until recently most historians have taught that the Saxon menace impinged on Wiltshire from the south-east, though archaeological evidence does show Saxons on the upper Thames at a quite early date. If at the time of the building of the Wansdyke Saxons were in control to the north and Britons to the south, there is the odd fact that Bath is north of the line. And Bath, as well as Cirencester and Gloucester, is generally supposed to have fallen to the Saxons as a result of the Battle of Deorham (Dyrham) in 577. It is all very puzzling.

Perhaps Geoffrey Ashe is right in suggesting, in his book *From Caesar to Arthur,* that there were two Saxon invasions, one before and the other after Arthur. The first penetrated Britain from sea to sea, via the Thames valley, but the invaders were chased out by Arthur and his cavalry. Later, after his death, the new invasion came from the south, from Cerdic and his men landing in Southampton Water. When this second group arrived

at the Wansdyke, taking it in the rear, they knew nothing of its purpose
or origin and so attributed it to their god Woden – hence 'Wodens-dyke'
or Wansdyke.

I am impressed by the picture of the English countryside towards the
end of the Roman era as drawn by Alfred Duggan in his novel, *The Little
Emperors.* He makes a Roman refugee from London travel up the Thames
in a canoe for more than a month, between Staines and the Cotswolds,
without seeing a soul.

'The whole valley was a dense tangle of thorn and scrub, uncultivated',
he writes. 'The Celts, with their light ploughs and badly tempered axes,
had no incentive to clear the forest from this stiff clay, flooded every
spring ... The country had not changed since the days of Caractacus;
possibly it had never been trodden by the foot of man.'

This tallies completely with what we know of the Saxon settlement of
Wiltshire. The prehistoric and Romano-British sites of villages are almost
all on the downs. They are hill villages. The Saxon villages, on the other
hand, were almost all valley villages, as they are to this day. A glance at
the map will show them strung out along the chalk valleys like beads in a
necklace, leaving the downs empty. The 'cheese' country of the
north-west, however, probably remained in its primeval condition, much
as Duggan describes the Thames valley, to a later date, its dense forest
yielding only gradually to the axes of Saxon farmers.

For me the interest of this obscure period lies in the fact that it holds
the origins of familiar places. The villages which I explored on my bicycle
as a boy and where I played cricket and football seemed about as
permanent as the Rock of Ages. They had been there from time
immemorial. But there must have been a time when the first settler laid
down his hearth-stone and put a fence around his farmstead. I find it
intriguing to conjecture how and when this happened.

Let me digress to engage in a little speculation about the district I
know best, the south-eastern corner of the county, where I was born in
the village of Pitton. Pitton first appears in written documents about the
year 820. Excavation of a Romano-British burial site on the downs above
the village has shown that it was still inhabited by a peasant community
about 350. At that time there were villas, or country estates, studding the
country between the downs and the fringes of the New Forest – one,
perhaps more, at Farley, one at East Grimstead, and a very large one at

West Dean. In the villas Romanised Celtic gentry would be living, while the hill-top village was inhabited by rather poor peasants, the outlines of whose fields we can still see on the hillsides by the Roman road nearby. Doubtless in addition to paying their taxes the villagers were forced to keep a section of the road in repair. We know that they were poor because their coffins were held together with the minimum number of nails — six, I believe. On the other hand, they were buried in coffins, not slung into a hole in the ground. Hobnails from long-decayed leather reveals that they were buried with their boots on. And some of them had had a coin placed in their mouth, to pay the ferryman for taking them into the Underworld. They were poor but they were not slaves.

Now let us see how the few events of which we have any record in the succeeding centuries might have affected this humble community.

In 367 Britain was swept by an invasion of wild Picts, Scots, Saxons and pirates of every kind, who defeated the Roman armies and pillaged at will for a year or two. Eventually peace was restored, but irretrievable damage was done. The local villas may well have been ruined at this time. The last Roman legion left Britain in about 425, but life went on much as usual under Romanised Celtic rulers.

Soon after 450 Saxons were present in some force in the upper Thames valley, and they may have advanced to the Severn, giving cause for the construction of the Wansdyke, about this time. From about 505 to 538 is the era of Arthur, under whom the British staged a revival. All through these events the southern or downland part of Wiltshire remained firmly in British hands. In this period there was evidently a flourishing monastery at Amesbury, which is recorded as one of the 'Three Perpetual Choirs of Britain' (the others were at Glastonbury and Llan Iltud Vawr in Glamorganshire). 'In each of these choirs there were 2400 saints, that is, there were a hundred for every hour of the day and night in rotation.' The numbers are probably exaggerated, but one gets the idea.

In the middle of the Arthurian peace in 519, a Saxon war-leader with a Celtic name, Cerdic, fought and won a battle against the Britons at a place called 'Cerdics-ford'. This Cerdic had landed from Southampton Water twenty-five years earlier. The battle is placed by most historians at Charford, near Downton, in south Wilts, though another theory puts it at Chard, in Somerset.

'From that time forth the royal offspring of the West Saxons reigned',

1 *Salisbury Cathedral from the south-west*

says *The Anglo-Saxon Chronicle,* indicating that this marked the beginning of the West Saxon state. And when the West Saxons resumed their advance in 552, with Arthur safely in his grave, their first major victory occurred near Sorbiodunum. At this time the Perpetual Choir at Amesbury disappears from the scene. The conquest of what is now Wiltshire was completed by 577, when the British were defeated in the battle of Deorham, on the Wiltshire/Gloucestershire border.

In the wake of the armies came the settlers. We can visualise them paddling up the rivers in their boats and forming settlements along the banks. Along the Avon, the Bourne, the Ebble, the Wylye and the Till, the Saxon villages, with names familiar to us, were founded. But not to the same extent along the Nadder. There we find villages, such as Fovant and Teffont, which have kept their ancient Celtic names. The Nadder is different from the other south Wiltshire valleys in that it has a greensand and limestone subsoil. Probably in early times it was densely wooded.

What happens when an invading army appears? The local residents take to the woods, with anything they can carry. Some are caught and killed, but some survive, to creep back to their homes when the way seems clear. The hill-top village above Pitton was, it seems, never re-occupied. Its limits evidently served in due course as a boundary mark for the Saxon parish of Winterbourne Earls. But Winterslow, another hill village adjacent to the same Roman road, seems to have had a continuity of occupation. Probably any survivors from the Pitton village settled with their kinsfolk in Winterslow. On what terms is not known. They may have been slaves of a new Saxon overlord. More likely, living as they did on a hill site with poor soil and no stream, they were allowed to carry on as independent though impoverished peasants.

The nearest Saxon village would be Alderbury, on a ridge above the Avon a few miles south of Salisbury. Between it and the hill-top settlement of Winterslow lay a great forest, the mediaeval forest of Clarendon. In the ensuing centuries Saxons from Alderbury gradually extended their holdings into this forest. They probed around its eastern edge, founding first the hamlet of Whaddon, then the villages of East and West Grimstead, then, finally, Farley, the 'far meadow'. Until towards the end of the nineteenth century these were all, ecclesiastically, chapelries of Alderbury.

So was Pitton, but its story seems to have been different. My

2 (above) *Cathedral Close, Salisbury.* 3 (below) *The College of Matrons, Salisbury*

conjecture is that it was settled from Winterslow and annexed to Alderbury at a later stage. Its mediaeval history is intimately linked with Clarendon, then a royal forest, and it seems to have been populated, at least in part, by foresters, keepers and other satellites of the royal demesne. Its very name, Putta's town, may mean that it belonged to a man named Putta or it may signify that this is where the royal mews were situated, for Putta means 'a hawk'.

Two other clues to the remote past exist. Pitton church stands on what was originally a roughly circular site, surrounded by yews and at the edge of what was in earlier times the only permanent spring in the valley. It bears all the hallmarks of a pagan sacred site and may well have been so regarded by the inhabitants of the hill-top village.

And there is the evidence of local tradition. Pitton and Farley have within the past hundred years or so been welded into one parish, a state of affairs now amicably accepted but formerly a cause of much friction. Within living memory there was intense rivalry between the two villages. An old Pitton resident once told me,

'We marry with Winterslow people but not with they down at Farley.'

An examination of the parish registers indicates that that is more or less true.

If ever a Farley child appeared in Pitton the boys would follow it and chant,

Farley jigger,
Lousy wigger,
Dirty little humbug!

The Farley children had a similar rhyme for the Pitton ones. It is evidence of folk memory lingering long.

Once when I was wondering whether any of the local families were directly descended from the old Romano-British inhabitants of the district it occurred to me to try the test of pronunciation. I recited aloud the names of some of the long-established families of Winterslow and the neighbouring villages and found that quite a number of them bore striking resemblances to common Latin names, as, for instance:

Gay . . . Gaius.
Noyce . . . Gnaeus.
Yeates . . . Aetius.
Ambrose . . . Ambrosius.

Titt . . . Titus.
Is this entirely fancy, I wonder?

So much for speculations about origins. From the sixth or seventh century onwards Wiltshire takes shape as the county we know, with virtually all of its towns and villages comfortably established. During the Saxon era it was the heartland of the kingdom of Wessex. Wilton still proudly proclaims itself as the 'Capital of Ancient Wessex', as indeed it was, though so were several other West Country towns, for the Saxon court tended to be nomadic.

The Saxons had just over two hundred years to settle in and become Christian and civilized before the Danish horror descended upon them. The barbarities of the Saxon invasion were repeated, though this time intensified, for the Danes, to begin with, had their minds exclusively on pillage and murder rather than settlement. Wessex, the strongest of the Saxon kingdoms, was one of the last to receive their visitation, but when eventually, in 871, they penetrated the kingdom in force they had eliminated the other Saxon states and could give Wessex their undivided attention. At the same time they had so devastated northern and western France that there was little left there worth pillaging, so the Northmen's army, 'the Host' as contemporary documents call it, was reinforced by massive detachments of freebooters from the Continent.

Early in 871 the West Saxon army fought and defeated the invaders at Ashdown, which was somewhere on the downland ridge overlooking the Vale of the White Horse, in Berkshire. Two months later the Northmen were in Wiltshire, trouncing the West Saxons at the battle of Marton, which was probably Marden, in the Vale of Pewsey. Worn out by the struggle and hardships, Ethelred, the king of Wessex, died and was succeeded by his brother Alfred. In May the Northmen were in south Wiltshire, defeating Alfred in a battle near Wilton. Alfred then bought peace with a massive tribute, which persuaded the enemy to leave Wessex in peace for six years.

In 877 they struck again. Their knock-out blow came at Christmas, well past the usual campaigning season, when Alfred and his courtiers were feasting at Chippenham. Alfred had to ride hard to save himself, and his followers seemed to have dispersed, some to remote western strongholds, some overseas. The doom of Wessex seemed complete.

Alfred's place of refuge was the tiny islet of Athelney, in the Somerset marshes. From there he kept an eye on the Northmen all that winter, while laying plans for a comeback in the spring.

At Easter he met the levies of Wiltshire and Hampshire who had gathered secretly at a place called Ecgbright's-stone, which is thought to have been near where the county boundaries of Wiltshire, Dorset and Somerset meet. The army welcomed him 'as one risen from the dead'. At their head he undertook a two-day march to meet the Northmen's army. The chronicles record that the West Saxons camped for the first night at a place called Icglea and encountered the enemy at another called Ethandun. The conventional interpretation is that Ethandun was Edington, in Wiltshire, not far eastwards from the White Horse carved on the hill above Westbury. An old theory, now discountenanced, held that the White Horse was cut to commemorate Alfred's victory. Icglea could have been Westbury Leigh or, more likely, Cley Hill. This version of events, however, does not seem to me to be at all satisfactory. The identification of Ethandun with Edington, on the Polden Hills in Somerset, makes much more sense. I have elaborated on this alternative in my book *Somerset*. As a loyal Wiltshireman, I deplore having to pass to a neighbouring county the honour of being the scene of one of the great decisive battles of the world, but, as an honest chronicler, I cannot help it.

The subsequent peace treaty was signed at Wedmore, in Somerset. Thereafter Wiltshire was left in peace for more than a hundred years, the heartland of the new realm which Alfred and his successors forged.

The formative years of the West Saxon kingdom saw the conversion of the Saxons to Christianity. *The Anglo-Saxon Chronicle* records that in the year 634 'Birinus preached baptism to the West Saxons, under King Cynegils'. The king was baptised in the following year. The church in Wessex was an independent foundation, owing apparently nothing to Canterbury, for Birinus was sent direct from Italy to Britain by the Pope. He founded the first Wessex bishopric at Dorchester, in Oxfordshire.

There were Christians in Wiltshire, however, before the time of Birinus. They were Romano-British who owned allegiance to the old Celtic church at Glastonbury. That town and the region around it were conquered and added to the domains of the West Saxon kings in the year 658, but by then the West Saxons were Christians and so the transition, as far as ecclesiastical affairs were concerned, was comparatively painless, and British abbots continued to rule at Glastonbury.

The interest of all this to Wiltshire was that the addition of so much new territory made the old bishopric of Dorchester unwieldy. In 705, therefore, it was dividied between the bishopric of Winchester, which took all east of the Forest of Selwood, and the bishopric of Sherborne, which took all west of the Forest. Selwood in those days was a vast amorphous tract of wooded country, forming a broad boundary zone between Wiltshire and Somerset but extending well into both modern counties.

In 709 the bishopric of Selsey, comprising Sussex, was split off the see of Winchester, but otherwise the ecclesiastical arrangements remained unchanged till the country started to settle down again after the Danish invasion. Then, in 909, the see of Winchester was divided, Winchester retaining what are now Hampshire and Surrey, while Wiltshire and Berkshire comprised a new bishopric with its seat at Ramsbury.

This Wiltshire village was the headquarters of a bishopric for 166 years, during which three of its bishops were later promoted to be archbishops of Canterbury. In 1075 the see was united with that of Sherborne to form the bishopric of Sarum, with a cathedral at Old Sarum.

Ramsbury was thus an important ecclesiastical centre in the heart of Wessex in the prosperous tenth century, when the kings of Wessex were busy reclaiming the rest of England from the Danes. Odo, the first bishop of Ramsbury, was a right-hand man to Athelstan, grandson of Alfred and one of the greatest of the West Saxon kings, who rebuilt and generously endowed the monastery at Malmesbury.

Although most of the warlike action in the tenth century occurred in central and northern England, it was to Wiltshire that kings and bishops often returned for parliaments and synods. Edgar, who has a good claim to be considered the first undisputed king of all England, held a council at Sarum in 960; and it was at Calne, in 978, that the memorable episode occurred when the floor collapsed under a Council meeting, precipitating most of the chief men of England into the room beneath and killing or maiming many of them, except the saintly Archbishop Dunstan, who was miraculously preserved by a beam beneath his chair.

The good times came to an end in the following century, when Wiltshire bore the brunt of Danish invasions in 1003, 1006, 1011, and 1014. After the death of the unfortunate king Ethelred the Unready, war continued for two years between his successor, Edmund Ironside, and the

Danish King Canute, with Wiltshire as a prominent battleground. Sherston, near Malmesbury was the scene of one battle.

The Norman invasion in 1066 saw a wholesale change of ownership of Wiltshire estates. Some landowners managed to hold their lands, but many more were dispossessed in favour of William the Conqueror's followers. The county quickly became studded with gaunt Norman castles. None now remains, but the castle mounds on which they stood are still to be seen at, among other places, Devizes, Old Sarum and West Dean. Malmesbury, Marlborough, and Trowbridge had important castles, and others (some of later date) were at Serrington and Sherrington in the Wylye valley, Castle Combe, Wardour and Ludgershall.

It was at Old Sarum that William held a great council in 1086 at which he made arrangements for the Domesday Book to be compiled. By this council feudalism was firmly established in England.

The era of peace was short-lived. After the death of Henry I in 1135 civil war soon broke out between his daughter, Matilda, and Stephen, and once again Wiltshire was a cockpit for the rival armies. The war swayed this way and that, with Wilton, Devizes, Marlborough and other towns changing hands several times. It must have been a terrible period for the ordinary people of Wiltshire. *The Anglo-Saxon Chronicle* states:

'Every powerful man made his castles and held them against the King ... and when the castles were made they filled them with devils and evil men. Then they seized those men who they supposed had any possessions, both by night and day, men and women, and put them in prison for their gold and silver, and tortured them with unspeakable tortures ... Many thousands they killed with hunger. I neither can nor may tell all the horrors and all the tortures that they did to the wretched men of this land. And it lasted the nineteen winters while Stephen was King; and ever it was worse ... When the wretched men had no more to give they robbed and burnt all the villages, so that you might go a whole day's journey and you would never find a man in a village or land being tilled. Then was corn dear, and meat and cheese and butter, because there was none in the land. Wretched men starved of hunger; some went seeking alms who at one time were rich men; others fled out of the land ... They said that Christ and his saints were asleep.'

When we learn that a Baron FitzGilbert of Marlborough had the reputation of being the worst robber-baron of them all we can imagine the ordeal of the common folk of Wiltshire.

Nevertheless, it could not have been all disaster, for two important religious houses, Bradenstoke Priory and Farleigh Abbey, were founded in those stormy times, and several towns, including Devizes and Wilton, won charters to hold markets or fairs.

Much of Wiltshire, away from the chalk downs, was in early days covered by dense forests, the most important of which were Savernake, Selwood, Chute, Harewood, Clarendon, Cranborne Chase, Pewsham, Braden, Melksham and Groveley. In all of them the strict Norman forest laws applied. A favourite hunting-ground of Norman and mediaeval kings, and especially of Henry II, who restored order after the appalling anarchy of Stephen, was the Forest of Clarendon, in the south-eastern sector of the county. There the kings had a hunting-lodge which in time grew into a great palace, at one time reckoned to be the second largest building in England, only surpassed by the great palace at Westminster. Here in 1164 Henry II called a council which worked out the Constitutions of Clarendon, setting out the roles of Church and State, and here too he quarrelled with Thomas à Becket on that very matter.

From that time onwards Wiltshire was allowed peace. Even the Wars of the Roses were fought out elsewhere. The general atmosphere is illustrated by the fact that, in an age of fortified towns and castles, mediaeval Clarendon Palace is a rambling and virtually unfortified place, the forerunner of the Tudor manor-house. It had only one tower, and few of the buildings were more than one storey high.

The villages of Wiltshire developed slowly and normally through the long feudal centuries. Churches and manor-houses were built. Local incidents, such as the slaying of a boar, were blown up and became legendary. The last wolf in the county, in Clarendon Forest, was not killed until about 1327, but by a century or so later nearly all the woods themselves had been enclosed, were parcelled out by banks and hedges, some of which can still be traced, into neat blocks and were subject to strict management.

Wiltshire's towns, too, were immersed in domestic affairs. Their annals are filled with accounts of lively encounters between personalities, as prosperous merchants rose to prominence and felt themselves capable of defying not only each other and the local lord but even the king. Much of the prosperity of the merchants was, of course, derived from the wool trade. The extensive chalk downs of Wiltshire were splendid sheep country. At first the wool was exported, but in the later Middle Ages a thriving weaving industry developed in many Wiltshire towns and villages, particularly Salisbury and the towns of north-western Wiltshire. The Church increased in power and wealth. Vast estates were owned by religious establishments, such as Wilton and Malmesbury, and some very fine churches were built, including, of course, Salisbury's superb cathedral.

The gradual progress towards a more free society, to replace feudalism, was accelerated by the unrest which followed the Black Death, in which the county probably lost between one third and one half of its inhabitants. In the reign of Henry VI Bishop Ayscough of Salisbury was murdered at Edington by peasants in revolt. The impact of this rebellion was, however, only temporary. Real revolution came in Tudor times, with the dissolution of the great religious establishments. There was a general scramble by wealthy laymen for their great estates, many of which have remained ever since in the hands of the families which then acquired them.

New ideas and the discovery of new lands across the Atlantic were at that time setting the country in a turmoil, and religious fanatics were abundant. Yet it is probable that the changes were not welcomed by most of the people, for Wiltshire was still predominantly rural, and country-dwellers appreciate beyond anything else a stable background, which was what the ecclesiastical landlords had provided. One aspect of the change which caused much distress was the sudden cessation of the Church's almsgiving services to the poor. The hordes of penniless beggars who infested the countryside in Tudor times became an increasing problem and gave rise to the enactment of a series of poor laws.

All the Tudor kings and queens visited Wiltshire. The Seymours, a daughter of which family, Jane, married Henry VIII, had their family seat at Wulfhall, near Savernake, and the wedding may have taken place there. During the next reign the Seymours wielded regal power during the minority of Edward VI. The return to Catholicism under Mary I produced several Protestant martyrs from Wiltshire, including John Maundrell and his companions, who were burned at the stake at Salisbury in 1556, and Bishop Latimer, who suffered in London but was for a time rector of West Kington.

The reign of Elizabeth I saw the building of many of the great country houses that are still the glory of Wiltshire, among them Wilton House and Longleat.

Much fighting took place in Wiltshire during the Civil War. Salisbury, Marlborough and other towns changed hands several times, and an important battle, in which the Royalists were the victors, occurred on Roundway Down, near Devizes. The siege of Wardour Castle, in which Lady Blanche Arundell with fifty retainers held out against a Parliamentarian army of thirteen hundred men, was an epic of high courage.

Wiltshire has a number of stories, which we shall see in later chapters, concerning the adventures of Charles II when he was a fugitive trying to escape to the Continent. Among the Wiltshiremen who had links with him at that time and who rose to prominence and wealth after the Restoration were Sir Stephen Fox and Sir Christopher Wren.

Although some Wiltshiremen joined the rebel cause and fought at the battle of Sedgmoor in 1685, Monmouth's rebellion did not greatly affect Wiltshire. The armies of both James II and William III passed through the county in 1688, but no battle resulted. Wiltshire was assuming its now familiar role of a corridor, along which traffic passes on its way east or west.

In the peaceful years that followed the upheavals of Stuart times Wiltshire became one of the most important industrial counties of England. Iron was mined, canals were dug, and mills and factories sprang up in many of the western and central towns, cloth-weaving being still the main industry.

The first railway in the county was begun in 1825. As the Industrial Revolution developed and factories moved to the north of England, Wiltshire found new prosperity in the railway works which were established at Swindon, soon to become by far the largest town in the county.

Early in the present century the Army came to Wiltshire and by degrees acquired vast tracts of land, mostly on Salisbury Plain. Most men who have served with the British Army have spent at least some time on the bleak chalk uplands around Larkhill, Bulford and Warminster.

Ironically, the military territory can now be considered one of Wiltshire's great conservation areas. During and since the Second World War the agricultural revolution resulted in the ploughing up of hundreds of square miles of primeval downland. Fields of tall wheat and waving barley now flourish on land which used to be thought not worth cultivating, where rabbits, wheatears and stone-curlew shared a lonely realm with innumerable sheep. The wild-life of the chalk hills has been driven to seek a refuge on the well-protected Army estates, where neither plough nor public can penetrate.

Agriculture still retains its position of dominance over much of the county. The old division between chalk and cheese has become blurred, for many of the big chalkland farms now keep large herds of Friesian cows. But the county is, in general, intensively farmed, and the old agricultural markets flourish.

A feature, common to most counties, in the post-war years has been the extension of commuterdom to towns, villages and even outlying farms. Cars and motorways have made it possible for businessmen to live in Wiltshire and to travel to work in London, Bristol, Bath or Southampton daily. Many other country properties have become week-end cottages or havens for retired folk. So the character of the countryside has changed, and farming people have become a minority in villages where they were once supreme. The transformation probably causes more good than harm, for the newcomers bring not only new money but new ideas, broadening the culture and horizons of once isolated communities.

TWO

The Grey Plain

A day of rain! November sun gleams wan
In western heavens beneath the lowering pall
Of sadly-sailing mist-clouds, a pale ball,
Seemingly washed and faded. A lone man
Trudging the tarmac road which metes the span
Of the wide Plain from Mere to Ludgershall
Now hastens the next storm-wind to forestall
And does the distant mist-wraith dully scan.
Stonehenge sits grey upon the greyish turf,
Gloomy against the grey November sky;
Grey, on that grey grass ocean, lacking surf,
Far more majestic than in bright July.
For Stonehenge, in its last, grey, aged phase,
Needs the environment of fading days.

The mood of this rather depressing sonnet, which I must have written in a fit of rare despondency, is to a degree confirmed by a pleasant little oil-painting by the talented Salisbury artist, Eric Brown, which hangs on my study wall as I write. It depicts a simple scene — a hill-top clump of beeches which acts as a focus for the downs rolling away like ocean waves beneath and columns of cumulus clouds marching across the Wedgwood blue sky above. All the lines are soft and curved; all the colours are pastel. There is nothing harsh or vivid anywhere.

Spring comes late to the exposed uplands. When primroses, violets and wood anemones are responding to the March sunshine in valley woods, the downs remain as lifeless and austere as ever. Grain ripens quickly on the thin soil, and chill winds begin to winnow the stubble on the rounded hills long before valley farmers are ready for Harvest Home. Yet there are summer days when one could ask for nothing better than to lie on one's back on the short, upland turf, watching a pinpoint skylark unwinding her chain of song from the deep blue zenith.

I speak with prejudice. I am a child of the Plain. I was born in, and spent more than fifty years of my life in, the last village on the south-eastern rim of the chalk downs. Their wide panoramas were my familiar background. 'The wind', I once wrote, 'which is never tranquil here, and the dreamy distance play tricks with our vision, till the whole landscape seems to be heaving before our eyes, the troughs being elevated and the crests sinking as the restless sea breathes and tosses. That company of gulls winging across the near valley is a wisp of blown spume.'

I feel identity with that other Wiltshireman, John Aubrey, who was one of the first to try to express in words the enchantment of the high downs.

'The turfe', he said, 'is of short sweet grasse, good for the sheep, and delightfull to the eye, for its smoothness like a bowling green, and pleasant to the traveller; who wants here only a variety of objects to make his journey lesse tedious; for here is ... not a tree, or rarely a bush to shelter one from a shower.

'The soile of the downes I take generally to be a white earth or mawme. More south, about Wilton and Chalke, the downes are intermixt with boscages that nothing can be more pleasant, and in the summer time doe excell Arcadia in verdant and rich turfe and moderate aire, but in winter indeed our air is cold and rawe.'

The Plain as I remember it *was* as smooth as a bowling green. It was made so by the nibbling of innumerable sheep and rabbits. Their incessant trimming of the wiry downland grasses gave the attractive little flowers of the chalk downs a chance to flourish. Milkwort, eyebright, squinancywort, rock-rose, viper's bugloss, lady's finger, tormentil, wild thyme, sheep's scabious, carline thistle, harebell, rest-harrow, autumn gentian — their very names are music. The downs were studded with age-old ant-hills, in which in summer young partridges scratched and dust-bathed, finding invaluable protein food. Wheatears nested in shallow, disused rabbit-holes and were among the commonest birds of the downs. Stone curlew, the near relations of the great bustards which were long ago a feature of the Plain, arrived from Africa to begin nesting, on bleak, stony hill-tops, before the end of March; in September they would assemble by the score in the evening twilight, to carol in musical chorus as they prepared for their return migration. In late summer butterflies were abundant — chalk-hill blues, small coppers, Adonis blues, small blues, green hairstreaks, skippers, marbled whites, heaths and the lethargic red-and-black burnet moths.

One half of the circle of the horizon around my native village of Pitton was occupied by deciduous woodland; the other half, to the north and east, by the swelling downs. In my father's day there had been no boundary to the downs till one started to descend the distant scarp to Devizes or Westbury, In his youth, in the late 1880s, he had escorted sheep across its thirty-mile breadth without encountering any barrier in the form of hedgerows, fences or cultivated fields. A few years before my birth, however, the Army had come to the Plain and had been enclosing large sections of it. New encampments sprang up on the bare downs, at Larkhill, Bulford, Porton, Warminster, Tidworth and on tracts of featureless land which had been nameless. Heavy guns rumbled, tanks churned up the ancient turf, generations of infantry underwent training, farmhouses were battered into dereliction, and one village, Imber, had to be entirely abandoned.

During and after the Second World War an even more far-reaching revolution hit the Plain. The development of chemical fertilizers, particularly new balanced compounds, the availability of tractors and heavy agricultural machinery, and the needs of a hungry populace acted together to transform the downland. The plough bit into square mile after square mile of thin chalk soil which had formerly been considered valueless, and the new techniques ensured that worthwhile crops were reaped.

At the end, nearly all ploughable land was bearing crops. Fences had been erected, water supplies had been taken to the fields, and the Plain had become one of the most intensively farmed areas of England. Most of the surviving downland was on hillsides too steep to plough, with one exception. That exception was the Army-occupied land. It is in the Army territory that the wildlife of the Plain — the wheatears, stone curlew, badgers, butterflies, woodlarks, weasels and the old chalkland fauna and flora — is now concentrated.

Even here, however, there are changes. The character of the old downland, with its short, clipped turf, owed much to the activities of rabbits and sheep, both of which have largely vanished. Rabbits disappeared under the onslaught of myxomatosis in 1953 and the following years. There are still flocks of sheep on the marginal lands around Army territory, but they are inadequate to restore the downland to its former state. So the shorter downland grasses and their associated miniature flowers have been smothered by coarser growths, and these rough grasses are in their turn being suppressed by bushes and brambles. Much of the military land has become a wilderness of scrub.

Nevertheless, of the 100,000 or so acres of chalk downland still left in England, Wiltshire has about three-quarters, and Wiltshire naturalists, led by the Wiltshire Trust for Nature Conservation, are wide awake to the need for preserving as much of it as possible.

Probably the major change that occurred between John Aubrey's time and mine was the introduction of beech trees to the chalk downs. If Aubrey can be relied upon, the only beeches in Wiltshire in his time were in Groveley Wood, though he speculates that there might once have been many. Writing in the second half of the seventeenth century he says,

'About the middle of Groveley Forest was a fair wood of oakes, which was called Sturton's Hatt. It appeared a good deal higher than the rest of the forest (which was mostly coppice wood) and was seen all over Salisbury plaines. In the middle of this hatt of trees (it resembled a hatt) there was a tall beech which overtopt all the rest.'

He adds that the 'hatt' was cut down by the earl of Pembroke in 1654.

The hill-crest clumps and the long shelter belts of beeches which are now a prominent feature of the chalk hills owe their existence to the landscape planning which accompanied the enclosure acts of the eighteenth and nineteenth centuries.

The settlements formed by the Saxons in the chalk country were all in the river valleys. Each chalk stream was occupied from mouth to source by a line of farms and manors, each with a short sector of river which usually included a mill. Each would have a riverside pasture, usually flooded in winter, and the house and farmstead would be by a road, just above the flood line. Ascending the hill away from the river, the farmer would have another meadow or so, then a belt of arable fields, and then he would come to the open down. When Thomas Davis in 1801 prepared his survey of Wiltshire for the first Board of Agriculture he recorded that the downs were common lands, belonging to the lord of the manor but on which the tenants had grazing rights for sheep and, in some instances, cattle. The sheep were run in a parish or common flock, tended by a professional shepherd. After describing the arrangements Davis, slipping in a comment on human nature, writes:

'This is the ancient custom of managing the sheep stock in the district; but latterly, as the value of stock has become more known to a South Wiltshire farm, the tenants of common fields have introduced the practice of folding their separate flocks on their own lands, thereby placing their sheep under the immediate care of their own servants, rather than entrusting them to a common shepherd, whose neglect or partiality made his attentions inadequate to the care of the flock.'

Davis was, of course, writing during the Napoleonic Wars, which gave an impetus to enclosures and which indeed resulted in much of the downland being temporarily ploughed (soon to relapse to its original state). The general principle guiding the enclosure acts was to divide the land of the parish between every resident who had rights there. The lion's share went, naturally, to the lord of the manor; a small farmer who had grazing rights for a cow, a dozen sheep and some geese would be awarded land in proportion, probably an acre or two. Wealthy landlords were thus confirmed in the exclusive ownership of extensive estates, a development which many of them celebrated by the embellishment of their property in various ways. Some laid out broad new parks and surrounded them by precinct walls; some erected hill-top monuments, towers and more extravagant 'follies'; some indulged in landscaping on a grand scale, using their estates as a vast canvas and not hesitating to move whole villages to improve the visual amenities. We shall encounter examples of all these activities as we explore Wiltshire.

An incidental but fairly general feature of the enclosures was the division of the enclosed land into fields, usually rectangular, with hedges to mark the boundaries. Previously unenclosed farmland had been managed according to the feudal open-field system. The land around a village was split into about three large segments, each subdivided into long, unfenced strips of roughly an acre apiece. The village farmers, according to their status, would hold a number of strips in each of the fields. The cropping programme was immutable. Each year one of the big fields grew wheat, one barley and the third lay fallow. In the autumn an automatic switch occurred. For the next year the wheat field of the previous year grew barley, the barley field lay fallow, and the fallow field was devoted to wheat. The arrangement embodied a primitive system of crop rotation, and allocation of strip-fields ensured that each man would have his share of the good and the poorer soils, but the rigidity of it clamped down on any attempts at improvement.

If then we try to imagine the chalklands of Wiltshire as John Aubrey saw them, three hundred years ago, we shall visualise a landscape not unlike much of central Europe, including northern France and Germany, today. The villages would be clustered in the valleys, each farmstead with its home paddocks, and each cottage with its enclosed garden. There would be water-mills and water-meadows, orchards and rick-yards, hops and periwinkles entwining the garden hedges. Surrounding the village would be a zone of arable land, open and hedgeless and divided into corrugated strips, or baulks. There most of the villagers would be working. These cultivated fields would slope up to the interminable downs, rolling away on every side in majestic immensity. Aubrey found them smooth and completely devoid of trees and bushes.

The village open-fields were the feature most affected by the enclosure acts. They were parcelled out rectangularly into fields usually of about ten acres, their boundaries being specially-planted hedges of hawthorn, or quickset. Beyond, the downs remained as they had always been, except those which were ploughed for a few years at the time of Napoleon. But the landscape artists with unerring eyes marked the highest knoll or crest of the estate and adorned it with a beech clump. In many instances long curving belts of beeches led the eye up to the crowning glory. It was imaginative workmanship, and the Wiltshire landscape owes much to the artists.

Some downland villages, such as Imber, Chitterne and Tilshead, were like islands in an ocean, or oases in a desert. Most, however, were strung along a valley, wedged together as tightly as possible. A feature of the chalk downlands is therefore the remarkable elongated shape of parishes and farms. Some parishes are no more than half a mile broad but extend

4 (above) *Thatching repairs in Durnford village,* 5 (below) *'The Porch House', a half-timbered fifteenth-century building in Potterne*

four or five miles to the crest of the downs on either side of the stream. Half a mile broad and eight or ten miles long! Even these narrow strips were in earlier ages subdivided. Thus, in the Bourne valley, Winterbourne Dauntsey, which itself is a typical elongated parish, was split longitudinally into Winterbourne Dauntsey and Winterbourne Monachorum. Its neighbour, Winterbourne Gunner, was divided into Winterbourne Gunner and Winterbourne Cherborough.

The name 'Winterbourne' refers to the seasonal nature of the upper reaches of chalk streams. In summer these dry up. Springs start to bubble or seep up into the dry courses in November or December, and the brooks are at their highest level in February. How far up their valleys the streams rise in midwinter depends on the rainfall of the previous summer and autumn.

Pitton has a 'winterbourne', locally known as 'the springs', which traditionally rose on average once every seven years. That is only an average, for they have been known to rise in successive years, and, on the other hand, they have sometimes not appeared for more than ten years. Their incidence in this valley is so erratic that no adequate channels exist, and in a year of high water widespread flooding of fields, gardens and even cottages results.

The streams of Salisbury Plain are crystal clear. Fish gliding over their gravel beds are as visible as the reflections of birds overhead. Even when one flows past a muddy farmyard it purifies itself in a remarkably short space.

The streams were used not only to turn mills but, until very recent times, to irrigate the riverside pastures. It was winter irrigation, against frost, and was practised to ensure an early bite of spring grass for sheep. A hundred years ago the entire course of a chalkland stream from source to mouth, was margined by a network of irrigation channels.

At the point where the river entered his land a farmer would dig a side carriage, along which water could be diverted to a strategic point at the head of his meadows. There he constructed a hatch, from which a grid of parallel ditches led to the far end of the meadows. They were there collected again into a single channel, through which water was returned to the river, for the next man downstream.

The ditches were four or five yards apart and at two levels, alternately, one two or three feet higher than the other. The top level ditches were known as 'carriages', the lower ones as 'drains'. When the hatches were opened, the water flowed into the carriages until it brimmed over the lips and trickled down the sloping sides into the drains. Considerable skill was needed to plan the channels so that the water overflowed evenly for the entire length of the meadow. When the system was functioning properly the surface of the pasture was covered by an inch or two of gently-flowing water.

The flooding, or 'drowning', of the meadows began in December. In a severe winter, when the rest of the countryside was in the grip of iron frost or lay buried in snow, the water-meadows were oases of greenery, and incidentally havens for numerous waterfowl. By March, when the hatches were finally closed, the lucky farmer had a splendid growth of grass. Before chemical fertilizers were in general use, he could have his sheep out to grass at least a month before the upland farmer.

Thomas Davis gives the credit for Wiltshire's water-meadows chiefly to a Squire Baverstock, of Stockton, who laid out many of them in his district between the years 1700 and 1705. Local traditions, I have heard, say that 'Dutchmen' were responsible for the original planning. John Aubrey knew about what Davis calls 'the flowing meadows' fifty years before Baverstock's time. He writes:

'The improvement of watering meadows began at Wylye, about 1635, about which time, I remember, we began to use them at Chalke. Watering of meadows about Marlborough and so to Hungerford was, I remember, about 1646, and Mr. John Bayly, of Bishop's Down, near Salisbury, about the same time made his great improvements by watering there.'

Water-meadows fell into disuse in the depressions which hit agriculture from 1874 onwards and especially after the First World War. They were essentially for use by sheep, the clumsier hooves of cattle doing too much damage to the delicately-adjusted channels. Sheep virtually vanished from the Wiltshire scene in the late 1920s and early 1930s and with their passing, the water-meadows, except for a few in the Avon valley, fell into dereliction.

Manipulating and controlling water-meadows called for considerable expertise. The old countrymen who practised the art were known as 'drowners' and were allegedly web-footed! They spent their contented lives pottering about the meadows, adjusting levels here, clearing away obstructions there, repairing hatches and culverts, catching vermin and just leaning on fences and watching the water.

Drowning meadows would probably be an economic proposition again nowadays, especially if one could inherit a water-meadow laid out ready for use. Laying out a meadow from scratch would be a formidable undertaking, though modern digging machinery could be used. But the maintenance of the system would present difficulties. A gap of a generation or two has occurred during which the traditional lore has not been passed on, and this more than anything else has prevented a revival of water-meadows.

The plateau that is Salisbury Plain is tilted gently towards the south-east and is drained by five rivers, spread like the fingers of a hand. Their general confluence is in the vicinity of Salisbury. The frontier of the Plain is particularly well marked, by an impressive scarp, on the north and west, but the rampart is gashed by two of the rivers the sources of which lie beyond the confines of the Plain.

The Avon, which is generally held to be the head river, rises in the Vale of Pewsey, breaks through the escarpment at Upavon and pursues a direct southward course to Salisbury.

The Wylye, which probably carries as much water as the Avon, rises near Warminster and cuts obliquely, from north-west to south-east, across the Plain. At Stapleford it is joined by the little river Till, which flows southwards for a few miles, through Winterbourne Stoke and Berwick St James, from Shrewton. In wet winters the springs rise as far upstream as Tilshead — a deceitfully-named place if ever there was one, for 'Tilshead' does not mean 'the head of the Till', as it ought, but is derived from 'Tidwulf's hide', intimating that here in Saxon times was the farm of a man named Tidwulf.

Flowing due east in the next valley south of the Wylye, the river Nadder differs markedly from the other four. This is because most of its course lies through greensand and limestone country rather than chalk. The Nadder valley is broader than the others, its villages spread over a hilly and well-wooded countryside rather than clinging to a narrow funnel amid chalk hills. There are lakes, waterfalls, forests and much small scenery. The Nadder joins the Wylye at Wilton, and their combined waters flow on to mingle with the Avon at Salisbury.

Over a formidable range of chalk hills along the southern edge of the

Nadder lies the secluded, hidden valley of the little river Ebble or Chalk. It rises near Berwick St John and joins the Avon south of Salisbury, at Bodenham.

To the east of Salisbury the equally small river Bourne comes in from the north-north-east to join the Avon at Milford.

Although Salisbury Plain and South Wiltshire are roughly synonymous, in few places does the county boundary coincide exactly with the natural watershed of the five rivers. In the extreme south the isolated village of Tollard Royal is near the headwaters of a tributary of the river Stour and would more naturally be part of Dorset. In the west, around Stourton and Kilmington, the meadows drain into the Blackmore Vale, which again belongs to the Stour. In the south-east Pitton, Farley, the Grimsteads and Dean are in the valley of the Deanbrook, which flows into the river Test. Such minor anomalies of drainage, however, do not deter the residents of all these villages from regarding themselves as true Wiltshiremen and from looking towards Salisbury as their market and shopping town and their spiritual home.

With one exception, every village of south Wiltshire lies in a river valley. Even Imber, Chitterne and Tilshead occupy the floor of downland valleys which meander down to the Wylye. The exception is Winterslow, a hilltop village by a Roman road east of Salisbury and probably inhabited continuously since Roman times.

South Wiltshire has one notable source of building stone, the quarries of Chilmark, in the Nadder valley. The quarries have been worked from at least early mediaeval times and supplied the stone for Salisbury Cathedral. In none of the other valleys is there any building stone at all.

The Nadder valley therefore has a wealth of attractive stone farm-houses, rectories and even cottages and barns, but the farther one travels from Chilmark, into the other valleys, the rarer such features become. The distant Bourne valley is particularly poor in this respect; only the wealthiest residents could afford the transport of cart-loads of stone from so far away.

In the border zones of the Plain and in the Nadder valley and the vicinity of Groveley Forest, where trees were reasonably plentiful, many of the buildings are half-timbered, but the central parts of the Plain lacked even that material. The cottages, garden walls and some of the bigger houses there are built of chalk cob.

Chalk cob is an ingeniously conceived material. In a district which lacked building stone it was simply dug from the subsoil. Cartloads of rubbly chalk were mixed with water, chaff and horsehair and trodden into a sticky paste, which was slapped into position by a 'mudwallers' prong' and allowed to set. The rough heap which represented a wall was trimmed into shape by means of a hook and a wooden saw.

Provided the top of the wall is protected against rain, either by the roof of a house or, in the case of a garden wall, by a special little roof of its own, chalk cob will last indefinitely. When eventually its term of life is over, frost and rain disintegrate it quickly. It can then be carted away and spread over cultivated fields to supply lime to the soil. That has been the fate of most cob buildings through the centuries. The layers of flint that constitute the foundations are taken for similar use elsewhere or for roadbuilding. The chalk cob floor can be dug up or ploughed. Soon the very site has been forgotten.

There has been much speculation devoted to the problem of where the builders of Stonehenge, Avebury and other prehistoric monuments in the chalk country lived. Here are these great monuments that have endured for more than three thousand years, yet never a trace of domestic buildings in the vicinity has been found. Excavators have been inclined to assume timber buildings and have probed for post-holes. Anyone investigating the site of a chalk cob cottage would find no post-holes. What could be more likely than that the art of building in this one easily available local material was practised on Salisbury Plain in the days when Stonehenge was new.

The last buildings of chalk cob were built in the first decade of the twentieth century. During the First World War a few of the surviving practitioners were pressed into service to give instructions in the old craft to soldiers on Salisbury Plain. Apparently it was thought that cob-walling might have a military application, in the construction of temporary fortifications. Nothing came of it, however, and I suspect that no expert in cob-walling now survives.

The complementary craft to mud-walling is thatching, which still happily flourishes. Forty years ago this was easily the commonest roofing material in every part of the Plain, being used for hay-ricks, corn-stacks and mangold-heaps as well as for cottages, barns and farmhouses. It was the cheapest method. Wrote one Palsgrave in the sixteenth century:

'I am a poor man; sythe I can not tyle my house, I must be fayne to thatch it.'

Nowadays from being a poor man's necessity it has become a perquisite of the affluent. Thatching has become a luxury trade. The material, the skill of the craftsman, and the insurance premiums, are all expensive.

In the old days there were two types of road on Salisbury Plain. There were the valley roads, which were narrow lanes meandering from village to village and leading mostly in the general direction of Salisbury. And there were the downland roads, which were not really roads at all but simply a sense of direction. On the vast panorama of the Plain navigation by sun, stars or compass would have seemed as natural as at sea.

Present-day enthusiasts anxious to preserve old rights of way make much of the old green tracks of the high downs, but such tracks are no more than tokens or compromises. A traveller on the Plain, in its primeval state (which, as we have seen, lasted to within living memory), would simply set his course in the right direction and go straight to his destination, there being virtually no obstacles to deflect him. A 'track' could be twenty, forty, a hundred yards wide; it was no more than a zone of downland over which a wayfarer passed when going from one place to another. It was trodden more by flocks of sheep, grazing as they went, than by human feet.

Two comments on the ancient freedom of the downs seem worth recording. One is that the downland track from Salisbury to Whitsbury was, until towards the end of the nineteenth century, marked by little heaps of chalk at regular intervals. They were for the guidance of the Whitsbury carrier on dark nights and were known as 'chalk lights'. As his cart drew abreast of one he could dimly discern, by the carriage lanterns, the ghostly white outline of the next ahead.

The other explains the series of deep, roughly parallel ditches on either side of Roman roads and other old tracks on chalk hillsides. As long as a vehicle was traversing the open downs it went where it willed, but when it arrived on the edge of a scarp leading down to a town or village it tended to gravitate to a track used by some predecessor. A drug-shoe or some other braking device would be fastened to a rear wheel, in order to steady the descent. The process gradually wore a deep cleft in the hillside. When the ruts became too formidable, that track was abandoned, and another struck out a few yards on one side or the other. So in time there were perhaps as many as twenty tracks, like the delta of a river, converging on a road at the foot of the hill. In the course of centuries, rain coursing down these channels deepened them, till now some of them are twelve or fifteen feet deep. Probably the most easily accessible and most noticeable to the motorist are those by the main road that descends from Savernake Forest to Marlborough, but similar phenomena are to be found in dozens of places on the chalk downs.

Salisbury Plain would seem to be ideally suited to the construction of a great motorway. Here are no natural obstacles and almost unlimited space. Yet opportunities galore have been missed. Most of the through roads cling to the valleys, weaving around the villages, to the frustration and exasperation of both motorists and villagers.

The one imaginative exception was to concentrate on developing the A 303, which runs past Amesbury and Stonehenge, as the main highway from London to the West, in preference to the A 30, which passes through Salisbury, though even there most of the distance lacks dual carriageways, and there are still bottlenecks to be circumvented. The main road from Southampton to Bristol, however, still insists on negotiating the tortuous, village-strung Wylye valley, when a little forethought could have taken it along a parallel course two or three miles away, on the downs.

The most glaring example is the A 30, formerly the main road to the West and still carrying an immense amount of traffic. For most of its course in Wiltshire it is a two-way road, with little opportunity for passing and with bad corners at Barford, Fovant, Donhead and several other places. It creeps along the edge of the Nadder valley, as though it were afraid to venture out into the light, whereas it might be striding along the crest of the great range of hills to the south. For, ironically, the old highway – the Shaftesbury turnpike – does strike out along those hills. It is still there, a broad green trackway, steering straight as a Roman mile for the fourteen miles or so from Harnham to the edge of Donhead, with never a village or corner to check the traveller. In a dry summer much of it is still passable for cars which can take a few jolts and bumps. Why the highway authorities preferred the congestion of the valley to this glorious upland sweep of countryside is beyond the comprehension of ordinary mortals.

THREE

Salisbury

The story of Salisbury begins not with the present city in its setting of riparian meadows but with the fortified hill-top of Old Sarum, two miles to the north. Here in pre-Roman times was a defensive earthwork, perhaps only a single encircling rampart and certainly not nearly as elaborate a fortification as exists now.

Under the Romans its importance increased, due no doubt to the fact that at least three major roads and probably a number of minor ones converged on it. In the Antonine Itinerary it is referred to as 'Sorbiodunum' or 'Sorviodunum'. There is no general agreement about the meaning of the word. It has been variously interpreted as 'dry down', 'river fort' and, the present favourite, 'battle hill'. It was evidently a moderately important centre in Roman times, but lacked the status of a provincial capital. Its exact location is, however, uncertain. So few Roman remains have been uncovered by excavations at Old Sarum that archaeologists tend to think that the Roman town must have been outside the ramparts, perhaps down by the ford across the Avon.

The Anglo-Saxon Chronicle records that in 552 the West Saxons under Cynric fought and defeated the Britons at Searo-burh, which is Old Sarum. The name later becomes 'Saresberie', with the 'r' changing to 'l' in mediaeval times. Little is known of the story of the hill fort under the Saxons for four hundred years. There are brief references in Saxon annals to grants of land to a church at 'Sarisbyrig' by King Ina in 720, to King Alfred improving its fortifications, and to King Edgar holding a parliament there in 960. By 1003 it was a sufficiently important town to have a mint and to be sacked and burnt (probably) by King Sweyn's

Danish army.

The first Norman monarch, William the Conqueror, seems to have regarded Sarum with special favour. It was here that he held the final muster of his victorious army in 1070, before disbanding them to go and possess their loot, in the form of English estates. It was here, too, that he called his council together in 1086, to establish the feudal system in England and, as part of the plan, to initiate the compilation of the Domesday Book. At Sarum, according to *The Anglo-Saxon Chronicle,* 'he was met by his councillors; and all the landsmen that were of any account over all England became this man's vassals as they were; and they all . . . became his men and swore him oaths of allegiance that they would against all other men be faithful to him.'

Meantime Old Sarum had become the seat of a bishopric. The last bishop of Ramsbury, Bishop Herman, had since 1058 been bishop of Sherborne as well, thus uniting again the old see of Wessex. In 1075 the royal council decreed that bishoprics should be removed from small towns and villages to larger centres, and apparently as a direct consequence Herman decided to make Sarum the seat of his combined diocese. The new cathedral was started there in the same year and was consecrated by Herman's successor, St Osmund, in 1092. Within a few days it was struck by lightning and remained partly ruined until restored by the next bishop, Roger, at some time after 1102.

Roger was a warrior-bishop typical of his age, and as his actions have much to do with the present site of Salisbury we will briefly sketch his career. Like so many of the energetic Normans, he was a great builder. Before he became bishop of Salisbury he had been chancellor of England and at times ran the country when King Henry I was absent overseas. On being appointed to the bishopric, he built strong castles not only at Sarum but at Malmesbury, Sherborne and Devizes as well. All went well for a time after Stephen succeeded Henry I, but then the king became suspicious of Roger, whom he arrested and imprisoned. All the bishop's estates were confiscated and never restored, though Roger himself was let out of prison, to die as a result of his treatment, about a year later.

The next bishop, Jocelin, was a mild and somewhat inadequate man for those turbulent times. Under him the fatal dual allegiance of the hill-top town, which had begun when Stephen had seized the castle, became established by custom. Like so many hill forts, Old Sarum consists of a series of terraces surrounded by concentric ramparts. Of them the innermost was occupied by the castle, with its towering keep and deep dungeons. Around that was a broad plateau on which the cathedral and satellite buildings had been erected. Separated from it by yet another deep ditch was another plateau, protected by ditch and rampart. The lay citizens of Old Sarum seem to have occupied sites on the two outer terraces, though excavations suggest that there was much vacant land within the fortifications. Perhaps many of the early mediaeval houses were outside the walls.

So, whenever there was friction between king and clergy, which was most of the time, one of the chief scenes of bickering was Old Sarum. The garrison had the advantage. Not only did they hold the castle on the highest ground and protected by its own dry moat but they also occupied a section of the second terrace and naturally had a claim to oversee all the fortifications.

The climax of the quarrel came in the stormy reign of King John, when the clergy prepared a petition to the Pope, asking leave to be allowed to abandon the ecclesiastical property at Old Sarum and to move to the more hospitable Avon valley. Some of their evidence strikes us as being exaggerated to the point of ridicule, though their basic case was genuine enough. They submit:

'Being in a raised place the continued gusts of wind make such a noise that the clerks can hardly hear one another sing, and the place is so rheumatic by reason of the wind that they often suffer in health.

'The Church, they say, is so shaken by wind and storm that it daily needs repair, and the site is without trees and grass, and being of chalk has such a glare that many of the clerks have lost their sight.

'Water, they say, is only to be got from a distance and often at a price that elsewhere would buy enough for the whole district.

'If the clerks have occasion to go in and out on business they cannot do so without leave of the Castellan; so that on Ash Wednesday, Holy Thursday and on Synodal and Ordination and other solemn days, the faithful who wish to visit the Church cannot do so, the keepers of the Castle declaring that the defences would be endangered.

'Moreover, as many of the clerks have no dwellings there, they have to hire them from the soldiers, so that few are found willing or able to reside on the spot.'

Old Sarum is now so essentially a grassy place that it requires an effort of the imagination to visualise its former bare appearance. When the entrenchments in the chalk were first cut, the glare of the sunlight on them could conceivably hurt the eyes, though the blindness of 'many of the clerks' must be an exaggeration. But one can sympathise with the clergy when they testify to harassment by the soldiery, especially as tradition relates one incident:

At Rogationtide the bishop and his clergy all went down to St Martin's (afterwards one of the parishes of New Sarum) for the usual perambulation of the bounds. On their return they found the gates barred against them and the ramparts crowded with laughing, jeering soldiers. All appeals were in vain, and the unhappy company had to spend the night in the ditches around the town.

Such indignities could not be tolerated. The Pope, appealed to, granted permission for the cathedral and chapter to be moved, so down to the meadows they went.

Several legends survive as to how the new site was chosen. One, related by John Aubrey, says that the bishop (Bishop Poore) first considered purchasing a plot of land from the Abbess of Wilton, who evidently owned much of the land in the district.

'Thereunto he rode severall times to the Lady Abbesse of Wilton to have bought or exchanged a piece of ground of her ladyship to build a church and houses for the priests. A poor woman at Quidhampton, that was spinning in the street, sayd to one of her neighbours, "I marvell what the matter is that the bishop makes so many visits to my lady; I trow he intends to marry her." '

No satisfactory conclusion was reached, however, and the situation was altered by a dream in which the bishop was told to build his church in Merrifield, or Merefield. On making enquiries as to where that might be, he found that it was already his own property, so the problem was solved.

Another legend says that the site was decided by an archer who stood on the ramparts of Old Sarum and shot an arrow into the air. Where it fell, the cathedral was built. As the distance is a good two miles, one could wish to have been there to see that notable exploit.

The site was near the confluence of the combined waters of the Wylye and Nadder (which had joined at Wilton) with those of the Avon. It was a spacious, pleasant meadow, but subject to flooding, which continued to be a nuisance down to modern times. In 1635 clergy had to ride into the cathedral on horseback to conduct the services, the water being too deep for wading; and there are those alive who saw the nave under water in January, 1915. The town itself, which grew up just outside the cathedral precincts, had a grid of water-channels along the middle of every street and was known in mediaeval times as 'The Venice of England'.

Work began on the new cathedral in 1219 and went on for about forty years, which is a remarkably short time for building a cathedral. In consequence, it is a pure example of the Early English throughout, not an amalgam of a number of styles, as in so many other cathedrals. It was consecrated in 1258, the cloisters, chapter house, old deanery and several other houses being completed during the next half-century. The spire, which was not part of the original plan, was begun in 1334.

Much of the attraction of Salisbury cathedral, though it is a superb building in its own right, lies in its perfect setting. In the quiet cathedral close, barricaded against the busy commercial world by an intact mediaeval wall, a rectangle of fine houses, some contemporary with the cathedral and others noble examples of Queen Anne and Georgian architecture, stand respectfully at a distance from the great church. From almost every side, therefore, one can view it across a foreground of daisy-spangled lawn and elm trees. The Close is even able to absorb the influx of modern motor traffic (partly because there is limited parking space and no through traffic is allowed) and remains an oasis of peace.

In the incessant feud at Old Sarum between the garrison and the clergy the civilian population evidently sided with the bishop. When therefore the latter determined to move to the valley, it was not long before the townsfolk came to a similar decision. There was no delay. The migration began even before the foundation stone of the new cathedral was laid, for as early as 1219 the new town was granted permission, by the king, to hold a market.

One of the oldest streets in Salisbury is New Street, the houses of which back against the Close wall. High Street is a continuation of the road which leads, through High Street Gate, into the cathedral precincts. The lay-out of the town is a notable example of mediaeval town planning. Salisbury did not grow up gradually, over the centuries, but was planned as an entity which did not alter much until the present century. It was laid out on a grid pattern, much like a new American or Canadian township.

the blocks being known as 'chequers'. Some of them still bear their mediaeval names. Penny-farthing Street, for instance, is said to have been the chequer where the builders of the cathedral pitched their tents when they went on strike for a penny-farthing a day! Culver Street is said to be derived from the Latin word for a dove, in reference to the prostitutes, colloquially known as 'doves', who resided there! Ivy, Swayne and Barnard were mediaeval worthies who have their names commemorated by streets.

To begin with, one of the chief sources of stone for the new town was Old Sarum. The old buildings there were simply pulled down and the stones re-used. The garrison, in their austere castle, must have had second thoughts, after their initial exultation, as they watched the town disappearing. For them it was an empty victory. The castle remained for several centuries after the town was abandoned but in time suffered much the same fate, much of the stone being used in the reign of Edward VI for building Wilton House.

The cathedral itself was constructed mainly of the splendid grey-green stone from the quarries at Chilmark, brought to Salisbury by cart. It is a pure product of Wiltshire. Elias of Dereham, an 'incomparable artificer', is usually given credit for the design of the building, though he may have been the ecclesiastical administrator (he was a canon) rather than the architect. A name associated with his is Nicholas of Ely, who was a master mason and probably had charge of much of the work. No doubt, too, the dean William de Wanda, and the cathedral treasurer, Edmund Rich (afterwards canonised as St Edmund of Abingdon), were deeply involved.

Elias of Dereham had close associations with the bishopric of Winchester, and in planning Salisbury's new cathedral must have borne in mind the fact that in 1107 the central tower of Winchester cathedral, built like Salisbury on marshy ground, had collapsed in ruins. The knowledge must have been a factor in his decision to plan Salisbury without a spire and with only a stumpy tower.

His successors were bolder. Under Bishop Wyvil the plan was conceived of adding both tower and spire and was carried out, with astounding audacity, by his architect, Richard of Farleigh. There must have been many moments when the builders feared that the tower was going to topple like Winchester's. In spite of reinforcing the pillars on which it was to stand, until they were solid walls six feet thick, the edifice started to slip. The enormous weight, for the spire weighs 6,400 tons, pressed the foundations at one corner deeper into the soft earth, with the result that for most of its history it has been 28 inches out of the perpendicular. Careful watch is kept on it, but it seems to have finished settling long ago. Even so, if we stand beneath the great fluted pillars of Purbeck marble which support its weight we shall see them warped and bending, like the knees of an old man, beneath their colossal burden. Two great inverted arches were hastily put in at the crossing of the eastern transept when the slip began, and these probably saved the cathedral.

The people of Salisbury, like most devout Christians of the Middle Ages, wanted a carillon of bells to complete their great church. That brilliant architect, Richard of Farleigh, appreciated the danger. The spire was too delicately balanced to cope with the vibrations of a peal of bells. So, before even the building of the spire was started, he made arrangements for the bells to be housed in a separate belfry, well away from the cathedral.

His bell tower, or campanile, stood at the north-eastern corner of the cathedral green, where its foundations may still be traced in the grass in a dry summer. It rose three stories high and was surmounted by a wooden tower and unimposing spire. In it were hung twelve bells.

After the Reformation the bell tower was neglected and allowed to become ruinous. The ground floor was used in the eighteenth century as an alehouse, and a favourite prank of the youth of the town, after they had enjoyed a convivial evening down below, was to climb up into the belfry and 'jamble' the bells. A riotous Whitsuntide Fair used to be held in the neglected churchyard. Instead of the smooth lawns of the present-day, the immediate surroundings of the cathedral consisted of a jungle of mouldering tombstones collapsing at drunken angles into thickets of weeds. Inside the cathedral itself, the damp nave (for its floor is below the level of the outside ground surface) was congested by more tombs and memorials, scattered about haphazardly.

The place badly needed tidying up, and in 1777 Bishop Barrington resolved to do so. He gave a free hand to the architect James Wyatt, who set about his task with a dictatorial ruthlessness. Until recently, few writers have found a good word to say for Wyatt. He has been criticised for demolishing the two beautiful Hungerford and Beauchamp chantries,

for destroying many of the tombs in the nave of the cathedral and for
arranging the remainder in straight, regimented lines, for pulling down
the campanile and, worst crime of all, for smashing such
thirteenth-century glass as remained in the windows. Had he been alive to
answer his critics he could have retorted that the chantries, splendid
though they were, did not match the Gothic purity of the main fabric;
that the present symmetrical arrangement of tombs and monuments is
better than the old; and that the campanile was no great loss. Anyone
who has seen a picture of the campanile against the background of the
cathedral will probably agree. We may, however, share the indignation
which has been expressed about the destruction of the glass and wonder
how a gifted architect could endorse the payment of money to one 'Berry
ye glazier about beating the fine painted Glass Window at Sarum to
pieces to save the Lead', although some modern commentators have
pointed out that it was doubtless dark and increased the gloom of the
cathedral interior. On the credit side, Wyatt cleared away the jumble of
tombstones in the churchyard, levelled and raised the surface and laid
down the lawns which we now admire. His contemporaries did not
admire them. When he suggested the scheme for renovating the
churchyard he met such furious opposition from the townsfolk that he
temporarily withdrew it. Then, when the storm had subsided, Bishop
Barrington brought in an army of workmen who completed the whole job
in a single night. When the citizens discovered what had happened they
protested so vigorously that Bishop Barrington had to leave the city and
was made bishop of Durham. But, happily, what had been done could not
be undone, and we who have inherited can appreciate his improvements.

Planned as an entity from the very beginning, the development of
Salisbury in the thirteenth century was rapid. For this it owed much to the
construction, while the cathedral was being built, of two new bridges, one
over the Avon at Fisherton (which existed as a village before Salisbury
was founded) and another, a little lower down the river, at Harnham.
Abandoned by its citizens, the commercial prosperity of Old Sarum was
doomed and soon dwindled, but for many decades the rival market town
of Wilton fought a vigorous rearguard action. Rightly complaining that
they had historical priority, the citizens of Wilton even went to the
lengths of waylaying merchants on their way to Salisbury and forcing
them to attend Wilton market instead. A compromise by which Salisbury

had markets on Tuesdays and Saturdays only was reached, but even so Salisbury continued to expand and flourish at the expense of Wilton. Until the 1950s Salisbury's Tuesday market attracted buyers and sellers of farm livestock from much of southern England, while Saturday was a shoppers' market, when countryfolk came in to do their week's shopping and browse amid the market stalls. As for Wilton, it had at last to endure the indignity of having as its postal address: Wilton, near Salisbury.

Salisbury's central market square, spacious though it is, is perhaps only a quarter of its original size. It extended to the street which is now known as New Canal and westwards, across Minster Street, to the banks of the Avon. From the very beginning it was planned to cope with an abundance of trade. Most of the encroachments on it, however, are of early date, the Ox Row, the Fish Row and the adjacent streets possessing some of the oldest houses in the city.

In the 1920s, when I was a boy, the market day division of space between the various kinds of livestock was still observed. In one section of the central square one could find poultry in wire pens, in another pigs, along by the Ox Row pens of sheep, and in a corner a miscellaneous collection of rabbits, ferrets and guinea pigs. Cattle and horses were sold in the private yards of the three local auctioneers. At an earlier date a section of the market was reserved for cheese, a speciality discontinued by the 1920s though the name is still used. The fine mediaeval Poultry Cross was presumably the recognised place for selling poultry. Before the business of selling livestock was taken over the by the auctioneers pigs were displayed for sale in what is now a bus park by New Canal and which is still referred to by older countryfolk as the Pig Market. In mediaeval times the cattle market was at Barnard's Cross, now an undistinguished little residential street, and it seems that the cattle were generally taken to be slaughtered by Fisherton Bridge, for at various times during the Middle Ages the city passed laws forbidding butchers to dump the offal into the river there.

Change came rapidly with the development of motor traffic after the Second World War. A new market place was laid out on what was then waste ground by the river on the outskirts of the town. The pigs, sheep and small livestock departed from the central market square, leaving it for use as a car park, and the auctioneers vacated their private premises. A second cattle market day was established on Fridays, for attested cattle

7 (above) *Longleat House from the east.* 8 (below) *Wilton House from the south-east*

only, but as most cattle became attested the Friday market gradually eclipsed the Tuesday one. Now the impressive new market place, so recently constructed, has had a great segment sliced off it to make room for a new by-pass.

Around the old market place the mediaeval city was laid out in three parishes. One was the parish of St Martin, based on the old village of Milford, a new church on a probable Norman foundation. The central and chief church of the city, apart from the cathedral, was that of St Thomas of Canterbury. The present edifice dates largely from the fifteenth century and has over the chancel arch an impressive Doom painting of that date. The third church, that of St Edmund of Abingdon (who was an early treasurer of the cathedral), was originally built in the thirteenth century and rebuilt in the fifteenth. Established in the first place for use by a college of priests, who resided nearby in a park adjoining College Street, it is now regarded as one of the redundant churches of the city and at the time of writing a new use is being sought for it.

Although the citizens of Old Sarum had no hesitation in accompanying their spiritual father to his new home in Salisbury, that did not deter them from quarrelling with him. The story of Salisbury throughout the Middle Ages is one of almost incessant squabbles between the townsfolk and the bishop, though with frequent interludes of violent bickering among the citizens themselves.

One of the reasons for the unrest was the very prosperity of the city. Although a thriving market town, its main commerce was in wool. It was a natural collecting centre for wool from the vast sheep-walks of Salisbury Plain, and in the early Middle Ages Salisbury's merchants were engaged in a flourishing export trade to the mills of Flanders. Later, under Edward III and succeeding monarchs, England developed its own weaving industry, and, again to the forefront, Salisbury became a great wool-manufacturing town. Its exports were now of finished cloth instead of raw wool. Southampton was its main shipping port, and there Salisbury merchants enjoyed special privileges, including reductions in tolls and customs.

The Salisbury merchants naturally became very wealthy. Evidently they dabbled in every form of trade. The Brokage Books of Southampton show that goods despatched to Salisbury were ultimately destined for not only Salisbury itself but Yeovil, Taunton, Bristol, Bradford-on-Avon,

9 The Tithe Barn at Bradford-on-Avon

Shepton Mallet, Frome and even such distant places as Coventry and Ludlow. They reveal, too, Salisbury as a customer for enormous quantities of wine and such commodities as woad and alum, used in dyeing.

The citizens bred by this abundant trade were an independent, cantankerous lot. One of the most notable, John Halle, defied not only the bishop but also the king. Shut up in the Tower of London for recalcitrance, he was again elected mayor of Salisbury in defiance of the instructions of the king, Edward IV. On release, he straight away took office and proceeded to throw his weight about as before. His splendid town house still survives, the Hall of John Halle, now the Gaumont cinema. The house of another mediaeval merchant, John a'Port, is now a shop in Queen Street. The halls of two of the city guilds, the tailors and the joiners, are to be seen in Penny-farthing Street and St Ann Street respectively, and Church House, in Crane Street, has some features of the original fifteenth-century building, thought to have been the home of another merchant, William Webb.

Of the older city inns, the Old George was once Salisbury's leading hostelry and exhibits some fine fourteenth- and fifteenth-century timbering. The Haunch of Venison and the King's Arms are likewise mediaeval, as is the impressive half-timbered Beach's bookshop at the corner of High Street and Crane Street.

Within the Close wall, which was constructed in the fourteenth century largely of stones from the old cathedral at Old Sarum, the best mediaeval buildings, apart from the cathedral, are the Bishop's Palace and the Old Deanery. There was, however, extensive rebuilding here from Stuart times onwards, and most of the finest buildings, including the North Canonry, Mompesson House and the Matrons' College, are seventeenth- and eighteenth-century.

On the outskirts of the city two venerable buildings probably ante-date the cathedral itself. St Nicholas' Hospital, which is tucked away by the river near Harnham Bridge, was originally established, perhaps by Bishop Herbert Poore, as a hospital for the sick poor. It is now an old people's home. The Old Mill at Harnham, with a rare Queen roof, is said to have housed the archives of Old Sarum while the new cathedral was being built. Incidentally, the quick way from the centre of Salisbury to the Old Mill is by the river path over Long Bridge, from which Constable painted his masterpiece, 'The Rainbow'.

Salisbury has an excellent museum, cramped for space but, at the time of writing, with hopes of a move to a larger building. Its collection includes two mediaeval 'props' of the annual processions of the mediaeval Tailors' Guild, – the Giant, a twelve-feet high figure with negroid face and flowing robes, and the Hobnob, a kind of hobby-horse who used to prance among the crowds, snapping and causing merriment. There is also much prehistoric material, from the barrows and megalithic monuments of the Plain, and a fine display on Wiltshire's bird, the great bustard.

I find it difficult to stop writing of Salisbury, my home city, in the vicinity of which I lived for more than fifty years. Bishop Wordsworth's School, within the Close walls, was my old school, and, sitting now in my study, I can close my eyes and visualize almost every house in the old city. When I revisit it nowadays, however, I find it hardly recognisable. The mid-twentieth-century custodians of Salisbury's heritage have given it really cavalier treatment. Streets existing from the time of the first planning of Salisbury have been obliterated, old chequers have been re-designed to accommodate new car parks, mediaeval houses have been gutted and their bare beams left exposed to a winter's rains, roads which were once main thoroughfares have become cul-de-sacs, and a new concrete elevated way poises, unfinished, over the roof-tops of the long-suffering city.

Nevertheless, Salisbury is as prosperous as ever. There being no town of comparable size for many miles around, it is still the shopping centre for a huge rural area, including the populous military establishments of Salisbury Plain. It still has its weekly markets (and its annual pleasure fair in mid-October). Tourists in increasing numbers invade it, especially on wet summer days when the beaches of south-coast resorts are uninviting. Its Arts Theatre has a company of high calibre. And its suburbs continue to expand, though the tendency nowadays is to treat the villages as residential suburbs. The city's ancient woollen trade has gone, and there are no big factories, but a number of light industries provide employment.

FOUR

The Valley of the Salisbury Avon

Ignoring for the moment the little streams of the Vale of Pewsey which are the headwaters of the Avon and which converge to break through the barrier of the chalk downs at Upavon, we can divide the valley of the Salisbury Avon into three well-marked sectors. The upper Avon covers its course from Upavon down to Amesbury; the middle Avon from Amesbury to Salisbury; and the lower Avon, from Salisbury to the Hampshire border at Downton.

With Salisbury as a focal point, it will be convenient to travel southwards from the city to look first at the lower Avon. We have a choice of two roads, one on either side of the river. The main road, leading to Bournemouth, is on the western side, and a minor one zigzags among the farms and over the hills on the east. There is no other public bridge across the Avon until one arrives at Downton.

The absence of bridges had much to do with the economy and development of south Wiltshire before Bishop Bingham built his two bridges at Salisbury, soon after the foundation of the new city. Until that time the Avon imposed a considerable barrier, to the advantage of Wilton, which had little competition as a market town west of the river.

Crossings were by fords, the most important of which are remembered by the names they gave to villages. Stratford, by Old Sarum, is the ford where a Roman road, or 'street', crosses the river. Britford, immediately south of Salisbury, is the 'ford of the Britons'; Longford, nearby, the 'long ford'. Just beyond the Hampshire boundary Charford is by some authorities identified as 'Cerdic's ford', where, according to *The Anglo-Saxon Chronicle,* the West Saxon leader Cerdic defeated the

Britons in the year 519.

Stratford rightly belongs to the middle section of the valley, but the others are all south of Salisbury and below the confluence of the Avon with the rivers Wylye, Nadder and Bourne. The Avon here is a broad and stately river, flowing clear and deep over gravel beds, and the wonder is that there are any fords at all. One suspects that they must have been usable only in summer and that even so hardy travellers must have been soaked up to their armpits.

Britford, though a quiet and undistinguished village, must be one of the oldest in the county, for it is mentioned at least as early as A.D. 670 Its church of St Peter is Saxon, part of it perhaps ninth century, though there are more recent additions.

Longford is not a village at all but a great estate, the home of the earls of Radnor. Its nucleus is a splendid mansion which looks like a castle and is called a castle. It stands by one of the loveliest reaches of the tranquil river, its eastern walls washed by the water, and long lawns and formal gardens forming an impressive vista along the bank. A fine stone bridge, privately owned, here spans the Avon and ties together the broad estates which extend on either side.

Longford Castle has an interesting though entirely peaceful history. It stands on the site of a mediaeval manor-house acquired by a country gentleman, Sir Thomas Gorges, in the time of Elizabeth I. In 1584 he married Helena, widow of the Marquis of Northampton and a lady-in-waiting to the Queen. Prompted by her, Sir Thomas set about replacing his somewhat modest manor by a much grander house.

The ground plan is unusual. It is triangular, with a tower at each corner. It is said that Lady Gorges based it on an heraldic sign she found on an old coat-of-arms, representing the Trinity, but another suggestion is that it evinced a secret hankering after the old Catholic religion (though whether a lady-in-waiting to the Queen would either have or provide evidence of having such an adherence seems to me very doubtful).

The ambition of Sir Thomas, or, perhaps more accurately, of his lady, was not equal to his resources. In the middle of the work the money ran out! But Lady Gorges rose to the challenge. Among the posts that Sir Thomas held was that of Governor of Hurst Castle, on the Hampshire coast, and during the wreck of the Spanish Armada one of the Spanish vessels was driven aground there. Lady Gorges asked the Queen if she might have the wreck, which request was graciously granted. What the Queen did not know, but Lady Gorges apparently did, was that the foundered vessel was one of the Armada's treasure ships, laden with silver bars. Ample booty was recovered to pay for the building of Longford Castle.

The estate was bought by the Huguenot family of Bouverie in 1717 and has remained in their hands ever since. The second earl of Radnor considerably enlarged the castle, and a new façade was added in the nineteenth century, but the nucleus is much as the Gorges planned it. Over the years the Radnors have accumulated a magnificent art collection, including paintings by Holbein, Rubens, Van Dyck, Reynolds, Gainsborough, and Murillo, as well as much fine furniture.

Alderbury, the village on the eastern side of the 'long ford', has a Saxon name, supposedly derived from a woman named Aethelwaru, but is on the site of a settlement certainly occupied in Roman times. Numerous prehistoric flint tools have also been found there. A steep hill from the centre of the village down to the river is known as Silver Street, said to be derived from the Latin 'Silva Strata'. It is recorded that oaks from Alderbury were used in the building of Salisbury Cathedral, but these could well have been felled in the forest of Clarendon (for which see Chapter 7).

Alderbury's inn, the Green Dragon, is generally agreed to be the original of the Blue Dragon, in Dickens' *Martin Chuzzlewit*. Dickens stayed there while collecting material for the book, and an old lady who died this century remembered ferrying him across the river. The owner of a property by the river is still supposed, I understand, to keep a punt handy to ferry people across to a right of way to Britford on the other side. The inn at Whaddon, a hamlet in Alderbury parish, is the Three Crowns and is said locally to owe its name to the fact that King Edward III, hunting in the forest with the kings of France and Scotland who were his prisoners, had lunch there. An alternative theory, however, is that the 'three crowns' were those of the three kings, or wise men, who visited the stable at Bethlehem.

An echo of the way in which certain families became closely identified with certain villages is found in the Alderbury couplet,

> *Alderbury without a Prewitt*
> *Is like figgetty pudden without suet.*

Two miles downstream from Alderbury, on the same side of the river and splendidly situated on a plateau overlooking the broad valley, is Trafalgar House. A noble brick house, it was built in 1814 in gratitude for Nelson's victory at Trafalgar and was given to his brother, the first earl Nelson. There was irony in the gift, for the brother was no great friend of Nelson's, who doubtless would have much preferred the grateful nation to have been a little more generous to Lady Hamilton.

Oddly, local folk always refer to the place as Trafal*gar*, — the accent on the last syllable in the correct Spanish way.

Downton, southernmost outpost of Wiltshire in the lower Avon valley, is older than Salisbury. It appears in history in the seventh century as a gift from the West Saxon king, Kenwalch, to the bishop of Winchester. A later bishop of Winchester built a palace or castle here in the twelfth century and also laid out the plan of the little town much as it is now. The main street of Downton is at right-angles to the main Salisbury–Bournemouth road and skirts a spacious and attractive green. The bishop designed it as a new town, and throughout the Middle Ages it enjoyed a modest prosperity, though no more than that. It failed to grow much and towards the end of its career was a 'rotten borough', sending two members to Parliament until disenfranchised by the Reform Act in 1832.

Its importance in Saxon times is illustrated by the tradition that The Moot, an impressive earthwork in the garden of a seventeenth-century house, is a Saxon meeting-place. An attractive corner of a pleasant village, The Moot is a series of concentric earthworks, with steep banks and small in size, in a setting of rook-haunted tall trees and crowned by a classical summerhouse. Though it may well be Saxon, it could, alternatively, be the groundworks of a Norman castle or it could be prehistoric; there is little to date it.

Downton used to have two fairs, one in April and one in October. Buyers from Wiltshire, Hampshire and Dorset used to frequent these events to purchase livestock, especially ponies, brought in from the New Forest. The spring fair, on 12 April, was remembered when I was a boy as Downton Cuckoo Fair, because cuckoos arrive in southern England about that date. 'On April 12th,' old people told me, 'they used to open the Forest gate at Downton and let the cuckoo through!' So they paid tribute to Downton's position as the gateway to all the chalk country and particularly to Salisbury Plain.

Modern Downton has a tannery and several other small industries, and early strawberries are grown in the adjacent fields. Tourist traffic along the busy Bournemouth road has a tendency to halt at The Bull, a well-known fishermen's inn. Its sign is a reminder that it gets its name from a bull trout.

At Downton we can cross the river again and, having arrived at the county boundary, turn northwards towards Salisbury. Although Wiltshire has no more villages in this direction, it used to have. The downland parishes of Martin and Whitsbury were transferred to Hampshire during the nineteenth century. They are in the wedge of chalk country that thrusts westwards from the Avon into the heart of Cranborne Chase, and the late Mr Morley Hewitt, who spent many years excavating the great Roman villa near Rockbourne (next village to Martin), used to speculate on the possibility of this being an Imperial stud farm for the Emperor's horses, with boundaries much the same as those of the modern parishes of Martin, Rockbourne and Whitsbury. If so, history has tended to repeat itself, for in the present century Whitsbury has become widely known for its training stables.

Whitsbury is a place of very ancient origins. It had a Roman villa, and a sixth-century bard, Taliesin, is said to have lived in a cell nearby. The Hampshire Women's Institutes' folklore book, *It Happened in Hampshire,* states that the old Romano-British name for Whitsbury is Hall Cynvelly, though the source of the information is not given.

Martin, a typical downland village, with much thatch and cob, is the one on which W. H. Hudson based Winterbourne Bishop, in *A Shepherd's Life.* In the 1930s I used to know quite well the family with whom he stayed and many of the Martin folk with whom he talked when collecting material for the book. Martin Down is one of the few surviving commons in the chalk country of southern England.

Before we pass through Salisbury on our journey through the central sector of the Avon valley, one outstanding landmark due south of the city must be mentioned. It is Clearbury Camp, a conspicuous hill (altitude 468 feet) crowned by a towering clump of beeches and encircled by a formidable earth rampart. My boyhood home being six miles due north-east of Clearbury (which we always pronounced 'Clybury'), the Camp was regarded as our local barometer; when Clearbury was shrouded in mist rain was imminent.

Back in 1925 a Herefordshire man, Alfred Watkins, wrote a book, *The Old Straight Track,* in which he propounded the theory of leys, or landmarks linked by straight lines. It attracted little attention at the time but in recent years has enjoyed a vogue, and it is being conceded that his ideas on sight lines may, after all, be sound. South Wiltshire has one rather remarkable ley, as defined by Alfred Watkins. A map will show that Stonehenge, Old Sarum, Salisbury Cathedral and Clearbury Camp are all on a straight line.

*   *   *

The lovely middle section of the Avon belongs to the villages of Woodford (Upper, Middle and Lower), Durnford (Great and Little) and Wilsford, with Stratford-sub-Castle as sentinel at the gate. They are quiet havens, entirely agricultural and residential and having the inestimable benefit of no main road. The highway from Salisbury to Devizes bounds over the downs to the west of the valley, that from Salisbury to Marlborough via Amesbury over the downs to the east. Those who venture into the middle Avon are fortunate if they possess leisure for following meandering lanes that are as tortuous as the river. They will find innumerable temptations to pause, time forgotten, by deep pools overhung by willows or on little stone bridges where a man may sit well occupied in watching the duck and moorhens among the water-weeds all through a summer afternoon.

One could hardly imagine a more perfect trout stream. John Evelyn would find it little altered since his visit to his uncle at Great Durnford in the seventeenth century, a village which he found 'in a valley under ye plaine, most sweetly watered, abounding in trouts catched by speare in the night, when they came attracted by a light set in ye extreme of a boate.'

Of the numerous fine mansions and country houses in this lovely valley the best known is probably Heale House, Woodford, former home of the Hyde family, where Charles II hid for a few days when escaping from the Battle of Worcester. He must have felt reasonably safe here, for he rode off one day on a sightseeing trip to Stonehenge.

In earlier times the bishops of Salisbury had a palace, of which not a trace remains, at Woodford. The site is occupied by Court House, where until the 1860s an ancient Court Leet, a court of Anglo-Saxon origin which had power to try petty crimes, met regularly. Miss Edith Olivier, in her collection of Wiltshire stories entitled *Moonrakings,* records that other old customs kept up at Woodford within the memory of old people still living there in the 1920s were May Day celebrations and a Mumming Play.

Another of her stories is of Netton, a hamlet of Woodford on the opposite side of the river. It was once a thriving village, much larger than it is now, having, among other industries, a wool store which employed thirty or forty people. She also recalls:

'There used to live up the lane an enterprising old lady, by name Eliza Harding, and when the drovers came down the lane with the sheep she would have ready outside her house a small table with cakes and bread and cheese, and by the side a cask of ale, so that the drovers could stop and partake of light refreshments, also to exchange news, for it was not necessary at that time to have a licence to sell ale.'

Woodford church was reconstructed in 1845 but retains its ancient stone tower. The pleasant church of St Andrew at Great Durnford, home of the Tryon family, still has its Norman nave and chancel, with typical rounded arches. Wilsford was, for some time before his death in 1940, the home of Sir Oliver Lodge, one of the pioneers of radio and, in later years, of psychical research, but his handsome house has since been burnt down.

It is hard to find anything to criticise in this delectable valley, but that irascible though shrewd tub-thumper of the 1820s, William Cobbett did so. Riding southwards down the valley in August 1826, he recorded his indignant thoughts in his *Rural Rides.* The scenery, he acknowledged, was magnificent — 'villages, hamlets, large farms, towers, steeples, fields, meadows, orchards and very fine timber trees scattered all over the valley'. What he objected to was the contention, held by some of the politicians of his day, that the countryside was overpopulated and that the only remedy was emigration. So he engages in some rough-and-ready calculations. From the source of the Avon in the Vale of Pewsey down to Salisbury, he reckons, there are 29 parishes with a total population of 9,116 persons. These countryfolk are raising enough food to feed 45,580 persons accustomed to a reasonable standard of living, or 136,740 at the subsistence level at which the villagers themselves were fed. From the size of the churches he concludes, not necessarily correctly, that the Avon parishes had once had far greater populations. In some instances, he says, the church porches would hold all the present inhabitants, 'even down to the bedridden and the babies'.

So he came to the Accursed Hill, as he calls Old Sarum, a deserted place which was still sending two members to Parliament but was destined not to do so much longer. Standing beneath the ramparts, he found himself 'swelling with indignation against the base and plundering and murderous sons of corruption'. His memory was too short to recall, probably, that one of the 'sons of corruption' would have been the first earl of Chatham, William Pitt, and his even more able son, who had been one of England's greatest Prime Ministers. The Earl had entered Parliament as member for Old Sarum, the seat having been purchased, with an estate at Stratford-sub-Castle, by his father, Thomas Pitt, who had amassed a fortune in the East India trade. Pitt, incidentally, is still a well-known local surname.

The Post Office Directory for 1867 records of Old Sarum: 'A tree, near Stratford, was the place of nominal election for the borough of Old Sarum, but, almost immediately after the Reform Bill, a violent wind blew down the principal part of the tree; its decaying stump is still much visited by the curious; several large arms of it were broken down and carried as trophies by the exulting populace, when the passing of the Reform Bill disfranchised the borough.'

After the tree had entirely disappeared its site was marked by a stone.

*　　　*　　　*

The link that joins the middle and upper Avon is the little town of Amesbury, now usually approached and by-passed (to the profound relief of its residents) from east or west by traffic on the A 303. In the present century it has enjoyed considerable prosperity not only through tourists (Stonehenge is only two miles away) but from the military occupation of the Plain, just to the north.

Amesbury is one of the oldest inhabited sites in all Britain. Its name is supposed to be derived from Ambrosius, the fifth-century Roman-Briton who first checked the Saxon invasion and who was the predecessor of Arthur. An old Celtic poem speaks of the 'Three Perpetual Choirs of

Britain', which existed in pre-Saxon times. One was in Glamorgan, one at Glastonbury and the third at 'Ambresbury'. 'In each of these choirs there were 2400 saints, that is there were a hundred for every hour of the day and night in rotation.' The numbers may well be exaggerated, but the poem testifies to the early existence of an early religious establishment at Amesbury, dedicated to raising ceaseless praise to God. In the Arthurian legends Queen Guinevere is said to have become Abbess of Amesbury after the death of the King. Tennyson describes how the sorrowing Queen arrived at Amesbury and how the nuns

> *. . . took her to themselves and she*
> *Dwelt with them, till in time their abbess died.*
> *Then she, for her good deeds and her pure life,*
> *Was chosen abbess there, and abbess lived*
> *For three brief years, and there an abbess passed*
> *To where beyond these voices there is peace.*

Later her body was taken by Launcelot to Glastonbury, where presumably it would be safer from the advancing Saxons.

In 980 Amesbury again had an abbey, founded by Queen Ethelfrida as a penance for her treacherous murder of her step-son, King Edward, at Corfe Castle. It lasted throughout the Middle Ages, to the time of the Reformation, though with some vicissitudes. Henry II, for instance, found the nuns had become so dissolute that he turned them all out and replaced them with a more disciplined set. It was not a large abbey but enjoyed the patronage of a succession of kings and queens. Many royal ladies retired there, and some were buried there.

At the time of the dissolution of religious houses in England Henry VIII evicted the nuns and gave the property to Sir Edward Seymour, afterwards Lord Protector Somerset, who pulled down most of the buildings and erected a house on the site. He did not, however, demolish the old Abbey church, which still survives as the parish church. Though with traces of Saxon and Norman work and with much subsequent renovation, the fabric is basically thirteenth-century. Its dedication is to St Mary and St Melorus. The explanation of the association with the latter obscure saint is that he was chosen by conscience-stricken Queen Ethelfrida, as meeting a fate similar to that of her own murdered step-son. Melorus was a fifth-century lad killed by his uncle.

The great house built by the Somerset family lasted only just over a hundred years. It was then replaced by another, designed by Inigo Jones. For a time it was the home of the Queensberry family and, under the Duchess of Queensberry, wife of the third duke, a country retreat for court poets and authors, including John Gay, who spent much time there and probably wrote *The Beggar's Opera* in an ornamental grotto in the grounds. Another rebuilding took place when the Antrobus family acquired the property in 1840, the house then built being still known as Amesbury Abbey.

Amesbury, small though busy and cowering by the river banks, is somewhat eclipsed in the history of our nation and in modern appreciation by its august environment. All around it, on the undulating downs of Salisbury Plain, are reminders of a long-past age when this was the metropolis of the land. Tumuli cluster thick on the downs, and Stonehenge is only one, though the greatest, of a bewildering galaxy of monuments and half-obliterated memorials to lost civilisation.

When the greater part of Britain was thickly clothed in forest, the chalk downs were probably open grazing country and therefore a natural attraction to early man. In the long prehistoric centuries all the green tracks of what was later to become England converged on the broad prairies of Salisbury Plain. All roads, in fact, led to the neighbourhood of Stonehenge.

The literature of Stonehenge is bewildering in its volume and variety. Beginning in the twelfth century, when Henry of Huntingdon described it as the second wonder of England 'where stones of wonderful size have been erected after the manner of doorways, so that doorway appears to have been raised upon doorway, nor can any conceive by what art such great stones have been so raised aloft, or why they were there constructed', it ranges through the exuberant fancies of Geoffrey of Monmouth and the hardly less romantic speculations of a succession of distinguished visitors from the sixteenth to the nineteenth century to the sober assessments of archaeologists in our own day. One of the latest contributions is that of Dr Gerald Hawkins who, in his book *Stonehenge Decoded* (published in 1965), propounds the theory that the stones were erected by a people with a remarkable degree of astronomical knowledge. Using an IBM computer, he showed how the Aubrey holes just inside the perimeter of the encircling ditch of Stonehenge could be, and in his opinion probably were, used as a similar computer for predicting eclipses.

'It is eerie but not really surprising', he writes, 'to find that Stonehenge could be put in motion to predict our modern movable feasts', of which he gives Easter as an instance. I find his calculations convincing, though it is fair to admit that they have been strongly challenged.

Let us look at the whole galaxy of barrows and assorted earthworks that cluster around Stonehenge in the central Plain. The oldest of all are the long barrows, of which there are about a dozen within ten miles of Stonehenge. The latest dating, by means of radioactive material, suggests that the Neolithic farming folk who constructed them were on the Plain as early as about 4000 B.C. The barrows are made of rubbly chalk and are long, low mounds, now grass-grown. Most of them are over a hundred feet long, and one near Tilshead, known as 'Old Ditch', measures 380 feet. They are usually broader and higher at one end, and it is at this end that burials are found. Some have stone chambers, approached through a gallery, and some have stone floors. Many have been used for a number of burials, though whether all were made at one time or at intervals has not been determined. The fact that some barrows contain skeletons in which death has been apparently caused by a blow to the skull indicated that these were probably sacrificial victims, killed to provide attendants for a chieftain on his journey into the land of shades. Some of the barrows, however, including the very large and impressive one on the downs above Winterbourne Stoke, hold only one burial. A few flint implements and fragments of pottery accompany some of the burials.

Far more numerous than the long barrows (twenty times more numerous, suggests Mrs M. E. Cunnington, in *An Introduction to the Archaeology of Wiltshire)* are the round barrows. The map on the cover of the official Guide to Stonehenge shows how they cluster as thick as daisies on a lawn on the downs around the great stones. Normanton Down has a group of thirty; the downs above Winterbourne Stoke, near the large long barrow, twenty seven.

The round barrows are of three types, namely, the bowl barrow, which is a simple mound, shaped like an inverted bowl and often surrounded by a ditch; the bell barrow, which also has an encircling ditch but separated from the base of the mound by a wide lawn or terrace; and the disc barrow, which has only a tiny mound at the centre but otherwise resembles a bell barrow. All three types are found around Stonehenge.

Bowl barrows usually contain only one burial; bell barrows most often have a number, apparently of warriors; disc barrows are normally the graves of women.

The round barrows belong to a later age than the long barrows, being the work of Bronze Age men who evidently first arrived in Britain about 2000 B.C. Some of those excavated have proved to be archaeological treasure-stores, yielding bronze weapons, tools, armour and ornaments, as well as beads of amber, jet and faience (the last-named the product of Egypt and found in twenty three excavated barrows). In at least eight, gold has been found, though in small quantities, indicating that it was regarded as very valuable. An elderly woman, interred in a round barrow near Stonehenge, had as a personal ornament a disc of amber framed in gold.

Stonehenge itself belongs to approximately the same era as the round barrows. Its building covered about four centuries, estimated by some authorities to have been between 1900 and 1500 B.C., by others between 1800 and 1400 B.C. It was thus contemporary with the golden age of the Minoan civilization of Crete. The pyramids of Egypt are a thousand years older.

The first structure at Stonehenge consisted of a circular enclosure, its perimeter marked by a deep ditch with a bank on either side. There was a gap in the north-eastern sector, aligned to the midsummer sunrise. Parallel banks and ditches on either side of a track about 35 feet wide led to this entrance. In this approach way, about 100 feet outside the great circle, stood a huge stone, the Heel Stone. It is a sarsen stone, of the type still found lying on the Wiltshire downs, particularly near Marlborough, about 20 feet long and weighing approximately 35 tons. Several smaller stones were erected near the entrance.

Of the encircling banks the inner one was by far the bigger and more impressive. A few yards inside it, at intervals of about 16 feet around the entire perimeter, were pits, from 2 to 4 feet deep. Soon after they were dug, these holes, which are known as the Aubrey holes after the antiquarian John Aubrey who first noticed them, were filled in again with rubbly chalk. Most of those which have been excavated have been found to hold cremations. There are fifty six of these evenly-spaced pits. Dr Gerald Hawkins maintains that they are Stonehenge's computer. He writes:

'If six stones, spaced 9, 9, 10, 9, 9, 10 Aubrey holes apart, were used, each of them moved one hole counterclockwise each year, astonishing power of prediction could have been achieved. With six stones, three white, three black, the Aubrey hole computer could have predicted – quite accurately – every important moon event for hundreds of years.'

Perhaps a hundred or two years after the first phase of Stonehenge was completed a second period of activity occurred. The builders were, it seems, a different race from the original ones. They are known to archaeologists as the Beaker people. It was they who were responsible for the first stone circles within the outer bank. They brought the so-called 'blue stones' from some distant place, generally supposed to be the Prescelly Mountains in Pembrokeshire, though old legends say Ireland.

Again there occurred a gap of perhaps a hundred years, and then yet another race took a hand in the building of Stonehenge. They pulled down the blue stones and replaced them with huge sarsen blocks, from the same source as the Heel Stone, the largest of which weighs about 50 tons. The general design was a circle of somewhat smaller stones (though they weigh about 25 tons each), capped by lintels to form a continuous circle. Within it were five great trilithons, arranged in a horse-shoe shape. Later, but probably soon after the main edifice was finished, the dismantled blue stones were re-erected, in a circle and horse-shoe within the sarsen circle. The largest blue stone was placed before the central trilithon but has since fallen down and, in its recumbent position, has been dubbed (no doubt incorrectly) the 'Altar Stone'.

Such are the elements of Stonehenge. Without a guide book it is not easy to understand the pattern of the stones, as many have fallen down and many are missing. Some were broken up, perhaps in mediaeval times, for use as building stone in a countryside singularly short of that commodity; and souvenir hunters with hammers have wrought their share of havoc. Sufficient remain, however, to make Stonehenge one of the most impressive prehistoric monuments in Europe, and a still increasing number of tourists comes every year to marvel at the great stones.

Until Professor Hawkins advanced his theory questions about Stonehenge were more often prefaced by 'How' rather than 'Why'. How were these great stones raised? And how brought, in the first place, from the Marlborough Downs or, in the case of the blue stones, from distant Pembrokeshire? The official answer is they were brought as far as

10 (above) *Old Wardour Castle. 11* (below) *The village of Castle Combe*

possible by water, bound to rafts. For the remainder of their journey they were hauled by human muscle-power, on wooden rollers. The great upright stones were erected by the expedient of digging a pit near their base and pulling them up by ropes. And the lintels were raised by ramps supported by timber scaffolding. Models in Salisbury Museum illustrate how these operations were presumably carried out.

Unlike the stones at Avebury (see page 139) most of the stones of Stonehenge have been carefully shaped. The uprights have projecting tenons over which mortices in the lintel stones fit, and their top surface is slightly concave, to give greater security to the lintels. The lintel stones, too, fit into each other, and are curved to form an accurate arc of the great circle. With such colossal stones, the construction is an astounding feat of engineering, both in design and execution. One inevitably asks, Who were these people who could perform such prodigies with only stone tools? (Although the final phase of Stonehenge belongs to the Bronze Age, the working of stone would not have been done with bronze tools.)

The official answer is that they were the people known as the Beaker folk, who arrived in southern England from the Low Countries about 1700 B.C. Says Professor R. J. C. Atkinson, in the official guide book;
'Though relatively few in numbers, they seem to have established themselves as masters over the native population. It is against this background of a rich commercial aristocracy, dominated by a dynasty of commanding chieftains, that we must see the building of Stonehenge III.'

In his book *Stonehenge of the Kings*, Patrick Crampton enlarges on this concept and attempts to reconstruct a picture of the kind of society in which the builders of Stonehenge lived.

One interesting detail is worth mentioning. In 1953 the carvings of a bronze dagger and bronze axe-heads were found on one of the great stones. The dagger is almost identical in appearance with contemporary daggers found at Mycenae, in southern Greece. It seems to confirm a widespread belief among archaeologists that the builders of Stonehenge knew about and were influenced by the architecture of ancient Greece, though there are some who think that the flow of ideas was in the other direction.

As for the Druids, they come nowhere in the picture, in spite of the modern cult that has adopted Stonehenge and holds a ceremony there at sunrise on Midsummer Day. The Druids were a Celtic priesthood who

12 A peaceful stretch of the River Avon near Amesbury

seem to have appeared in Britain no earlier than about 250 B.C., when, of course, Stonehenge would be 1200 or 1300 years old. There is, of course, the possibility that they took over the old sacred site, but there is no evidence one way or the other. The association of the Druids with Stonehenge in literature is due to the imaginations of a number of antiquarians from the seventeenth century onwards.

Local folklore has, naturally, been busy with Stonehenge. The most widely-known story is that the stones were erected by the Devil in a single night. As he flew through the air, the Devil boasted that no-one would ever know how the stones had got there. Upon which a friar, who was hiding in a ditch nearby, could not resist retorting, in broad Wiltshire:

'Ah, that's more than thee canst tell!'

The Devil, surprised, dropped the stone he was carrying into the brook at Bulford, where it still is. Then, in a rage, he seized one of the great stones and hurled it at the fleeing friar, whom it hit on the heel. That, says the legend, is why the Heel Stone is so called, and the mark of the heel can be still seen upon it (though I have never been able to find anything like it).

Perhaps the only conclusion that one can draw from this is that it does seem to indicate a conflict between Christianity, represented by the friar, and an older religion, represented by Stonehenge.

From Stonehenge a long curved trackway, the greater part of it discovered by aerial photography in 1923, leads down to the river near Amesbury. It is thought that this is the way along which the stones were dragged, and later it may have been used as a processional approach.

Another notable feature in the vicinity of Stonehenge is the Cursus. It is an elongated earthwork about a hundred yards wide and $1\frac{3}{4}$ miles long, extending west to east about half a mile north of Stonehenge. The enclosing bank and ditch are low and shallow and have been partly obliterated by ploughing. The Cursus (a name given to it in the eighteenth century) is probably contemporary with the earliest phase of Stonehenge, but its purpose is obscure.

On a little plateau above the Avon and by the main Salisbury–Marlborough road, two miles north-east of Stonehenge, is another prehistoric feature discovered from the air in the 1920s. It is Woodhenge, a circular edifice enclosed by a bank and a ditch, inside which are six concentric rings of post-holes. The timber posts which they contained seem to have supported a large circular building, orientated, like Stonehenge, along the axis of the midsummer sunrise. Near the centre was found a small cairn containing the skeleton of a three-year-old child, whose skull had been split, evidently as a sacrifice. Meagre remains of pottery and other artefacts indicate that Woodhenge is contemporary with the earliest phase of Stonehenge.

A mile or so away, on the outskirts of the village of Durrington, Durrington Walls (which now lends its name to a telephone exchange!) is a thirty-acre enclosure bounded by a bank and a ditch and containing more than one circular structure, with post-holes for timbers, much on the lines of Woodhenge. Another extensive earthwork, called by eighteenth-century antiquaries 'Vespasian's Camp' though it is not known to have had any connection with Vespasian, is situated on a terrace above the Avon overlooking Amesbury Abbey. Of the many relics of prehistoric man on the wide military territory of the Plain, north of Stonehenge, one of the most ancient is a small earthwork, consisting of two concentric circles and known as Robin Hood's Ball, about midway between Shrewton and Figheldean. The latest date suggested for it is 3500 B.C.

Before leaving this region of awe-inspiring antiquity, our attention may be captured by a constellation of rounded clumps of trees on the north side of the road between Amesbury and Stonehenge. They are like the rounded beech clumps one sees on the crests of chalk hills, but they are much closer together and there are many more of them. Local tradition, which calls them the Trafalgar Clumps, says that they were planted to commemorate the Battle of Trafalgar and that they represent the battle plan of the British and French fleets, with each clump marking the position of a ship.

Serving as a link between relatively modern and goodness knows how ancient times, Durrington used to celebrate Old May Day (13 May) with perhaps significant ritual. Miss Edith Olivier sets down, in her book *Moonrakings,* the words of an eye-witness of the festivities, recounted to her in the early decades of the present century:

'The custom in the olden days was for the men and women of Durrington to have a sort of fair at the Cross Stones on Old May Day. First of all, the men went to the downs and got a may bush and then to the Nag's Head Inn for the May-pole. They tied the bush to the top of the May-pole, and chained the pole to the top of the Cross Stones. All this happened the night before, when it was dark.

'In the evening of Old May Day they danced around the Cross Stones to the music of concertinas and whistle-pipes. They also had cakes and barrels of beer to eat and drink.'

At Durrington now we are in the heart of Army territory. To the west the once-empty Plain is occupied by the military complex of Larkhill, with artillery ranges and tank training areas beyond. To the east the equally large Bulford Camp sits in the broad vale beneath Beacon Hill, on the other side of which it links up with the barracks at Tidworth. The Old Marlborough Road, which, like the Shaftesbury Drove, once struck out a much more direct course to its destination than does its valley-confined successor, is now but a grassy memory, but the road from Bulford to Tidworth under Beacon Hill permits a good view of the Bulford Kiwi. This imposing figure of their national bird was carved on a chalk hillside by New Zealand troops stationed here in the First World War.

North of Durrington the downs close in on the Avon till the valley is so narrow that in places one could almost throw a stone across it and there is hardly enough level ground in the bottom for a cricket field. The military occupation of the downs now hems in the Upper Avon villages more tightly than ever.

The chief villages of this sector of the valley are, progressing from south to north, Milston, Figheldean, Netheravon, Fittleton, Enford, Chisenbury and Upavon. Milston was the birthplace of Joseph Addison, his father being rector there. At Netheravon Sydney Smith spent two years as curate, so poor he could afford meat only once or twice a week. All the villages have pleasant little churches illustrating virtually the entire range of English ecclesiastical architecture. It was near Netheravon that William Cobbett (see also page 85) once saw 'an acre of hares'. He records that he went out into the fields above the village with his host, Mr Hicks Beach: 'His son took a gallop round, cracking his whip at the same time; the hares (which were very thickly in sight before) started all over the field — ran into a flock like sheep; and we all agreed that the flock did cover *an acre of ground.*' Now the downs above Netheravon and Upavon are occupied by extensive airfields.

Upavon, where we emerge from the claustrophobic valley into the broad Vale of Pewsey, was once a market town. In mediaeval times it had a weekly market and two annual fairs; also a small Benedictine priory.

On a hill above Upavon the extensive Casterley Camp, of the first century A.D., covers 68 acres. Mrs M. E. Cunnington in *An Introduction to the Archaeology of Wiltshire* offers this comment:

'In some cases tradition may still linger of the removal of the village from the hills to its present position in the valley. When Casterley Camp was excavated (in 1909 to 1912), local men from Upavon were employed, and they took it as a matter of course when signs of former habitation were unearthed, because they said they had always heard that the village used to be on the hill. It is difficult to disentangle genuine tradition from suggestion carried by written word or word of mouth, but in this case it may have been genuine, because before the site was excavated no-one would have thought of describing it as that of a deserted village.'

FIVE

The Wylye Valley

The volume of water carried by the Wylye can be little if at all inferior to that of the Avon. It mingles with the Avon just across the meadows from Salisbury Cathedral and for the last three or four miles of its course is reinforced by the Nadder, which joins it at Wilton. Wilton, which is said to have given its name to the county, is the town on the Wylye, so the river can claim to be the mother stream of Wiltshire.

Wilton's own claim to be the ancient capital of Wessex is justified. It could, in fact, be said to have been the first capital of all England, for here in the year 838 the West Saxon king Egbert was formally acknowledged as overlord of all the English kingdoms. The place is recorded as being 'the royal borough of Wilton'. No doubt it was an important town which had grown gradually to that status through unchronicled centuries. There is a suggestion that it may have been a pre-Saxon town, known by the British name of Caer Guilion.

Throughout the Middle Ages the town was dominated by the great Abbey of Wilton, which had been endowed with vast estates by a succession of monarchs, beginning with King Egbert, who founded a Benedictine priory there. Saxon kings had a palace at Wilton. The daughter of one of them, King Edgar, was educated at Wilton, where her mother was Abbess, and was later canonised as St Edith. In its heyday Wilton is said to have had either twelve or thirteen churches. For comparison, Salisbury in its early centuries had four, including the cathedral.

Decisions fraught with destiny are often lightly made. When the Bishop of Salisbury, weary of Old Sarum, approached the Abbess with a request for land on which to build his new cathedral, the Abbess evidently considered the matter for a time, but then, presumably seeing no reason why she should help a rival ecclesiastic out of a difficulty, decided, 'Let the Bishop build his cathedral on his own land.' Which is what he did, to the eternal detriment of Wilton. The two towns were too close to each other for both to flourish, and as Salisbury's prosperity grew Wilton's declined.

Wilton Abbey suffered like every similar establishment at the time of the dissolution of monasteries. Pensioned off with £100 and some property, the Abbess retired with her thirty one nuns to Fovant, and the Abbey and its home estates were given by the king to Sir William Herbert, first earl of Pembroke. To the Pembroke family it has belonged ever since.

Like so many of his contemporaries who similarly inherited monastic property, Sir William pulled down most of the abbey and built for himself a new house with the stones. For the next century or so Wilton recovered some of its old-time glory. Charles I was one of a succession of monarchs who, as is recorded of him, 'did love Wilton above all places, and did come here every summer'. Elizabeth I was here with all her court in 1573. Thirty years later it was the turn of James I, before whom, it is claimed, Shakespeare's company here gave the first performance of *As You Like It*. Wilton, under the benign rule of the earls and countesses of Pembroke, achieved a reputation as a Utopia in the west, and not only because here Sir Philip Sidney, brother-in-law to the second earl, wrote his book *Arcadia*.

The original designer of Wilton House, now a lure for countless summer tourists, was Hans Holbein, a friend of the first earl, who, however, died before the work was executed. The ground plan remains substantially his work, and his superb porch has survived, but much of the edifice was destroyed in a fire in 1647, which, however, left the way clear for an even greater architect, Inigo Jones, and his pupil and son-in-law John Webb to exercise their genius. Much of their work remains, though many of the finest rooms were demolished by that ruthless Wyatt who pulled down the Salisbury campanile and tidied up the cathedral. The rooms now seen by visitors are not only beautiful in themselves but are furnished with superb eighteenth-century chairs, cabinets, tables, mirrors and other furniture. The collection of paintings is one of the finest in the south of England and includes works by Reynolds, Rubens, Tintoretto, Rembrandt, Van de Velde and, above all, Van Dyck, who was greatly admired by the fourth earl. The splendid house is set spaciously in formal gardens and centuries'-old lawns, leading to delectable riverside walks — the very place for tranquil relaxation on a hot summer afternoon.

Outside the precinct walls of the great park, modern Wilton finds itself a bottleneck on the A30 road, its congestion relieved only by the development of the roughly parallel A303 as the major highway. Nowadays it has little industry beyond agriculture and its accessories, except for its world-famous carpet factory, still happily flourishing. Wilton carpets owe their origin to the enterprise of one of the earls of Pembroke, the eighth, who brought over skilled weavers from France. Thwarted in his efforts to do so legitimately, by the French king, Louis XIV, who was jealous of his profitable monopoly, the Earl proceeded to smuggle over his coveted weavers in a giant cask of Canary wine.

Wilton was a natural site for an important weaving industry, being able to draw unlimited supplies of good wool from Salisbury Plain. It had possessed generations of weavers earlier, though not of the same calibre and skill as the earl's immigrant Frenchmen. To the present day Wilton's autumn sheep fair is one of the great events in the agricultural calendar of the West Country, though it has shrunk somewhat since its zenith in the mid-nineteenth century, when it often attracted an entry of nearly 100,000 sheep.

Wilton is also an important military centre and during the Second World War had the headquarters of the Southern Command at Wilton House. To an earlier association with the Army the town owes its remarkable Italian-style parish church, for it was built through the enthusiasm for Byzantine architecture of a Russian-born countess of Pembroke and her son, Lord Herbert of Lea, who was War Minister at the time of the Crimean War.

The church strikes a note of incongruity in this ancient town, but it is a very impressive edifice, with an equally imposing interior rich in mosaics and marble. Of much greater antiquity, though restored in the nineteenth century, is the little flint church of Fugglestone St Peter, on a corner site by the Great West Road. Fugglestone and the adjacent Bemerton, between Wilton and Salisbury, were ministered by saintly George

Herbert for three years up to 1632, when he died of consumption at the early age of forty. Here, perhaps inspired by the pastoral peace of the meadows over which he regularly walked between his two churches, he wrote his well-known paraphrase of the 23rd Psalm, 'The God of love my shepherd is', as well as a number of other favourite hymns.

Bemerton grew up around a ford, long disused, where the river was crossed by the Roman road from Durnovaria (Dorchester). On the downs above the village, in the year 1194, Richard I staged a magnificent tournament, one of the first to be held in England. Both Bemerton village and the down are now almost submerged in the suburbs of Salisbury, the twelfth-century event being commemorated by the name of a residential street, Tournament Road.

On the other side of the river, on the downs that are the watershed between the Wylye/Nadder and Ebble valleys, Salisbury 'Race Plain' is now the scene of some of the most important events in the racing calendar. The present races were instituted in 1722, but races of sorts were being run there nearly a hundred years earlier. Aubrey relates that 'Henry, Earle of Pembroke (1570-1601) instituted Salisbury .Race, which hath since continued very famous, and beneficiall to the city . . . This race is of two sorts; the greater, fourteen miles, beginnes at Whitesheet and ends on Harnham-hill, which is very seldom runn, not once perhaps in twenty yeares. The shorter begins at a place called the Start, at the end of the edge of the north downe of the farme of Broad Chalke, and ends at the standing of the hare-warren, built by William Earle of Pembroke, and is four miles from the Start.'

Aubrey further records that the four-mile course used to be run in 'five minutes and a little more' by Peacock, who was a 'bastard barb' and 'the most beautiful horse ever seen in this last age, and was as fleet as handsome.'

The home ground of South Wilts Cricket Club is at Bemerton. Although Wiltshire has no first-class cricket team it has an honourable cricketing history, extending back to the reign of George III, and in 1854 Bemerton was the scene of a notable match between South Wilts and All England, which the home team won by three runs.

Below the Race Plain are the villages of Netherhampton and Quidhampton, the latter having once possessed a mumming play of which the complete script has been preserved by Miss Olivier.

Following the valley of the Wylye upstream from Wilton we find ourselves travelling more north than north-west, past the hamlet of Ditchampton, which was once the home of my old friend and fellow-farmer, A. G. Street, and where in an earlier age the Knights of St John of Jerusalem had a priory. Like the other valleys of the Plain, the Wylye for most of its length (roughly eighteen miles from Warminster to Wilton) is narrow, with just room for a village and a road on either side of the river before the scarp of the downs has to be ascended. In consequence, the villages tend to be arranged in pairs, one on either side of the river, while two parallel roads, again one on either side of the river, run from end to end of the valley.

The first pair, upstream from Wilton, are South Newton (with its hamlet of Stoford) and Great Wishford. South Newton's church is relatively modern, having been reconstructed by the same Lord Herbert of Lea who was responsible for Wilton church, but the church of St Michael at Wishford is mediaeval, much of it dating from the thirteenth century. It has several interesting memorials.

One is to Sir Richard Grobham, whose chief claim to fame is that he slew a wild boar, one of the last to inhabit the district, after an epic chase that ended on the banks of the Wylye. Mortally wounded, the boar managed to swim the river, expiring on the far bank. Ever since, the owner of the meadows on the near side of the river has been able to claim a pitch of hay annually from the spot where the boar died. The chase took place in the reign of Elizabeth I. Sir Richard was steward to Sir Thomas Gorges, founder of Longford Castle (see page 59), and the Spanish Armada treasure ship that provided the capital for the building of Longford also evidently set up Sir Richard as lord of the manor at Wishford.

The second knight commemorated in a monument in Wishford church is Sir Thomas Bonham. Sir Thomas, having no treasure ship to fortify his fortune, which evidently was at a low ebb, was so alarmed at the prospect of increasing his family that, when twins arrived, he set off on a Crusade to the Holy Land (this was in the fifteenth century) and was gone for seven years. Obviously he was one of those unlucky persons for whom nothing ever goes right, for when he arrived back he was unshaven, unwashed and so shabby that even his wife failed to recognise him until he had had a bath. Calling off a marriage into which she was about to enter with another man, she resumed her wifely duties with Sir Thomas and within a year presented him with more additions to his family. Septuplets! They were all taken to church in a sieve to be baptised, and brass figures of all nine little children were set in the Bonham memorial, which can still be seen, though some of the children have disappeared. The sieve, too, was hung in the church for centuries, and John Aubrey, writing in 1664, says that old men then living had seen it there. A sieve with seven dolls in it used to be carried in the Wishford Oak Apple Day procession (see below). Oddly, a somewhat similar story is told of Upton Scudamore, farther up the river.

In the churchyard wall at Wishford is a series of stones inscribed with the price of a gallon of bread at various dates, selected to no obvious pattern and starting with 1800.

Wishford is, however, best known for its celebrations of Oak Apple Day, 29 May. These are supposed to commemorate a victory scored by the villagers of Wishford against an encroaching earl of Pembroke in a past century, who tried to interfere with their immemorial right to gather and cut wood in the Forest of Grovely on the hill above the village. In fact, the customs belong to a much earlier period and are probably a survival of a prehistoric festival of the green woods, such as was celebrated throughout much of Europe.

What happens is that very early on the morning of Oak Apple Day, long before light, all the inhabitants of Wishford are awakened by a 'tin-pan' band. The youngsters of the village patrol the entire place, making as much noise as possible to ensure that every resident gets up and performs his duty, which is to tramp a mile or so up the hill to cut green wood. Most of the villagers go with the purpose of cutting green boughs to decorate their houses and the church. Prizes are offered for the best decorated houses and also for the oak branches possessing most oak-apples. Some dedicated gardeners, however, with a commendable sense of occasion, take the opportunity of cutting bundles of bean-rods and pea-sticks.

In mid-morning a bus takes a party of villagers, dressed in Victorian costumes, to Salisbury Cathedral where they lay an offering of green oak boughs before the high altar. Then a cheer-leader raises the shout,

'Grovely! Grovely! Grovely! and all Grovely!'

to which the group responds. Afterwards they engage in a traditional dance on the lawn outside the west door of the cathedral.

In earlier times it seems that the dance was performed inside the cathedral, before the altar. When it was over, the Wishford people did not go straight home but joined in a somewhat riotous fair held in the Cathedral Close. In the staid Victorian era this was regarded as unseemly, so nowadays the fair, which is a village fête of the usual type, is held at Wishford, preceded by a lunch attended by local gentry and dignitaries, including, as a rule, the mayors of Salisbury and Wilton.

The lunch now is not centred around the 'fat buck' to which the villagers are traditionally entitled. The Wishford celebrations are based on a document, of which two copies survive, called *The Sum of the Ancient Customs belonging to Wishford and Barford out of the Forest of Grovely,* which states that the two villages are to have one fat buck every Whitsuntide, to be divided equally between Wishford and Barford. The rangers were to provide this, but if they did not the villagers could go and help themselves. As compensation, the villagers had to pay to the rangers one white loaf, one gallon of beer and a pair of gloves, or 'twelve pence in money'.

The sale of Midsummer Tithes is another ancient custom preserved at Wishford. The grazing rights on two small pastures, totalling about $4\frac{1}{2}$ acres, are sold by auction by a churchwarden just before sunset on Rogationtide Monday. He walks up and down the church path, between the gate and the church porch, and, using the church key as a hammer, knocks down the rights to the last bidder before the sun disappears below the horizon. The rights last from the date of the sale to 12 August.

The long swell of downland which is the watershed between the Wylye and Nadder valleys and is crowned towards its eastern end by the Forest of Grovely is studded with prehistoric earthworks. A Roman road, leading from Sorbiodunum to the Mendips, runs along its crest, striking a course amid tumuli, Celtic field outlines and an assortment of ditches of unknown purpose. There is a hill-top earthwork to pair with most of the villages of the Wylye. Grovely Castle looks down on Little Langford; East Castle on Hanging Langford; Bilbury Rings on Wylye; Stockton Earthworks on Stockton; while on the other side of the valley Codford Circle occupies a hill site above Codford, and Yarnbury Castle is an impressive and complex Iron Age fort close to the A 303 road on the downs between Wylye and Winterbourne Stoke. Until nearly the end of the nineteenth century a big sheep fair was held annually within the ramparts of Yarnbury, – always pronounced, incidentally, 'Yarnboro' by local people.

Down in the valley a mound by a former ford in the village of Sherrington marks the site of a strong mediaeval castle, and the churches are rich in memorials of mediaeval knights. Steeple Langford church has a tombstone decorated with the carved figure of a huntsman in a long gown, carrying a horn. He is supposed to represent Waleran, a favourite of William the Conqueror, under whom he was Ranger of the New Forest, though the tomb may be of a later member of his family. In Boyton church is the tomb of a Crusader, Alexander Gifford, whose family held the manor for hundreds of years in the Middle Ages. Another famous mediaeval family in these parts were the Lovels, who gave their name to Upton Lovell and who have monuments in the parish church. Codford St Mary possesses, besides the family tombs of the Mompessons, a pulpit that stood in the church of St Mary's, Oxford, at the time of the Reformation.

One of the loveliest of all chalk streams, the Wylye is a fisherman's paradise, its fishing rights jealously preserved. It is best enjoyed from the quiet lanes that meander along its southern banks; life on the other side of the river is made uncomfortable by the almost incessant traffic that thunders along the main road between Salisbury and Bristol. Where that highway is crossed by the A 303 the village of Wylye is, at the time of writing, watching its home meadows being ripped apart by giant machines constructing a major road roundabout and by-pass. Like the Avon, the Wylye is hemmed in, on the north, by the military territory of Salisbury Plain, and during the wars of the present century large temporary camps have been established at several places. Because of the proximity of the stone quarries of Chilmark, in the Nadder valley on the other side of the downs, the manor-houses of the Wylye are stone-built and handsome; and stone is used even in some of the cottages and barns.

William Cobbett, passing this way in 1826, was greatly impressed by the valley. 'Fine, very fine' he repeatedly calls it and says that from Heytesbury to Warminster it is 'singularly bright and beautiful'. But the beauty was marred for him by his encounter with a party of ragged men and boys who had walked twelve miles from Bradford-on-Avon to go nutting in the hazel woods near Heytesbury. He went without supper and breakfast 'in order to give these chaps a breakfast for once in their lives. There were eight of them, six men and two boys; and I gave them two quartern loaves, two pounds of cheese, and eight pints of strong beer'. He comments, too, that the valley was so depopulated that the church at Bishopstrow would hold the 2,080 people who lived between Warminster and Salisbury, though there were, in fact, twenty one village churches to accommodate them.

Where the Wylye valley broadens into a plain at the approaches to Warminster, Heytesbury, now by population only a village, was once a prosperous borough sending two Members to Parliament. It had a weekly market and a fair, on 14 May, which was still being held in the 1860s. It has a stone lock-up and some interesting almshouses, rebuilt in the eighteenth century on a fifteenth-century foundation.

Codford lies on the right side of the river to share in the business brought by the main road. Its inn, The George, was once the popular overnight call for carters taking waggonloads of corn to the great market at Warminster. Nearby is the old wool store, where bales by the hundred were stored as they came in from the big sheep farms of the Plain.

Stockton, a mile or so away but on the quieter side of the valley, has a documented history extending back to 901, when the lord of the manor was a nobleman named Wulfhere, and it is said that the boundaries of the parish were just the same then as they are now. Stockton is one of those villages which have been fortunate in its chroniclers, for the parson, the Rev. T. Miles, wrote a detailed description of it in 1847, and Mr Yeatman-Biggs, another resident, did the same about a hundred years later. Both record some of the old customs observed in the village. On Pancake Day the village children 'went a-shroving', singing a traditional song; May Day saw more celebrations; on Whit Monday the Stockton Club paraded, led by Stockton Band; 6 July was the date that Stockton Feast 'began a week of jollity'; several farmers gave Harvest Home suppers; and at Christmas Stockton was one of the villages which preserved a mumming play. Stockton House is a handsome mansion of Elizabethan or Stuart date, and the church was begun before Salisbury Cathedral.

On the outskirts of Heytesbury the long scarp of the downs north of the river becomes higher, steeper and more dramatic and swings away north-north-west. From its crest two mighty Iron Age fortresses,

Battlesbury and Scratchbury, look down on the Warminster plain. Battlesbury in particular is one of the most impressive earthworks in the county, with multiple ditches and ramparts. It is in the parish of the valley village, Bishopstrow, where, in an age long after the hilltop settlement was abandoned, St Aldhelm on a missionary journey stuck his staff into the ground while he was preaching. To the amazement of the congregation, the staff budded and in due course became the ancestor of a flourishing grove of trees — hence, it is said, the name 'Bishop's trow' or 'Bishop's trees', though an etymological dictionary says the derivation is 'Bishop's cross'. Still, St Aldhelm was here, and the church is dedicated to him.

My father, who was born in 1874, could remember Warminster as a great corn market. In the days before motor transport lines of waggons loaded with grain used to converge on the town, where the carters parked their vehicles along the broad high street. Farmers haggled with merchants in the street, selling their produce by the waggon-load instead of by sample, as nowadays. It was then much the same as Cobbett observed it in 1826, commenting:

'Everything belonging to it is solid and good. There are no villainous gingerbread houses running up, and no nasty shabby-genteel people; no women trapesing about with showy gowns and dirty necks ... A really nice and good town. It is a great corn-market; one of the greatest in this part of England; and here things are still conducted in the good, old honest fashion. The corn is brought and pitched in the market before it is sold; and, when sold, it is paid for on the nail; and all is over, and the farmers and millers gone home by daylight.'

The carters took longer on their homeward journey and often carried back waggonloads of coal, which was brought to Warminster from Radstock. John Aubrey, writing in the 1660s, also found Warminster 'the greatest corn-market by much in the West of England. My bayliff has assured me that twelve or fourteen score loades of corne on market-dayes are brought thither.' He adds that 'hither come the best teemes of horses', especially for work with coaches.

Warminster continues to be busy, not nowadays as an agricultural market town but as a shopping centre for the neighbouring villages and military establishments and a halt for travellers on the congested A36 road. Its broad main street, no longer deeply rutted by waggons, gives the town centre a spacious appearance. Most of the buildings are modern and undistinguished, though the church of St Lawrence has a fourteenth-century nave and the fine old grammar school, where Dr Arnold of Rugby was a boy, was built in the eighteenth century.

The harmonious name, Warminster, remains a mystery. According to the experts, it should mean 'the minster or monastery church by the river Ware or Were', but there is no trace of such a church, and residents argue about whether there was ever a river of that name.

At Warminster we have broken away from the enfolding chalk hills. Westwards it is fairly level travelling for the last three or four miles to the Somerset border. Corsley, on the boundary, has a splendid Tudor house where the brother of Sir Walter Raleigh lived and where Sir Walter was a frequent visitor. A couple of miles north of Warminster the village of Upton Scudamore was the mediaeval home of the Scudamore family, members of which lie in their knightly tombs in the Norman church.

If, however, we wish to continue following the Wylye valley we have to turn abruptly southwards just before we reach Warminster. We still have another seven or eight miles to go to reach the headwaters of the river, at the end of what is locally known as the Deverill valley. Here are four villages, reading from north to south, Longbridge Deverill, Brixton Deverill, Monkton Deverill and Kingston Deverill. Before we venture into this narrow coombe, we shall wish to see the lions of Longleat! Longleat House, the home of the marquess of Bath, whose family has for generations dominated all this part of Wiltshire, lies in beautiful wooded country on the Somerset border, south of Corsley. It is best viewed first from Heaven's Gate, a hill-top vantage-point, in June when the rhododendrons are in bloom. Years before the lions took up residence and the house was open to the public, a visit to Heaven's Gate to see the rhododendrons was a favourite week-end excursion for Wiltshire and Somerset folk. I remember going there by motor-coach one Easter Monday in the 1930s.

Longleat House stands on the site of a mediaeval priory of the Black Canons. At the time of the dissolution of religious houses it was bought by Sir John Thynne, who lived there till it was burnt down in 1567. He spent the next twelve years supervising the construction of the magnificent house which has been the home of his family ever since. It was built in the then newly-popular Italian style, and a descendant of Sir

13 (above) *The superb gardens of the eighteenth-century Stourhead House at Stourton. 14* (below) *Longford Castle*

John, the fourth marquess of Bath, employed Italian craftsmen to make the internal decorations and furniture match. In the eighteenth century the celebrated landscape gardener, 'Capability' Brown, was employed to lay out the formal gardens, orangery and terraces, which he did with his usual genius and, one imagines, a complete disregard of the cost.

During its long career, Longleat has been visited by a succession of reigning monarchs, beginning with Elizabeth I, and has offered hospitality to many well-known people. Among them was Bishop Ken, friend of the first Viscount Weymouth, who, on being deprived of his bishopric of Bath and Wells in the reign of William III and Mary, made his home at Longleat for twenty years, during which he wrote most of his hymns.

The present marquess of Bath, faced with the now familiar problems of maintaining a huge and elaborate house and park, pioneered, with James Chipperfield, the idea of turning the inner section of his estate into a wild-life park, in which visitors could see wild animals running free. The lions of Longleat have now become world-famous and, with the other large animals for which accommodation has been found, attract increasing numbers of tourists.

In the demesne village of Horningsham is a unique example of a style of architecture very different from that of Longleat House. It is Horningsham Old Meeting House, the oldest non-Catholic place of worship in England and perhaps the oldest Protestant chapel still in regular use in the world. A group of Scottish masons who were helping in the building of Longleat were encouraged by Sir John Thynne to erect this little thatched chapel for their worship, and the date they inscribed on it, 1566, is still easily legible. A row of cottages built for them still stands and is known as Little Scotland.

I have a small personal interest in the Old Meeting House, for on the occasion of its fourth centenary, in 1966, I mentioned in an article for a Canadian magazine the mystery of the missing communion set, which had been in use from the time of the founding of the chapel till about 1816. A new communion set was then purchased, and the old one — a rare link with pre-Reformation England — passed into the possession of the minister, Rev. Joseph Silcox, who soon afterwards emigrated to Canada, taking it with him. As a result of my article the communion set was located. It is on exhibition now in the Elgin County Historical Museum

15 The main street, Lacock

at St Thomas, seven miles from the Ontario town of Frome, of which Rev. Silcox was one of the founders.

Many visitors to the Longleat wild-life park find themselves approaching it by roads which give views of an imposing isolated hill. This is Cley Hill, an island outcrop of chalk which once stood like a beacon over the tangled Forest of Selwood. It is crowned by earthworks and tumuli and is a landmark for miles around.

It is on the highest ridge of Selwood that Henry Hoare of Stourhead erected in 1772 a tall triangular tower to mark the alleged spot where King Alfred mustered his army to fight the Danes in his Whitsuntide campaign of 878. *The Anglo-Saxon Chronicle* says that the rendezvous was at 'Ecgbrythes stane', from which Brixton Deverill is commonly supposed (though erroneously, according to some etymologists), to have derived its name. Whether or not Alfred's Tower marks the exact location, the army must have assembled somewhere among the woods of these frontier hills.

The largest village on the Wiltshire side of Selwood is Maiden Bradley. The 'Maiden' element in its name refers to a twelfth-century priory hospital for leper girls which stood on the site of Priory Farm. Bradley House was the home of the Seymour family, from whom came the dukes of Somerset who wielded almost royal power in the reign of Edward VI. Another scion of the family was Sir Edward Seymour, who was Speaker of the House of Commons in the reign of Charles II and whose impressive marble monument adorns the fourteenth-century church. General Ludlow, who commanded a Parliamentarian army and who was one of the judges at the trial of Charles I, was born at Maiden Bradley.

Probably because of its isolated situation, old customs lingered long at Maiden Bradley. Records exist of a ball game traditionally played on Long Knoll (a 945-foot hill nearby) on Palm Sunday, of a traditional village dance, of a riotous game intriguingly named Bumball Toopy and played in public houses, and a mumming play. The custom of beating the bounds was also observed until about the middle of the nineteenth century. The villagers must have needed the encouragement provided by a cart-load of food and ale which accompanied them on their perambulation, for the parish boundaries must measure the best part of twenty miles and climb to the tops of four or five of the highest hills in Wiltshire. If on their journey they happened to meet a stranger they gave him a meal, then stood him upside down in a shallow hole and beat his backside with a shovel, so that he would remember the whereabouts of the parish boundary, too.

The Deverills are quiet, secluded villages, hidden by the downs and clinging close to their little river, here called the Deverill rather than the Wylye. Sir John Thynne, who built Longleat, is buried in the church at Longbridge Deverill, on a wall of which hangs his helmet. Kingston Deverill has a pile of sarsen stones, which, like Alfred's Tower, is said to mark the spot where Alfred met his army.

Before we leave the Wylye we must penetrate its tributary valleys. These converge on the main stream from the north and provide the natural drainage system for much of Salisbury Plain. The only downland valley with permanent water is that of the little river Till, which flows from Shrewton through Winterbourne Stoke and Berwick St James to join the Wylye at Stapleford. Like other winterbournes, it is fed in winter by springs which rise much farther up the downland valleys; for several months a pleasant little stream meanders through the fields of Tilshead and Orcheston. Another winterbourne which carries water in some winters curves through Chitterne and extends as far up as the abandoned village of Imber.

Innumerable dry valleys lead down from the crests of the chalk hills to the central basin of Salisbury Plain. Normally, the porous chalk can easily absorb the rainfall. Occasionally, however, exceptional circumstances turn these converging valleys into swirling torrents, and the surprised motorist finds his way barred by a muddy flood, sweeping across a road on what he supposed were waterless downs. This happened to me in two places, near Hindon and Teffont, when this book was being written early in 1975, and the people of Chitterne were preparing to barricade their doors with sandbags. The most memorable of all floods on Salisbury Plain was that of 1841. It swept down through Tilshead, Shrewton and Winterbourne Stoke one winter afternoon and destroyed forty seven houses, as well as barns and other farm buildings. We will let the Rector of Headington describe it, in a sermon which he afterwards published as a pamphlet and sold to help the rebuilding fund:

'This aweful work of devastation occurred yesterday week, occasioned by the rapid thaw of the large quantity of snow which had fallen two days before. About five o'clock in the evening, the waters, flowing from the hills, began to rush in a torrent, several feet deep, down the vale of Tilshead, carrying along, by its resistless force, soil and shrubs and farming produce and parts of buildings; and gradually increasing in depth and strength of current, as it rushed rapidly along towards the villages below. This happened just before nightfall, so that the inhabitants became aware of their danger. Had the flood come two or three hours later, after they had gone to rest, it is impossible to say how many would have perished. But so sudden and unexpected was the rising of the waters that some few families were not aware of the dangers; and had at that early hour retired to bed, without the least foresight of the horrors that awaited them . . .

'When the next morning dawned, what a sight did they behold! Many cottages had been swept clean away, as if they had never been; not a trace or sign of them left. Others with their roofs fallen in, one or two walls and a chimney standing, large barns levelled, and nothing left but the foundation stones which supported them; walls and fences of every kind thrown down; rafters and thatch of houses floating and eddying in the torrent. The loss of property amounts to many thousands of pounds . . .'

Incidents of the great flood were long remembered. In his book *Round About Wiltshire*, published in 1907, A. G. Bradley says he had met an old man of Tilshead who had saved his sow from drowning by dragging her upstairs. When I repeated this story recently I was told by one of my readers that it was a woman, not a man, who performed this feat and that she was his great-grandmother. With the money raised by public subscription new cottages for the homeless were built at Shrewton and Tilshead. They still bear plaques commemorating the 'Aweful Visitation'.

Shrewton is a five-fold village, consisting of the parishes of Shrewton, Maddington, Orcheston St Mary, Orcheston St George and Rollestone. The parish fields extend from this hub like segments of a wheel. Of the five parish churches, all within a mile or so of each other, the oldest is the tiny one at Rollestone, which was built in the thirteenth century. The two Orcheston churches are seventeenth-century.

A prominent feature of Shrewton village is its stone lock-up, which until recently stood in such a vulnerable spot on a corner near the centre of the village that it was demolished on more than one occasion by tank and lorry and has now been moved back for its safety. This would not have pleased the eminent dowser, Guy Underwood, who maintained that it was sited on a spot indicated by hidden subterranean springs. The lock-up has generally been regarded as a cell affording cold lodgings for prisoners being escorted, on foot, between Salisbury and Devizes, though some writers have thought that it had a more local significance, connected with The Gibbet, about half a mile away.

Old guide books and even post office directories extol the 'long grass meadows' at Shrewton and Orcheston. Those at Orcheston totalled only 2½ acres, but, says Thomas Davis of Longleat, writing in 1811, 'the crop they produce, in some seasons, is so immense and of so good quality that the tithe hay of them was once sold for the sum of five guineas'. The grass is, in fact, the black grass, or creeping bent *(Agrostis stolonifera),* regarded nowadays as a weed. One supposes that here its reputation must have been achieved by comparison with the poor, thin herbage of the surrounding downs, though no doubt the grass grew luxuriantly in meadows subject to winter flooding.

Now an undistinguished downland village, Tilshead appears in the *Domesday Book* (1086), as a prosperous town, with sixty six burgesses. Dr W. G. Hoskins, in *Provincial England,* comments: 'It was one of the largest boroughs in Wiltshire, and it has been suggested that the only possible reason for a borough in the middle of the Wiltshire downs must have been the existence of sheep farming on a great scale all around it.' A vestige of its former prosperity is perhaps supplied by a recollection that Tilshead once had 'tutti-men', who presumably administered certain common and other rights, with considerable ceremony, much as the tutti-men of the ancient borough of Hungerford still do.

Imber, now a deserted village, was always one of the loneliest places in southern England.

> *Seven miles from any town,*
> *Little Imber on the down,*

says the old Wiltshire couplet. Now it is desolate as well as lonely, for, after gradually acquiring all the land for miles around, the War Department in 1943 demanded the evacuation of the village. The villagers understood at the time that their exile would be only temporary, but the exigencies of modern warfare persuaded the Army to keep it. Now cottages, farms and manor-house have fallen into ruin, aided by soldiers training in street fighting, the gardens are lost in weeds, no cattle walk the village lanes, no cats emerge from cottage doorways, and barbed wire enhances the desolation of the scene. The ancient church of St Giles is heavily protected against intrusion, and a service is held there once a year, but the Baptist chapel, though labelled 'Consecrated Ground', has been entered and ransacked. The public are admitted to Imber for the annual service and sometimes at other times, and when last I was there I found old anniversary hymn-sheets still littering the smashed pews of the chapel. Battered, abandoned and forlorn, Imber is no place in which to linger, and even if it were suddenly released by the Army I doubt whether many if any of the former inhabitants would want to return or whether new residents would want to live there.

Among the farming families of Imber were the Deans, one of whom has a stone commemorating an exploit of his on the downs between Imber and West Lavington. It is to be found, amid long grass, on the east side of the A 360 road just where the descent from the Plain to Lavington begins. The inscription reads:

'At this spot Mr Dean of Imber was attacked and robbed by four highwaymen in the evening of October 21, 1839. After a spirited pursuit of three hours, one of the Felons, Benjamin Colclough, fell dead on Chitterne Down. Thos Saunders, George Waters and Richard Harris were eventually captured and were convicted at the ensuing Quarter Sessions at Devizes, and transported for a term of fifteen years. This monument is erected by public subscription as a warning to those who presumptuously think to escape the punishment God has threatened against Thieves and Robbers.'

A version of the story that I have heard is that Farmer Dean challenged the highwaymen to a shooting contest. He threw his hat into the air, and he and the men shot at it in turn till his opponents had emptied their pistols. Mr Dean, however, had kept a charge in reserve and proceeded to hold up the highwaymen. When they ran away, he gave chase.

One of the interesting sidelights of the story is that the robbers seem to have been on foot.

SIX

The Nadder, The Ebble and Cranborne Chase

The anomalous character of the valley of the Nadder among the rivers of Salisbury Plain is due to its geological structure. From a base on the line Shaftesbury-Mere a wedge of limestone is driven deep into the chalk, its apex penetrating as far east as Barford St Martin. Between the towering crest of Great Ridge and Grovely to the north and the impressive scarp of chalk hills to the south, the Nadder villages are scattered over a broad vale of green meadows, abrupt wooded hills and gentle streams. In this well-watered land they do not need to cling to the river-banks, like the villages of the other valleys, but sit around haphazardly.

In the centre of the vale is the miniature town of Tisbury, an attractive little place of grey stone houses. An abbey stood here in Saxon times, but during the Middle Ages it was incorporated into the vast estates of the abbess of Shaftesbury. Fifteenth-century Place House, at the eastern end of Tisbury, was one of her possessions. Its splendid tithe barn, 188 feet long by 32 feet wide, with two porches and thirteen buttressed bays, is still used for storing agricultural produce. The barn has three threshing floors, where once men beat out grain with flails. When I was last there it was being used for pioneering operations in one of the latest techniques for storing grain, by refrigeration, – a happy blend of ancient and modern. The entrance to the farmyard is through two massive stone gatehouses, the outer one of which has two arches, one designed to admit a loaded waggon, the other a horseman.

The lovely church, in a delightful setting, dates only from the seventeenth century, though incorporating some Norman features, including the pillars that support the tower. In the churchyard a giant yew, split with age, is claimed by local people to be a thousand years old, which is quite possible. John Lockwood Kipling and his wife Alice, father and mother of Rudyard Kipling, are buried here. They lived in retirement in Tisbury on their return from service in India.

In status Tisbury vacillates between that of a large village and a small town. Having no established markets or fairs, it was for centuries overshadowed by its neighbour, Hindon. The railway, which established a station here but none at Hindon, brought a new prosperity to Tisbury, — a situation which has now changed, for Tisbury has no main road carrying traffic through it. In times past Tisbury has had stone quarries and a thriving cloth trade (as demonstrated by the local place-name, Tucking Mill); it possesses a street of shops, a depot for distributing agricultural goods and a factory (Parmiter's) for manufacturing harrows and other farm implements.

Nearby are the two castles of Wardour, the home for nearly four centuries up to 1944, of the earls of Arundell. The older castle, now a magnificent ruin, was built in the fourteenth century by a Lord Lovell, whose descendants held it until dispossessed during the Wars of the Roses. The Arundells, who bought it in 1570, were a celebrated fighting family whose members won renown on many overseas battlefields. The most famous of all, however, was Blanche, Lady Arundell, who conducted an heroic defence of Wardour Castle itself against a Commonwealth army in 1643. The odds were thirteen hundred besiegers against a garrison of twenty five men, but Lady Arundell conducted the defence with such spirit, backed up by her womenfolk who loaded muskets for the men, that the Castle held out for five days and five nights of the fiercest assaults. In the end, numbers told, and Lady Arundell agreed to honourable terms of surrender, which were broken as soon as the soldiers were safely inside the Castle. The place was thoroughly sacked, the loot being sent off to Shaftesbury in five cart-loads. Many priceless art treasures were destroyed, including paintings and 'one extraordinary chimney-piece, valued at £2,000, which they destroyed'.

Not long afterwards Lord Arundell, Lady Blanche's son, arrived on the scene and proceeded to besiege the Roundhead garrison which had been left in the Castle. The siege dragged on for a long time, until Lord Arundell, realising that the only way to force a conclusion was to sacrifice his inheritance, blew up much of the Castle. After the Civil War was over, he built a new house against one of the surviving walls, and this served as the family home until 1776. A new Wardour Castle, designed by James Paine and still standing, was then erected on a splendid new site on the other side of the park.

There is an intriguing sequel to the story. Old Wardour remains one of the most spectacular ruins in southern England. It has towering walls and battlements supporting no roof, stone stairways that lead to emptiness, trailing ivy, lawns studded with tall cedars, and a magnificent setting by a small lake . . . everything, in fact, that a ruin should have. After the new castle was built the Lord Arundell of the time used to take his guests across the park to see the ruins and regale them with its history. Often on summer afternoons they took a picnic, which they ate sitting on the lawns by the lake.

Further to enhance the attractions of this delectable corner, Lord Arundell decided to build a grotto — a fashionable idea at the time. On his estate, in one of the fields of Place Farm, Tisbury, stood a stone circle, resembling Stonehenge. Sir Richard Colt Hoare, describing in the early nineteenth century what it had been like, says it was 'a circular work with a vallum set around with stones, and a large stone placed erect in the centre.' According to Colt Hoare, Lord Arundell decided that the central stone was ideal building material for his grotto, so he caused it to be uprooted and carted to Old Wardour. It must have been a formidable task, for the stone was twelve feet high and four feet wide.

I visited Old Wardour a few years ago, in search of this stone. It was, in a way, easy to find. The grotto, which is extensive, forms one of the most prominent features of the Castle precincts. It is built against a steep bank, overhung by tall trees and separated from the front of the Castle by a wide lawn. There are tiny stone chambers, alcoves where one may sit and admire views of the Castle, a network of paths, and an abundance of great sarsen stones, honeycombed with age.

I examined a great stone, standing almost alone in a shrubbery, and decided that this must be the one I was looking for. Then I discovered another and was not so sure. And another. I made another study of the main part of the grotto and came to the conclusion that most of the stones would qualify.

Suddenly the solution occurred to me. Lord Arundell had not been content with one stone. He had carted the entire prehistoric stone circle to

Wardour for his grotto!

Searching for confirmation I eventually found it in another book of Colt Hoare's, a *History of Modern Wiltshire,* published in 1829. In a section about Place Farm, Tisbury, he writes:

'One of the fields is called "Lost Stones", and in the centre of it was formerly a circular work, with a vallum set around with stones. About the year 1792 Lord Arundell, employing the celebrated constructor of rock work, Joseph Lane, to form a grotto at Wardour, these stones were removed. In the centre of the original work, as far as I can remember it, stood three upright hewn stones of large dimensions, placed so as to form three sides of a square, and in the space between some human bones were found. These three stones were placed near the old castle at Wardour, and the bones deposited beneath.'

As far as I can ascertain, no-one in the present century has realised the significance of the grotto, which could repay a careful examination. Most of the stones resemble those of Avebury rather than those of Stonehenge, and some are honeycombed almost to the same extent as the Blowing Stone which stands not far from the Uffington White Horse, in Berkshire. The size and number of the stones in the grotto suggest that the circle was a larger and more important monument than has so far been realised.

The field name 'Lost Stones' has been forgotten, but some local people seem to have an idea as to where it was. A very large, flat sarsen stone in a hedge between two fields may offer a clue.

The Wardour estate features in certain dramatic episodes of local history in the eighteenth and early nineteenth centuries – the poaching wars of Cranborne Chase. Cranborne Chase was one of the great royal hunting forests of England. The hilly, wooded country along the Wiltshire-Dorset border was its heart-land, but its boundaries at one time bit deep into both counties as well as encroaching on Hampshire in the east. When the new Harnham Bridge was built (see page 51) the earls of Gloucester, who then held the hunting rights in the Chase, used to impale a stag's head on a pole at the bridge a fortnight before Midsummer and then throughout the summer would exact tolls on every waggon and pack-horse crossing the river. This was supposed to be compensation for disturbance to the hinds when they were dropping their fawns. All the severe Norman laws of the chase applied to the vast, thinly-populated country between Cranborne and Shaftesbury.

The gradual easing of those laws in later mediaeval times was helped here by the fact that for several centuries the Chase belonged to the Crown, who took, at the most, only an intermittent interest in it. During those years, especially on the Wiltshire side, the waste land was gradually claimed for cultivation, and new farms and estates were carved out.

Herein was a latent cause of friction, for the normal rights and interests of the farmers and landowners were at times in conflict with those of any owner of Cranborne Chase who cared to try to exercise his old forest rights. The earls of Salisbury attempted it when they were granted the Chase by James I, and much ill-feeling followed. For two centuries lawsuit followed lawsuit, and deer poaching developed into a kind of guerilla war, with occasional pitched battles fought. The climax came early in the nineteenth century with a determined effort by Lord Rivers, who had acquired the Chase, to re-establish the old rights. He failed, and at last the old quarrel subsided.

The essence of the argument was that the owners of Cranborne Chase had the right to hunt deer within its ancient boundaries and to clear away anything that interfered with their free movement. The ancient boundaries, however, included powerful estates of more recent origin; the earls of Arundell, for instance, took a poor view of the claim made by the Chase owners to hunt in Wardour Park. The nineteenth-century Lord Rivers went so far as to order all farmers within the old limits to pull down all their fences, so that the deer might wander at will over the farmland. And the incident which brought matters to a head was the action of a keeper who shot dead a dog which was quietly walking with its master, a farmer of Alvediston.

Poaching as generally understood and as practised in Wiltshire until earlier in the present century was a matter of a solitary countryman, or at most two or three, attempting to snatch a pheasant, hare or rabbit. Poaching in Cranborne Chase in the troubled years was very different. The instigators were not cottagers in search of an illicit meal but estate-owners and large farmers indignant at what they considered an affront. It offered excitement to several generations of hot-headed young country gentry. They organised bands of followers who, dressed in specially designed 'armour' of padded quilting and wicker helmets and armed with staves, fought battles with posses of keepers similarly equipped. With £30 the maximum penalty, it was good sport at little cost. When a law of George II stepped up penalties to a maximum of seven years' transportation for anyone caught twice, the gentry were deterred, but poaching continued as vigorously as ever under less affluent and more ruthless leaders. The fights became even more desperate, and murders occurred.

William Chafin, whose ancestor had been Chief Ranger in the Chase, wrote in his reminiscences in 1818:

'In or about the year 1738 a keeper of West Walk, whose name was Tollerfield, who had been to Fontmell church on the morning of Easter-day and had received the holy sacrament there, was way-laid and murdered as he was returning home in the middle of the day. He was soon found, quite dead, having been most dreadfully beaten and bruised with bludgeons or clubs, and his skull fractured . . .

Another murder of the like kind, and about the same time, was perpetrated in Lord Pembroke's Walk at Fernditch. One of his keepers was found dead, having been beaten in a most cruel manner with sticks or staves. One criminal alone was detected, although it is not doubted but many were accessory to the murder. This man, whose name was arraigned and tried at Salisbury, found guilty, and condemned to be hung in chains near the spot where the murder was committed; which sentence was duly executed. But, in the course of a few nights after, the gibbet was cut down, and the body carried away and thrown into a very deep well at some distance from the place. The weight of the irons carried it to the bottom, and it was not discovered till a long time after.'

So the dismal record goes on.

Towards the end of his book *Anecdotes and History of Cranborne Chase* Chafin, however, inserts a revealing and amusing episode:

'Another very old keeper attended the Chase Court, which was annually held at Rushmore, and was sworn to the truth of his presentment of all the Deer killed in a certain Walk, and how they were disposed of, to the best of his knowledge. When the Court was dismissed he joined others of his fraternity and told them that "he had taken the old oath, which he had done just threescore following years; but that he must not mind that, for he could have no peace nor content at home unless he made his old Jane's frying-pan hiss now and then; for she could not live without venison, having been so long used to it." '

Throughout the centuries from Norman times onwards the shadow of Cranborne Chase, with its feuds and forest rights, was a dominant fact of life in the valleys of the Nadder and Ebble. In even earlier times, Cranborne Chase and the adjacent valleys were 'different' from the surrounding countryside. The origin of the differences may perhaps be sought in Roman times, for Dr I. A. Richmond, in *Roman Britain,* states:

'It is calculated that under Roman rule the Cranborne Chase farmers were deprived of something like three-fifths of their yield, very different from the reasonable rates of taxation of one-twelfth or one-tenth which applied to other parts of the Roman world . . . The Belgae, who owned it, had been violently hostile to Rome and hard fighting had been required to conquer them. In these circumstances the terms of capitulation will not have been merciful, and there are numerous analogies in the Roman world for punishment of an obstinate resistance by the reduction of the hostile populace to serfdom.'

The excavations in Cranborne Chase, admirably conducted by General Pitt-Rivers in the 1880s, produced evidence of a dense population in Roman and pre-Roman times, in contrast with later times, when it became largely depopulated. There are echoes of past troubles in some of the legends which survive in the villages bordering the Chase, as at Patty's Bottom, a downland hollow in the hills above Bowerchalke, which Edith Olivier (in *Moonrakings*) states was 'supposed to have been the scene of a great battle between Romans and ancient Britons. Legend relates that the valley was filled with blood. On certain moonlight nights tramping is distinctly heard and horses without heads can be seen rushing madly about.'

It is interesting, too, that some of the villages deep in the woods of the Nadder valley retain their Celtic names. Some have seen in the Gawen family which held the manor at Alvediston for centuries in mediaeval times a link with the Sir Gawain who was one of the knights of King Arthur's Round Table.

We return to Wardour, which prompted this digression into the historical background of the district. It has one further claim to distinction. Somewhat surprisingly, in view of the attitude of the owners of Cranborne Chase, it is the home of English fox-hunting, the South and West Wiltshire Hounds having been active here as early as 1690.

On the other side of Tisbury Fonthill Park, with its villages of Fonthill

Bishop and Fonthill Gifford, is one of the great estates of southern England, the home of Lord Margadale. Here one of the streams which form the headwaters of the Nadder has been dammed to form a delightful lake, set amid tall trees and usually alive with waterfowl. Extensive and well-managed farms surround the park which is the nucleus of the estate and which still contains a few reminders, in the form of walls and tunnels, of the grandiose activities of a previous owner, the eccentric William Beckford.

This eighteenth-century millionaire was the son of a Lord Mayor of London, who had been a close friend of William Pitt and who had derived a vast fortune from West Indian estates. On succeeding to the family fortune, young William set about spending an income of £100,000 a year, which he did with marked success. In an age when estate-owners were vying with each other in erecting towers, Grecian summer-houses, grottoes and other follies Beckford went one better. The enormous house he built, 'Fonthill Splendens' as it was dubbed, was one huge folly. The great central tower he proposed to make as high as the cross on St Paul's Cathedral, and he pushed his army of workmen so vigorously, urging them on at night by light of torches, that shoddy workmanship caused it to collapse. Undeterred, he started again. It stood for a few years and then crashed, destroying much of the great house in its fall. He was then living at Bath, at a house from which he could see Fonthill tower, twenty miles away. His fortune had evaporated, though not so much through his extravagances as because of the abolition of slavery and consequent deterioration of his West Indian plantations.

One of his eccentricities of which traces still remain was the building of a wall twelve feet high around the estate. It was the result of a sudden decision when he felt outraged by the intrusion of a pack of hounds in cry after a fox one day as he was peacefully meditating in the park. He was, as a matter of fact, an able literary practitioner, his greatest work being an imaginative fantasy, *Vathek,* which has flashes of genius.

North-west of Fonthill the large village of Hindon, on the edge of the Nadder basin, is, unlike Tisbury and the Fonthills, a downland village. Hindon was deliberately planned as a town, by its owner, the bishop of Winchester, at the same time as the bishop of Salisbury was building his new cathedral in the meadows. It had a bailiff and burgesses, a weekly market and two annual fairs and sent two Members to Parliament until the Reform Act of 1832 but never became a prosperous town. Two-thirds of the place was destroyed by fire on July 2nd, 1752, after which Hindon was rebuilt in the Georgian style, though on the general mediaeval plan, one of the chief features of which is the broad high street.

Nearby are East and West Knoyle, the former the birthplace of Sir Christopher Wren, whose father was rector there and the designer of the ornamental plaster-work in the chancel of the church. Here, in lush pasture-land, the Nadder vale merges with that of the Stour — the Blackmore Vale of Dorset — the watershed being so ill-defined that it is impossible to tell at a glance which valley one is in.

In the far south-western corner of the county, the little town of Mere, whose name emphasises that it has always been a boundary settlement, stands on one of the headstreams of the Stour, looking south across the meadows though flanked on the north by some of the most imposing chalk hills of Salisbury Plain. Once as lonely and remote as a frontier town should be, Mere has lately become far too busy for its comfort, for since the A 303 has come to be regarded as the main highway from London to the West its narrow, sharp-angled streets are frequently, and especially at holiday week-ends, jammed with traffic. Normally adequate car parks, however, help to make it a popular mid-day halt for travellers, who find refreshment at the two handsome inns, the Ship and the Talbot, which face each other across the main street. The eye is caught by the ornate wrought-iron sign of the Ship, the work of a Mere clock-maker, Kingston Avery, in the early eighteenth century. A pleasant place of grey stone and a number of seventeenth- and eighteenth-century houses, Mere has also one of the finest churches in Wiltshire, dating partly from the thirteenth and partly from the fifteenth centuries. Its 100-foot tower dominates the town, though higher still is Castle Hill, on which in 1253 Richard, earl of Cornwall, built a castle, which has long since disappeared. At Mere white-bearded old William Barnes kept a small school and wrote his haunting poems about Blackmore Vale.

Zeals and Stourton, west of Mere and also in the Blackmore Vale, belong to Wiltshire, though very near the border. The lakes at Stourhead are the source of the river Stour which eventually finds its way into Christchurch Harbour. They form a part of the lovely park of Stourhead, with its fine eighteenth-century mansion, daffodil-showered lawns, summer-houses disguised as classical temples, thickets of rhododendrons and azaleas, rockeries, grottoes and numerous other features of landscape artistry created by the fertile imagination of the owner, Henry Hoare the Second. Somewhat incongruously, a central feature of the gardens is the Bristol Cross, which stood in the middle of Bristol for four hundred years from 1373. Now the property of the National Trust, Stourhead is a mecca for tourists and for local people at week-ends in blossom-time. The interior of the house is an Aladdin's cave for art lovers, among its most important treasures being a splendid collection of Chippendale furniture, Thomas Chippendale the younger having worked here for a time. In the early nineteenth century Stourhead was the home of Sir Richard Colt Hoare, whose histories of ancient and 'modern' Wiltshire are invaluable sources of information and who was one of the pioneers of scientific archaeology. It is true that his enthusiasm surpassed his skill, for in opening 379 barrows, mostly in Wiltshire, he destroyed much that would have been of value to better-equipped twentieth-century archaeologists, but he at least aroused the interest of local gentry in the prehistoric heritage of their estates.

From Stourton and Zeals the county boundary strikes south-eastwards across the Vale, skirting the hill-top town of Shaftesbury and hitting the chalk again on the towering ridge of Wingreen, 911 feet high. The natural geographical boundary should run along the crest, but at some time the parish of Tollard Royal, on the far side, has been incorporated into Wiltshire. Here we are again in the heart of Cranborne Chase. The royal personage referred to in the name of the village was King John who had a hunting lodge here. The lodge, much altered and known as King John's House, is now a private residence.

From the wind-battered beech clump on the top of Wingreen, now a National Trust property, paths and lanes lead along the ridge to Winkelbury Hill, which was once held by local people to be a favourite rendezvous of witches and where General Pitt-Rivers excavated a Saxon cemetery. From Wingreen, looking northwards, we gaze down on the headstreams of the Nadder in the extensive parishes of Donhead; from Winkelbury we see below us the village of Berwick St John, at the head of the Ebble valley.

Donhead is quite untypical of most Wiltshire villages. Far from being nucleated, it consists of ten or a dozen hamlets, either in the bottom of or perched on the scarps of steep coombes and approached by narrow,

16 (above) *Avebury Ring. 17* (below) *The White Horse on the Downs at Cherhill*

sunken lanes. Clear streams chuckle over stone beds and are dammed in places to form watercress beds. Exposed rock-faces of greenish stone are half-buried in hart's-tongue and other ferns and trailing ivy. The church of Donhead St Mary has several Norman and Early English features and a fine fifteenth-century tower. In this parish Wincombe Park, which has one of the sources of the Nadder, was for a time the home of the historian, Sir Arthur Bryant.

After passing through Donhead, the A 30 road from Shaftesbury to Salisbury, until recent years the main highway from London to the West, avoids the villages of the Nadder Vale, except the fringes of Fovant and Compton Chamberlayne, until it comes to Barford. Proceeding eastwards, one passes roads which lead off, on the left, to Wardour, Ansty (which still possesses a 70-foot maypole used regularly on May Day), Swallowcliffe and Sutton Mandeville. On the right, well back from the road, the downs which seal off the Nadder from the Ebble valley rise like a wall – an almost endless series of scalloped coombes. The steep, turfy slopes have offered a canvas which soldiers, who camped beneath them during the First World War, used to advantage, carving their regimental crests and other insignia, including a colossal outline map of Australia, deep into the chalk.

Compton Chamberlayne was for centuries the home of the Penruddocke family, a fact commemorated in the name of the village inn. The most celebrated member of the family was Colonel John Penruddocke, a devoted Royalist who in 1655 started an ill-timed revolt against the Puritan government. At the head of about two hundred horsemen he rode into Salisbury one March morning, arrested two judges and the sheriff and proclaimed Charles II king in Salisbury market-place. He received little support, however, and had to retreat to Devonshire, where he was captured and executed.

Barford and Burcombe are the last two stone villages of the Nadder, the valley of which here begins to be confined between ranges of chalk hills, like the other valleys of Salisbury Plain. Both are villages of ancient foundation, and Burcombe church still retains some Saxon work in the chancel walls.

In our survey of the Nadder vale we have by-passed a group of villages which lie under the northern downs, on the B-road that leads from Salisbury to Mere. Next to Barford, travelling westwards, is Dinton, a

18 The south side of the nave, Malmesbury Abbey

larger village than most in this valley and distinguished by a number of handsome stone houses, several of which belong to the National Trust. These include Philipps House, an imposing mansion set in a park and now let as a holiday home to the Y.W.C.A.; Lawes Cottage, where Henry Lawes, the composer, lived; and Little Clarendon. At Dinton was born Edward Hyde, who, starting life as the third son of a small landowner here, rose to be lord chancellor in the reign of Charles II and was made first earl of Clarendon.

The two Teffont villages, Teffont Magna and Teffont Evias, are attractive little places nestled along the banks of a clear stream which gushes, in considerable volume, from the earth where the chalk and greensand measures meet and tumbles down, among the gardens and trees, to join the Nadder. Each pleasant cottage by the side of the stream has its own private bridge to the front door, usually a stone slab. Teffont House, in Teffont Evias, is a handsome mansion dating from the reign of Henry VII.

Finally we come to Chilmark, where we might equally as well have started our exploration of the Nadder vale, for here are the main quarries of that splendid stone responsible for most of the architecture in south Wiltshire and in many places beyond the county boundary. The spire of Chichester cathedral is of Chilmark stone; so, of course, is Salisbury Cathedral, Wilton House and most of the great country houses in the vicinity. Chilmark quarries were worked by the Romans and were gradually extended in the course of centuries until they came to resemble a subterranean world. The main vault alone covers thirteen acres, and from it tunnels and corridors extend in all directions. The public cannot now, however, visit them, for they have for many years been used as a munitions store and are strictly guarded.

Chilmark is a good place to pause, for here the roadside hostelry, the Black Dog, an ancient inn with open hearths and much interesting cottage architecture, has a reputation for good food.

The least arduous way into the Ebble, or Chalk, valley from the Nadder is to veer south-west along the A 30, passing Whitesheet Hill where the old Shaftesbury turnpike descends from the ridge, and then to turn left to Berwick St John. There are other lesser roads from each of the Nadder Vale villages to its counterpart by the Ebble, but each involves a stiff climb over the rampart-like hills which are the frontier between the two valleys.

The villages strung out like a rope of beads along the narrow valley of the Ebble are, in order from west to east, Berwick St John, Alvediston, Ebbesbourne Wake, Fifield Bavant, Broadchalke, Bishopstone, Stratford Tony, Coombe Bissett (where the main Salisbury-Weymouth road crosses the valley), Homington, Odstock and Nunton, with Bowerchalke occupying a side valley to the south of Broadchalke. This secluded vale is bordered on the south by Cranborne Chase, with which its history is intimately connected. In mediaeval times much of the valley was Abbey land, belonging to either the abbess of Wilton or the abbess of Shaftesbury. At the time of the Dissolution, large sections of it passed to the earls of Pembroke, who are still among the chief landowners.

Broadchalke is the largest village in the valley and possesses a number of large and imposing brick houses. It is said that many of them were erected as winter residences for farmers from the Chase and other outlying farms who retreated hither for the sake of some social life during the dark months.

The Ebble valley, or Chalkbourne as earlier writers called it, is one of those fortunate districts with little history. Bishopstone, which has a fine fourteenth-century church, derives its name from the bishops of Winchester, who once owned the manor. The second element in the name Stratford Tony comes from Ralf Toni, who was William the Conqueror's standard-bearer at the Battle of Hastings and who was given the manor as part of his reward. Fifield Bavant's Norman church is one of the smallest churches in England, measuring only 35 feet by 14 feet.

An admirable little *History of Broadchalke* has been compiled by Mr H. M. Trethowan, who lives there. Though replete with fascinating details of life at various periods, it has virtually nothing of national or even regional interest to record. Lucky Broadchalke! How much more revealing of everyday life it is to read of the mediaeval village blacksmith who was fined one penny for any of his ploughshares that broke; of a freeman, Thomas Gawain, who in return for certain services was entitled to 'Christmas day dinner at the Abbey of Wilton and afterwards he could go on drinking as long as he could see without candles'; and of Edith Braunce who, having been given four ewes and two skeps of bees by the Church on condition that she supplied a one-pound candle every year, eloped with a man from Wilton, taking the sheep and bees with her.

Among the seventeenth-century residents of Broadchalke was John Aubrey, who had a small estate there and served for a time as churchwarden.

The Ebble valley seems to have been more densely populated in mediaeval times than at present. A number of hamlets that are now little more than single farms with workers' cottages were then quite populous villages. Croucheston, Flamstone, Faulston and Stoke Farthing are examples. The sites of several deserted villages can also be traced, and it seems likely that many of the hillside lynchets were carved out in those days of land shortage.

John Aubrey, who loved his little farm at Broadchalke, writes of the river:

'There are not better trouts (two feet long) in the kingdom of England than here ... The water of this streame washes well, and is good for brewing. I did putt in craw-fish, but they would not live here; the water is too cold for them.'

Nowadays the cool crystal stream has been laid out in watercress beds, on such a scale that the growers buy the elastic bands, with which they bunch the watercress, in half-ton lots.

The best churches in this valley are probably those of Broadchalke, Coombe Bissett (pleasantly situated on a bank looking across the main road to a duck-haunted pool and a picturesque barn), and Odstock, which has a fine Elizabethan pulpit. Odstock church has the distinction of a door which is never locked, the explanation of which is in the oft-told story of the gipsy's curse. The tale is set out in some detail in my book *The Folklore of Wiltshire*; I give here an outline.

Joshua Scamp was an honest gipsy who at the very beginning of the nineteenth century frequently camped with his family in a chalk-pit near Odstock. On one occasion his son-in-law borrowed a coat on a rainy night, went to South Newton and there stole a horse, leaving the coat to incriminate Scamp. For the sake of his daughter, Scamp refused to plead and was therefore condemned to death for horse-stealing and was hanged in public at Salisbury.

The event attracted much attention, for it was widely known that Scamp was innocent. The gipsy tribes in the region came to regard Scamp as a martyr and used to assemble at Odstock on the anniversary of his death. The celebrations, however, tended to centre around the Yew Tree

Inn and, as the years went by, became more and more uproarious. The villagers began to dread the annual visitation, and eventually the church meeting resolved to put a stop to it. They pulled up a briar rose that the gipsies had planted on Joshua's grave and locked the church door. Then they enrolled a posse of special constables to try to contain the explosion that they guessed would come.

They were right. The gipsies were furious. The climax of their indignation was the action of the Gipsy Queen who, perched on the churchyard wall, screamed out a stream of curses. She cursed the parson, the sexton, the churchwardens, a couple of renegade gipsies who had enrolled as special constables and, last of all, anyone who in the future should lock the church door.

One by one the curses worked out. The parson, of whom the Queen had said that within a year his voice should no longer be heard from the pulpit, had a stroke which affected his speech. The sexton, to whom it was predicted that death should come swiftly and suddenly, was found dead one morning at the roadside. The chief churchwarden, a prominent farmer, had his valuable herd of cattle destroyed by anthrax. A prophecy that no son of his would ever inherit the farm seemed to be justified by the fact that all his male children were born dead, and that, in the end, broken, he emigrated to Australia. The renegade gipsies mysteriously disappeared, though more than a hundred years later two skeletons, buried in a shallow grave on the downs, were thought to be theirs. In the present century two persons, a carpenter and, I believe, a curate, have both locked the church door and both have met an untimely death soon afterwards. After the second fatality, the church key was thrown into the river.

It is a dramatic story, around which I once wrote a radio play, *The Odstock Curse*.

On the downs above Odstock are two extensive yew woods, known as the Great and Little Yews. The sombre groves and avenues have the appearance of having been there from time immemorial. One boundary of the Great Yews is formed by a great earthwork known as Grimsdyke, which extends for some fourteen miles through the heart of Cranborne Chase. For much of its length it consists of a double bank with a ditch, five or six feet deep, between. It is generally supposed to belong to the period of the Saxon invasion.

On the other side of Odstock the once lonely downs towards Salisbury are now the site of Odstock hospital, where much pioneer work in plastic surgery has been done; while nearby is the common cold research station.

SEVEN

The Bourne Valley and the South-East

Although the Bourne valley is as long as any of the other river valleys of Salisbury Plain, the river Bourne carries a relatively small volume of water. For two-thirds of its length it is a winterbourne only. In winter its headwater springs rise in the pond at Burbage, but in summer the stream bed is dry everywhere north of Idmiston.

Burbage itself is best considered as a forest village. Savernake, now just to the north of it, once enveloped it on almost every side. Indeed, the two Collingbournes, Collingbourne Kingston and Collingbourne Ducis, were also forest villages in mediaeval times, for the extensive Forest of Chute here encroached on the valley from the east, over territory that is now as bare and treeless as any in Wiltshire. Although the Collingbournes are in a valley which leads directly south to Salisbury they were too remote to have any interest in that city until the era of motor traffic. Nineteenth-century directories record that carriers' carts from Collingbourne went to market at Marlborough and Andover, and when a railway came to link those two towns it established a station at Collingbourne Ducis.

Collingbourne Ducis, which derives its name from having once belonged to the duchy of Lancaster, had a church so old that it was in ruins at the time of the Domesday Book. It was rebuilt in the thirteenth century and holds the tombs of members of the Seymour family, who in the reign of Edward VI ruled England for a time but who, in the earlier age represented by the church memorials, spelt their name in the old Norman-French way – Saintmaur. An interesting mediaeval feature of the church is that its tower was adapted by some enterprising parson as a dovecot, with rows of specially-constructed nest-holes around the bells.

Of the two villages of Tidworth, about four miles south of Collingbourne, North Tidworth is in Wiltshire and South Tidworth in Hampshire. The county boundary here behaves in an erratic fashion, striking across the Bourne and excising for Hampshire a sizeable slice of territory east of the river, but there is, of course, no natural frontier between the undulating chalkland of Salisbury Plain and of the north Hampshire downs. Tidworth, once a typical downland village, with fine mansions in a setting of tall trees by the stream, is now a garrison town. It has barracks, cinemas, supermarkets and a military cemetery, with Tidworth House now an officers' club and the great natural amphitheatre nearby lending itself admirably to the spectacular nocturnal Tidworth Tattoo. I remember attending some of the last Tattoos before the Second World War, when special trains brought spectators from as far away as Cornwall and the Midlands. I believe that in 1938 the attendance topped 150,000. The support of army officers has much to do with the continuing activity of the Tidworth (or Tedworth, to give it its old name,) Hunt, which achieved considerable fame in the nineteenth century under its vigorous but eccentric master, Mr Assheton Smith, who lived at Tidworth Park.

On the downs to the west of Collingbourne, about midway between the Bourne and Avon valleys, is one of the few surviving downland villages of Salisbury Plain — Everley. Its name suggests that this, too, was once a forest village, for it is said to mean 'the glade of the wild boar'. It existed as long ago as the seventh century, when King Ina, according to local tradition, had a palace here. Before that the Britons of Roman and pre-Roman times had a fortified settlement on Sidbury Hill, about three miles to the south-east. Traffic now passes through Everley along the main road from Andover to Bath and Bristol, on a line approximately east and west. In former times the traffic flowed north and south, for the old downland highway from Salisbury to Marlborough runs through the village — the only village, indeed, which this well-routed road touched between Salisbury and the Pewsey Vale. Stage coaches passed this way and used Everley as a staging post.

Early in the nineteenth century Everley was subjected to a piece of arbitrary re-planning. The lord of the manor, Francis Astley, prompted by a new wife, decided that he wanted a zone of privacy around the manor house, so he pulled down the greater part of the old village, made a park on the site and rebuilt the village outside the precinct walls. Among the buildings then demolished were the old inn and the fourteenth-century church, the latter being the subject of a special dispensation by the bishop of Salisbury, on the grounds that it was 'in a serious and dilapidated state' and 'the present situation not being convenient'. A copy of an etching of the old church is still preserved in the new one. The parish registers contain interesting references to old customs which lingered long in this isolated village, including that of holding Christmas 'ales'. 'It was said there had been a custome long before, of makinge ye neighbourhood eat bread and cheese and drink beer at ye parsonage house on Christmas Day after evening praier', wrote a rector in 1610, and he strongly objects to continuing it, ostensibly because of its 'riotous' nature but more probably because he had to pay for the feast!

The reason why the old north-south highway through Everley is no longer used is that the way to the south has been blocked by military land. There are still living a few old people who can remember the days before the Army came to Salisbury Plain. The first incursion occurred in 1897, when the War Department bought a 300-acre farm near West Lavington. Between then and 1902 it acquired 43,500 acres of the Plain, including the chief estates of Tidworth, Bulford, Durrington and Ludgershall and the downland expanse which became the artillery ranges of Larkhill. The downland ridge between Tidworth and Bulford, culminating in Beacon Hill, is nowadays the heart of the Army domain.

Ludgershall, on the eastern side of Collingbourne and Tidworth, lies on the far side of the Bourne valley watershed, on the gentle slope inclining towards Andover. Nowadays an undistinguished little town, it has an impressive history, being a place of importance even in Saxon times. The Normans built here an imposing castle which dominated the countryside for several hundreds of years and played an important part in the civil wars of Stephen and Matilda. It has recently been excavated and opened to the public, with a resident warden.

In those days Ludgershall had regular fairs and markets, but later, after the castle had fallen into ruin, its prosperity declined. Cobbett, who visited it in 1826, described it as 'one of the most mean and beggarly places that man ever set his eyes on. The curse, attending corruption, seems to be upon it. The look of the place would make one swear, that there was never a clean shirt in it, since the first stone was laid. It must have been a large place once, though it now contains only 479 persons.'

Ludgershall was, in fact, a typical 'rotten borough' of those days, still sending two Members to Parliament but soon to be disenfranchised by the Reform Act.

The road south from Tidworth along the Bourne valley returns to Wiltshire at Cholderton, after a four-mile stretch in Hampshire. The church here, though consecrated only in 1850, has an interesting history. The rector in the 1840s, Rev. Thomas Mozley, found lying neglected on the quay at Ipswich an old oak roof of a church that had been destroyed at the time of the Reformation. So, as Cholderton church needed rebuilding, the rector went to immense trouble to fetch the roof from Ipswich and model his new church around it. The project cost in the end £6,000, of which the rector found £5,000 from his own pocket, an exercise which left him almost penniless.

In his account of the building Rev. Mozley relates how the work was held up for two months by a notorious poacher who, finding himself homeless because of his bad reputation, camped, with his wife and four children, in the church porch. 'With sailcloth he had made the small porch really a very comfortable apartment, though it was very cold. On Sunday he left a gangway. He had heard the old saying that if a man cannot get shelter elsewhere in his own parish he has a right to it in the church.' The village eventually got rid of the family by raising £20 or £30 to send them off to Canada.

At Cholderton is a grove of ancient yews reputed to be haunted and to have associations with 'the Druids'. The villages in this section of the Bourne valley, including Newton Tony, Allington and Boscombe, have an unusual number of ghost stories, many of which are told in my book *Folklore of Wiltshire*. Idmiston has a handsome church, parts of which date from the thirteenth century. At Boscombe the eminent and controversial theologian, Richard Hooker, was rector from 1591 to 1595, during which period he wrote four erudite books, *The Laws of Ecclesiastical Polity,* which earned him considerable fame. He was also a gifted preacher, his sermons being so popular that even in this remote parish he had to enlarge the church to accommodate the congregation. The church is much as it was in his day, and his rectory, haunted, still stands. Boscombe was the temporary home, too, of Dr John Smith, who, when recovering here from inoculation against smallpox, became fascinated by Stonehenge and wrote a lot of nonsense about it. Stonehenge is, indeed, only a few miles away over the downs, Boscombe parish having a common boundary with Amesbury. It used to be an easy walk over the springy turf, but now the way is barred by the giant aerodrome of Boscombe Down, testing-place of new types of aircraft.

Porton and Gomeldon, now populous villages, used to be hamlets or chapelries attached to Idmiston. An extensive tract of downland from Porton to the Hampshire border is occupied by Porton Experimental Station, a vast establishment primarily devoted to the conduct of hush-hush experiments of military significance. Though just what goes on there is secret, Porton has two ancillary roles of importance locally. One is that it is a major employer of labour and so provides a livelihood for a large proportion of villagers for miles around. The other is that it has incidentally preserved, and kept both plough and public away from, a splendid section of Wiltshire downland which in consequence is one of the best, though unofficial, nature reserves in the entire county.

South of Porton the Bourne valley is occupied by the villages of Winterbourne. Nowadays there are three of them, Winterbourne Gunner, Winterbourne Dauntsey and Winterbourne Earls, — all strip-shaped parishes each with a narrow section of river and a long ribbon of territory extending for miles on either side to the crest of the downs. Formerly each parish was split into two longtitudinally, so that in mediaeval times we had in addition Winterbourne Cherborough, Winterbourne Monachorum and the hamlets of Hurdcott and Ford (the last two still flourishing). All had mills, to which the waterless villages to the east used to send corn for grinding. The villages in effect merge with each other and are all known locally under the general name of Winterbourne.

The Winterbournes were fortunate in having a local historian, Mr C. H. Bray, who, from the 1930s to the 1950s, burrowed deeply into mediaeval records and produced a detailed history of the three parishes. They were important villages in the Middle Ages, Winterbourne Earls being part of the home estates of the great earls of Salisbury. Nowadays they are mainly residential, and the downs on either side, once empty, have been requisitioned for Army use, for an airfield and for a golf course.

Ford, the Winterbourne hamlet nearest Salisbury, derives its name from the former ford by which the Roman road from Winchester to Old

Sarum crossed the Bourne. Here in the thirteenth century lived Thomas
à Becket, then a parish priest at Winterbourne. When the king was in
residence at Clarendon Palace, a few miles to the south, Becket used to
walk over to officiate at services, and it is said that his path is still green.

The main A30 road from London to Salisbury crosses the Bourne at St
Thomas's Bridge — another memory of Becket and scene of many motor
accidents in the present century. Two villages, Laverstock and Milford,
occupy the river valley between the bridge and the confluence of the
Bourne with the Avon, three miles downstream. Both are of earlier
foundation than Salisbury, by which they have now been virtually
swallowed. The gaunt old lunatic asylum which once made Laverstock a
name of dread to generations of villagers in south Wiltshire has now been
demolished.

On the eastern side of the hill behind Laverstock is a hidden valley
inaccessible by any public road and occupied by farms on the Clarendon
estate. Here we are within the limits of the ancient Forest of Clarendon,
which once reached the eastern outskirts of Salisbury, as Cranborne Chase
did the southern. In fact, the infant city of Salisbury owed much of its
prosperity to the proximity of the Palace of Clarendon, a favourite retreat
of the kings of England from the time of William the Conqueror to the
Wars of the Roses.

The palace occupied a hill-top site on the eastern scarp of that hidden
valley and commanded a distant view of the cathedral. It probably began
its career as a hunting lodge in Saxon times, for a trial trench during the
excavations of the 1930s revealed traces of a building with a different
alignment below the Norman walls. Successive monarchs after William I
added to and improved it until in the thirteenth and fourteenth centuries it
was one of the largest and most magnificent residential buildings in
England, second only to the great Palace of Westminster.

The history of Clarendon Palace developed to a curious pattern.
Situated in a singularly peaceful part of the country, it offered a pleasant
haven to which the king and court could retreat and enjoy hunting in the
surrounding forests in uneventful times. This programme was reflected in
two notable characteristics of the palace. In an age of strong castles, the
palace was almost unfortified. It spread itself casually over about eighteen
acres and was, in some respects, a prototype of the later manor-house.
Also, it was occupied only at irregular intervals. Sometimes it was left

empty, apart from caretakers, for quite long periods, as, for instance, when a king was engaged in foreign wars or during domestic troubles. And, naturally, some kings had a greater affection for Clarendon than others. During the intervals when it was unoccupied the buildings often fell into disrepair or even became ruinous. Then a new monarch would demand that they be restored and enhanced. Consequently there are few buildings in England so fully documented as Clarendon Palace. From reign after reign detailed instructions and surveys are extant concerning work to be done there.

Early in the 1930s Dr Tancred Borenius, professor of mediaeval art at London University, who had been studying the documents conceived the idea of excavating the site and trying to match the records with the ruins. By permission of the late Mrs Christie-Miller, proprietor of the Clarendon estate, he began work in 1933 and continued for a couple of months or so each summer until interrupted by the outbreak of war. The half-finished task was never resumed.

The excavations made possible, however, the identification of the great hall, the royal quarters, the kitchens, the cellars, the royal chapel and several council chambers, including one known as the Antioch Chamber, because it was adorned by a huge mural depicting the combat of Richard I and Saladin before the walls of Antioch. Murals were, indeed, an important feature of Clarendon Palace. The best artists of the western world were hired to paint scenes of the campaigns of Alexander the Great, of the life and death of Edward the Martyr, of the miracles of St Catherine and a talismanic Wheel of Fortune. Fragments of the painted plaster, still retaining some of its vivid colouring were found during the excavations, as were many fine decorated tiles, also made and fired on the site.

Often in the course of the Middle Ages great affairs of state were debated and decided at Clarendon. Here Henry II and his contemporaries hammered out the Constitutions of Clarendon, which were supposed to regulate the respective powers of Church and State, and here too quarrels occurred between the headstrong king and the equally stubborn Thomas à Becket, who, as we have seen, was at one time a humble priest at Winterbourne. Here two prisoner-of-war kings, John of France and David of Scotland, dined and hunted with their captor, Edward III. Here, towards the end of the palace's career, Henry VI was confined in specially constructed quarters during periods of madness.

After the Wars of the Roses the parsimonious Henry VII made no attempt to restore the semi-derelict palace, and when, in the following century, Queen Elizabeth I came hunting in Clarendon Forest she and her party lunched in 'booths', the palace being then evidently too ruinous for even temporary occupation.

Doubtless it was used extensively as a stone quarry, and when the excavators began their work in 1933 little of the magnificent palace remained visible above ground. During the long years of neglect a dense wood had enveloped the site, so that it was possible to walk along a footpath within a few yards of the Great Hall and never know that a building had ever stood there. To that state it has again reverted. There is little to be seen, – apart from the fact that the site is private property.

Memories of the brilliant past of Clarendon, however, still linger in the district. Local people still tell tales of the ghosts of horsemen seen riding along a ridge which marked the road linking Clarendon with the Roman road between Sarum and Winchester. Near Alderbury shaped masonry from the dismantled priory of Ivychurch, the priests of which once attended to the spiritual needs of the court at Clarendon, can be seen built into the walls of a private residence. A fine chimneypiece in the Green Dragon inn at Alderbury (the 'Blue Dragon' of Charles Dickens) was probably taken from the priory.

Clarendon estate still retains its ancient boundaries more or less intact. They are much as they were in the thirteenth and seventeenth centuries, when surveys were made. John Aubrey, writing in about 1680, says;

'Clarendon Parke was the best parke in the King's dominion . . . This parke was seven miles about. Here were twenty coppices, and every one a mile round. Hunt and Palmer, keepers there, did averre that they knew seven thousand head of deere in that parke; all fallow deer.'

Hunt and Palmer are still remembered, having given their names to coppices within the forest. And a quite formidable deer-leap along much of the old boundary is a reminder of the deer (which are, incidentally, by no means extinct).

Clarendon Park occupies a wide arc of country due east of Salisbury and imposes a barrier between the city and the villages beyond. A few footpaths traverse it, but no public roads. On the far side of the estate is a ring of villages – Alderbury, Whaddon, West Grimstead, East

Grimstead, Farley and Pitton — once populated largely by retainers, keepers, rangers and others who earned a livelihood on the royal estate. Most of the cottagers were still doing so, either as employers of Clarendon Park or as independent craftsmen engaged in underwood work there, when I was born at Pitton.

Farley would seem to be an unlikely place in which to find a Wren-type church (in fact the architect was Alexander Fort, who like Wren had worked at Hampton Court and Kensington Palace). The village was the birthplace of Sir Stephen Fox, who was a contemporary and friend of Sir Christopher Wren, and no doubt this may have been how Fort came to be employed. Sir Stephen is said to have been a boy of poor parentage who by some means managed to secure a position at the court of Charles I. He accompanied Charles II into exile, contriving, in his capacity of household steward, to stretch the slender royal resources farther than was reasonably possible. After the Restoration he was rewarded with the post of Paymaster General to the Forces, which enabled him to accumulate a considerable fortune. Disappointed by the performance of his son, to whom he had looked to establish the dynasty of landed gentry he was bent on founding, in old age he married a second time. His new wife, a Lincolnshire heiress, delighted him by producing twin boys, one of whom in due course became the first earl of Ilchester, the other the first earl of Holland.

Sir Stephen maintained his links with his birthplace to the end of his life. Sir Stephen's sons acquired large estates in the district, the earl of Ilchester taking Pitton and Farley, the earl of Holland Winterslow, and the Ilchester estates passed into other hands as recently as 1912.

At Winterslow the earls of Holland made two attempts at creating a great park around a country mansion, in the approved eighteenth-century style. Both attempts were frustrated by fire, the second, in 1744, occurring when a ball to celebrate the completion of the building was in progress. After that the Holland family lost interest in Winterslow and transferred their resources to an estate nearer London, a decision which served their descendants well, for the residence they built was Holland House and the estate comprised Mayfair and much of the West End. At Winterslow one can still see the belt of beeches surrounding the home park and the gaunt old cedars in the middle. A new bungalow there in which I lived for a few years was said by villagers to be on the site of the

Holland House 'music-room'. When I asked for suggestions for a name
for the bungalow a local resident put forward *Foxland.* 'It's on land that
used to belong to the Foxes', she pointed out. So 'Foxland' it was.

The fields around Winterslow and Pitton abound in names which link
them with the West End of London — Piccadilly, Soho, Pimlico Firs.

Winterslow is really three villages — West, Middle and East (or The
Common) — with numerous outlying farms and hamlets. It is one of
Wiltshire's few hill-top villages and, sitting astride a Roman road,
probably has an unbroken continuity of occupation since Romano-British
times. Long before that, in about 1600 B.C., extensive flint mines were
being worked on Easton Down, and there are several barrows within the
parish. Excavations have revealed numerous Iron Age and Roman
remains on sites by the Roman road.

Ample material exists for a substantial book on Winterslow. There are
mediaeval documents relating to the three main manors, the records of the
Holland family and the work of archaeologists. Being left to its own
devices after the departure of the Hollands, the village bred a race of
sturdy, independent smallholders, who encroached on the old common
land, maintained resolutely traditional customs and became enthusiastic
nonconformists. Until within living memory it kept up its ancient
mumming play and other Christmas customs and the old rural industry of
truffle-hunting. It has ghost stories, a celebrated local witch (Lyddie
Shears) and associations with a number of literary figures, including
Rudyard Kipling and Hazlitt (who lived here for a time and who called
one of his collections of essays *Winterslow*).

At Old Lodge, a fine country mansion, now demolished, which stood
on the downs in what is now Porton Experimental Station, the Poore
family lived at the end of last century. At Winterslow they initiated
several remarkable experiments, including the establishment of a Land
Court, which was responsible for reclaiming much common land and
allocating it to smallholders on 999-year leases. They also started a
Winterslow weaving industry, which flourished for many years.

Winterslow Hut, on the main London-Exeter road in a downland vale
below Winterslow, was a famous coaching inn.

Although north of Pitton and Winterslow stretch the rolling uplands
of Salisbury Plain, to the west and south, as we have seen, lie the woods
that now represent the ancient Forest of Clarendon. This links with

another mediaevel forest, that of Melchet, and through that with the New Forest. Looking south from the hills of Winterslow one sees, as the horizon, the chalk ridge of Whiteparish and Dean Hills, but everything between appears to be forest, and the valley does indeed possess what is perhaps the largest unbroken area of woodland in the county (though the forests overlap into Hampshire). Here we have crossed the watershed from the valleys of Salisbury Plain. The little Deanbrook which tumbles out of Clarendon Lake and flows past East and West Grimstead finds its way into the Test. In the valley the chalk is hidden deep beneath strata of clay, gravel and sand, and a land-mine dropped in the woods near Grimstead in the Second World War penetrated into a measure that consisted almost exclusively of fossils. Two little streams that in winter bubble and chatter for a mile or two through the forest suddenly disappear in a kind of swallet, known as Pig Brook, and re-emerge in a chalk cutting at West Dean, a mile away.

West Dean straddles the county boundary; some houses have rooms in each county. Here in the seventeenth century the Evelyn family, of which John Evelyn the diarist was a member, lived in the manor-house, now destroyed. A remarkable collection of memorials to the family, in alabaster and marble, is crammed into the tiny Borbach Chantry, which was happily preserved when, in 1866, the attached church of St Mary was pulled down. It was originally erected in 1333 by the Borbach family and lies hidden in a wood on the opposite side of the road to the modern church. Nearby, also hidden by trees, is the castle mound, with surrounding dry moat, on which the castle of Waleran, Ranger of the New Forest and occupier of numerous manors in Wiltshire, lived at the time of the Domesday Book. Even earlier, the Deanbrook valley was a popular residential district in Roman times. No fewer than three villas, one of them very large, have been excavated in West Dean parish, and there are known to have been others at East Grimstead and Farley.

Whiteparish and Dean Hill would be a natural boundary between Wiltshire and Hampshire. It is the only commanding range (its highest point 512 feet above sea level) between Salisbury and Southampton, and it offers magnificent panoramic views in both directions. As boys we used to sit by the Pepperbox and claim to be able to read, with the aid of field-glasses, the names on the great ships in Southampton Docks. The Pepperbox, which crowns the summit of the hill and nowadays stands on

National Trust land and is a favourite summer picnic site, is an octagonal brick tower, with its door and windows bricked up. Its alternative name of Eyre's Folly gives a clue to its *raison d'être*. The seventeenth-century landowner who built it was said to have gazed down on the relatively new Longford Castle, clearly visible to the left of Salisbury Cathedral, and determined that, if he couldn't have a building as splendid, he would at least have one higher up. He was probably the Sir Giles Eyre who lived at Whiteparish and got into much trouble, being imprisoned and 'plundered by soldiers', for refusing to make forced loans to Charles I.

He has a memorial in Whiteparish church, which serves the large village of Whiteparish on the southern side of the hill. Here, in wet, wooded, meadow country, Wiltshire thrusts out a wedge to the very borders of the New Forest. Nomansland, which is a typical Forest village and was created about two hundred and fifty years ago by squatters, is just within Wiltshire, its houses looking across the road into Hampshire.

Nomansland is in the parish of Landford, which claims to have a history extending back to about 3,000 B.C., numerous flint implements of that date having been found at a site which was apparently a 'factory' in those days. There is Norman work in the parish church of St Andrew. The parish has extensive commons, some of which have been and are now being built on, and numerous hamlets and outlying farms and large houses. Lanes leading westwards pass through Hamptworth and Redlynch to Downton.

EIGHT

Savernake, Chute and the Pewsey Vale

Just as the south-eastern borders of Wiltshire are shrouded in woodland, so too forests canopied the central sector of its eastern frontier. Here the great mediaeval Forest of Chute extended over large areas of both Hampshire and Wiltshire and, in our own county, linked up with Savernake Forest. The border country in this district is wild, hilly and broken. North-west of Andover the land climbs in a long, gradual ascent to elevations of over 800 feet near Chute and Conholt, before beginning the descent, through tortuous downland valleys, to the Kennet. The hills of the divide are so steep and spectacular that a Roman road, which usually disregards natural obstacles, swerves in a broad arc to avoid a deep coombe which conceals the farm of Hippenscombe.

The section of the Roman highway which skirts this dramatic valley is known as Chute Causeway and is reputedly haunted by the ghost of a vicar of Chute who, during a visitation of the plague, persuaded the victims to go to a camp prepared for them on the Causeway, where he would see that they, or such of them as survived, were fed till the epidemic subsided. He then went away and left them to starve.

It is near Tidcombe that we first encounter that enigmatic earthwork, the Wansdyke, which carves an almost incomprehensible line right across central Wiltshire, past Bath, to the Severn Sea near Portishead. In places it is an impressive grass rampart overlooking a deep ditch; in others the earth has been levelled or incorporated into roads or field boundaries till its very identity has been lost.

The section of the Wansdyke near Tidcombe is the southern arm of the dyke, which splits into two at Bedwyn, the northern arm running eastwards to Inkpen Beacon. West of Bedwyn, or rather of the hill-top earthwork of Chisbury Camp, there is a gap, and we can pick up the rampart again in Savernake Forest.

Although one of the ancient forests of England, Savernake is no casual conglomeration of straggling woods, glades and thickets. It used to be but, like so many Wiltshire estates, it was taken in hand in the eighteenth century by landscape planners. As a matter of fact, that most celebrated of all landscape artists, 'Capability' Brown, had a finger in it, for on a visit to Savernake he was so struck by its 'capabilities' and talked so much about them that the owner, the Marquess of Ailesbury, was inspired to put his ideas into practice. What Mr Brown visualised was no less than the planning of the entire forest as 'one great Whole', and that is what the marquess did. The woodland was divided into segments by eight tracks which lead to the centre of the Forest, a magnificent Grand Avenue was planted with beeches and elms, giving an impressive vista from Tottenham House, former home of the marquesses of Ailesbury, to a towering column erected to celebrate the restoration to health of King George III.

The Esturmey family, from which the marquess of Ailesbury is descended, have been Hereditary Wardens of Savernake since the reign of William the Conqueror, who gave the position to one of his knights, Richard Esturmy, after the battle of Hastings. The present marquess, the twenty ninth hereditary warden, has written a fascinating book, *A History of Savernake Forest,* which reveals that throughout the Middle Ages the Forest was governed by the usual strict forest laws, giving rise to the natural reaction of poaching and encroachment. Even priests from Marlborough were not above 'taking a doe with a bow and arrow'.

In the middle of the fifteenth century, the estates passed through the female line of the Esturmey family to the Seymours, who were soon to play a leading role in the affairs of England. They made their home at Wulfhall, the site of which is about a mile from Great Bedwyn. It had, by the way, nothing to do with wolves but derived its name from being the hall of a Saxon named Ulfela. John Seymour, who died in 1536, was a courtier and friend of Henry VIII. On his visits to Wulfhall the king evidently met John Seymour's daughter, Jane. Whether things were carefully planned or whether the susceptible king acted on the spur of the moment we do not know, but he was at Wulfhall when Anne Boleyn was awaiting execution. Anne had her head cut off on 19 May 1536, and Henry was betrothed to Jane Seymour the next day and married her on 30 May. Within a week he was starting to flirt with other girls, and it may not have been altogether a tragedy for Jane that she died, twelve days after childbirth, in October 1537.

The child was, of course, to become king of England as Edward VI. He was only ten years old when his father died, and was for a time cleverly manipulated by his ambitious uncle, Edward Seymour, whom he made first duke of Somerset and Protector of the Realm. One of the duke's activities in his five years of power was to plan a superb mansion in Savernake, on the lines of Longleat House which his friend, Sir John Thynne, was then building. The two noblemen probably employed the same architect, John of Padua.

Unfortunately for the duke, he was executed on Tower Hill (on 22 January, 1552) before his plans could be put into practice, and the project was abandoned. His son and heir settled for the more modest mansion of Tottenham Lodge. This son, Lord Hertford, also fell into disgrace through unwise ambition, for he married Lady Catherine Grey, sister of the unhappy Lady Jane Grey, whom Queen Mary had executed. Lady Catherine was altogether too near the throne for the peace of mind of a reigning monarch, so she spent most of her married life in strict confinement, mostly in the Tower of London.

Meantime Jane Seymour's other brother, Baron Seymour of Sudeley, carried on intrigues on his own account. As soon as Henry VIII was dead he sent a proposal of marriage to Princess Elizabeth (afterwards Elizabeth I). When she rejected him he turned his attention to Catherine Parr, Henry's widow, and married her. Young Elizabeth was sent to be Queen Catherine Parr's ward, which gave the baron and Elizabeth opportunity to carry on what was evidently a lively flirtation, for once the Queen 'cam sodenly upon them wher they were all alone (he having her in his armes) wherefore the Quene fell out both with the Lord Admiral (her husband) and her Grace also'.

The family were certainly triers – Lord Hertford's grandson, William, married Lady Arabella Stuart, who had as good a claim to the throne as James I, but that affair too ended in tragedy, with Lady Arabella dying in the Tower of London. And before the end of the seventeenth century the male line of the Seymours had died out and the wardenship of Savernake passed through the female line to Lord Bruce, the eldest son of the earl of Ailesbury. By this time both Wulfhall and Tottenham Lodge, which had been the home of the Seymours, were in ruins, so a new Tottenham House was built. This mansion, enlarged and improved, still stands and is now a school. It was at this stage that the visions of Capability Brown were translated into reality and the Forest assumed its present status – a well-managed, superbly planned forest unit, sixteen miles round and comprising more than 4,000 acres.

Just before the Second World War the marquess of Ailesbury concluded an agreement whereby the Forestry Commission leased the Forest for 999 years, though leaving the wardenship with the family. The Commission now manages Savernake as a commercial unit, though with limits imposed on the planting of softwoods. Recently nature trails and picnic sites have been provided, and the resident deer are, of course, well protected. There are a few red deer in a small park near Tottenham House, but fallow and roe are quite plentiful.

The largest village in the Savernake neighbourhood is Great Bedwyn, which was once even more important if not larger than it is now, for it was one of Wiltshire's 'rotten boroughs', which used to send two Members to Parliament before the Reform Act. In various periods of history, as in the reigns of Alfred the Great and William the Conqueror, it has been royal property, and before that a Roman villa existed on a site nearby. The name is said by some to mean 'white barrow' or 'white grave', in reference to a supposed tumulus which no longer exists, but a more generally accepted derivation is 'from the name of a plant of the convolvulus type'. Perhaps significantly, Wiltshire villagers call traveller's joy or old man's beard 'bithywine', which is very near an eighth-century version, 'bedewinde', of the name of the village. Fourteenth-century Great Bedwyn church, with some splendid interior carving, holds the tombs of the Seymour family, including those of the short-lived Queen Jane, and of the admiral who married Henry VIII's widow.

Little Bedwyn, on the road to Hungerford, has an even more ancient church, partly Norman, with a magnificent spire and a great yew in its churchyard. The village nestles in a deep valley, and the enveloping hills are dominated by the formidable hill-fort, Chisbury Camp, which is said to derive its name from the early Saxon leader Cissa and which still has earthen ramparts fifty feet high.

Great Bedwyn is an exceptionally large parish, of over 10,000 acres, including within its boundaries the hamlets of Crofton, East and West Grafton, Marten, Wilton and, away to the south on the downs, Wexcombe. This last was the home of Mr A. J. Hosier, the agricultural genius who, in the grim days of the early 1930s, made a success of his downland farming by introducing such ingenious novelties as the Hosier milking bail and gates which were simple extensions of barbed-wire fences. A company founded for marketing his inventions still flourishes, under the name of Hosier, at Collingbourne.

It is at Bedwyn that we first make the acquaintance of the Kennet and Avon Canal, once regarded, and rightly, as a modern triumph of engineering but now a quiet backwater valued for sentimental reasons and for its recreational facilities. John Rennie was its designer and creator. An Act to authorize its construction was passed in 1794, and the Canal was opened on the last day of 1810. It cuts sheer across the centre of Wiltshire, from the Berkshire border near Hungerford to Somerset at Limpley Stoke. It has twenty-nine locks in a staircase just west of Devizes and at one time used to carry barges of up to 60 tons between London and Bristol. The canal's short period of prosperity was, of course, brought to an end by the coming of the railway. Recognising the danger, the Kennet and Avon Canal Company planned to build their own railway alongside their canal but were bought out by the Great Western. Canal and railway now run side by side for much of their course through Wiltshire, though diverging by a few miles in the Vale of Pewsey. The canal is now the haunt of fishermen, naturalists and canal enthusiasts, who have formed a Kennet and Avon Trust in an attempt to keep it in repair. Each year at Easter it is the venue for the well-publicised canoe race from Devizes to Westminster.

Before we turn west into the Pewsey Vale we should visit Froxfield, the last village in Wiltshire before reaching the Berkshire border. Otherwise an undistinguished though pleasant little place, it is memorable for its imposing quadrangle of buildings erected by a duchess of Somerset in the reign of James II. Entering through a gatehouse bearing the Somerset arms, one finds oneself on a spacious lawn, surrounded by red brick houses, and in the centre a small chapel. Known as the Somerset Hospital, they are almshouses for widows, the original bequest stating that they are for the widows of twenty clergymen and thirty laymen.

For all that it appears to be a flat, low-lying plain, the Vale of Pewsey is really an elevated plateau, at no point lower than 300 feet above sea level. It is a natural eastward extension of the valley of the Bristol Avon, into which river it seems its little streams ought to drain. Instead, they find a weakness in the chalk rampart that marks the southern edge of the Vale and plunge southwards across Salisbury Plain.

The Vale, about twelve miles long, is nowhere more than five miles across, from north to south. The wall of chalk hills along its southern border is steep and impressive, but the range that shuts it off on the north is more so. Here rise a series of towering, rounded hills – Martinsell, Huish, Knap Hill, Milk Hill, Tan Hill, the last two with altitudes of 964 and 962 feet respectively. From the summit of Tan Hill it is possible to see Salisbury spire, twenty five miles away. Within the Vale itself are several abrupt tumps, notably Woodborough Hill and Etchilhampton Hill, both over 600 feet high. The Vale has some of the richest farming country in the south of England, an underlying stratum of Gault clay being overlaid by fertile greensand. Most of the farms, except those in the centre of the Vale, have a slice of valley land linked with an extensive section of chalk down, thus getting the best of both worlds. William Cobbett, who stayed at a farm in the parish of Milton Lilbourne in 1826, calculated that the land of the parish produced annually about 3000 quarters of wheat, 6000 quarters of barley and the wool of 7000 sheep, besides pigs and poultry (and he saw no fewer than 300 pigs in one stubble-field) – enough, he declared, to provide 'bread for 800 families, mutton for 500 and bacon and beer for 207'. It would, he writes, 'be impossible to find a more beautiful and pleasant country than this'.

The villages of the Vale are quiet places, contented to have little history. Pewsey, the little town which gives the Vale its name, has a fine statue of King Alfred in its main street, as a reminder that it was once the property of Saxon kings. It was once bigger than Swindon and had a flourishing corn market, held on Tuesdays, and an iron foundry. The church is said to be built on foundations of sarsen stones, laid in Saxon times, and the roof of the organ chamber and vestry is, somewhat surprisingly, constructed of timbers from the roof of the old Augustinian priory of Ivychurch, near Alderbury (see page 122). The connection is explained by the fact that when Ivychurch was dismantled in 1889 the rector of Pewsey was Rev. the Hon. B. Pleydell-Bouverie, a member of the family of the earls of Radnor, who held the gift of the living of Pewsey.

Pewsey's church of St John the Baptist, its oldest parts more than seven hundred years old, is one of several fine churches in the Vale. The best is perhaps that of Chirton, dating from about 1170 and containing much superb Norman work, including an unsurpassed timber roof and splendidly carved doorway and font. There is no better Norman village church in all England. The churches of both Alton Barnes and Alton Priors are both very old, that of Alton Barnes being on probable Saxon foundations. Alton Priors church once belonged to a priory connected with Hyde Abbey. The little church at Manningford Bruce is partly Saxon and partly Norman. All Cannings church is of Norman foundation but has been subjected to additions and alterations in almost every subsequent century. Bishops Cannings has a handsome church, cruciform and in Early English style, with a fine tower and spire. Its organ was presented by a local man. William Bayley, who in the eighteenth century sailed around the world with Captain Cook. Patney church also has a little eighteenth-century organ.

Wootton Rivers church possesses a curious and somewhat improbable treasure – a clock made by a village genius. His name was Jack Spratt, and he was alive when Miss Edith Olivier collected material for her book *Moonrakings* in the 1930s. Having left school at the age of seven he worked on farms till he discovered his aptitude for mechanical work and particularly clock-making. Miss Olivier reports;

'In his house he has a grandfather clock which can play over a hundred tunes, and has twelve sets of chimes, a different one for each hour. The case is beautifully carved, a table knife having been used as the tool.'

Concerning the church clock, she writes:

'At the coronation of King George V (1911) the villagers met to consider how they might commemorate the event, and the idea of having a clock for the church was dismissed as too expensive a scheme. Mr Spratt quietly offered to make a clock himself, free of charge ... his only stipulation being that the people should do their part by providing the material he required in the shape of a few hundredweights of metal, any scraps of rubbish of iron, steel, brass or lead that they could find. Half-inclined to think it must be a joke, the villagers set to work and brought him their contributions of old reaping-machines, bicycles, chaff-cutters, pipes, bedsteads and even perambulators ... The whole work has the merit of being local, for, after some time spent in experimenting, the castings were made by a Pewsey firm from wooden patterns.

The chimes are probably unique. It is possible to tell the hours by the different chimes of the quarters, all the hours between twelve and six having different sets of quarter chimes, these being repeated between six and twelve.'

Mr Spratt used clippings from his wife's hair to make brushes for cleaning the intricate parts of his clocks.

The chancel of All Cannings church was rebuilt in 1867 by the Rev. Anthony Methuen and his sons as a memorial to Samuel Coleridge, the poet, who had lived with them in the rectory for a time fifty years earlier.

Another literary figure from the Pewsey Vale was the thresher-poet, Stephen Duck, who was born at Charlton St Peter in 1705. For much of his life he worked as a farm labourer, writing in such spare time as he had verses which eventually attracted the attention of local gentry. He was taken to London and lionised at Court, Queen Caroline appointing him Keeper of her library and granting him a pension. After a time the novelty wore off, and then Duck had to endure the shafts of snobbery and the machinations of rival poets. Being able neither to put up with the persecution nor to escape back to Wiltshire, he drowned himself.

Every year he is supposed to be commemorated by the 'Duck Feast', held at the Charlton Cat Inn. A toast is drunk to his memory by the participants, thirteen 'Duck' men, who drink from the Duck goblet. The chairman, known as the Chief Duck, wears a tall hat trimmed with duck feathers. The rent of a field, given in 1734 for the purpose by Lord Palmerston, is said to provide the money for the feast. There is something odd here. In 1734 Stephen Duck was only twenty-nine, with twenty-two years of life still ahead of him. I suspect that the Duck Feast is very much older than Stephen Duck.

Stephen was, incidentally, a fairly proficient poet, especially when dealing with themes of which he had some first-hand knowledge, such as threshing. Poor Stephen Duck! Did he sometimes wish, when among the books at Richmond, that he were back in the gloomy, dusty Wiltshire barn?

The hills that crowd in on the Pewsey Vale, and particularly those to

:he north, have generally dominated the life of the Vale villagers. Their nstinct was on highdays and holidays to take the hills. On Martinsell, for instance, a Palm Sunday Fair was held by the people of Wootton Rivers, :o be replaced later by a religious service. A huge fair, for cattle and sheep but attended by much sport and merrymaking, used to be held on Tan Hill, above All Cannings, on 5 August.

On Milk Hill, above Alton Priors, is what is reputed to be the oldest dew-pond in England, Oxenmere. A pond of that name was indeed mentioned as a reference point in a land survey of the year A.D. 825, and there is this pond, at the correct point of the parish boundary of Alton Priors. I am prepared to believe that a pond has existed there since Saxon times, but whether it can be considered the same pond is a matter of opinion. A dew-pond's life is, at the most, about 150 years, after which it has to be re-made, so Oxenmere must have been reconstructed many times.

Dew-pond making is, incidentally, an old Wiltshire craft, followed by generations of experts, among whom were the Smith family of Market Lavington. The late Mr Tom Smith made one as recently as 1938. Recently it has been revived, and when I last visited Oxenmere a few years ago a group of students were experimenting in the vicinity with various methods. 'Dew-pond is a misnomer. Keeping the ponds full has little or nothing to do with dew. The 'secrets' of the old craftsmen were concerned mainly with making the ponds waterproof, but, that aside, it was simply a matter of ensuring that the intake of water was greater than the loss by evaporation, and that was done by providing each pond with a catchment area much greater than the surface area of the water.

The slopes of the downs have also provided a canvas for those landscape artists who specialise in carved hill figures. The Vale has or rather had three white horses, one on Walker's Hill, a mile north of Alton Barnes, and two on a hillside south of Pewsey. None of them has any great antiquity. The Alton Barnes horse was carved in 1812, presumably inspired by the Cherhill Horse (see page 170), which it closely resembles. It was paid for by a local farmer, Mr Robert Pile, who is said to have parted with £20 for the work and then to have done most of it himself! He made a contract with a travelling painter, John Thorpe, who accepted both the commission and the cash and then promptly decamped. Thorpe was later caught and hanged, though whether for this or some other crime is not known. It is quite a large horse, 160 feet long by 166 feet high, and is a sprightly animal, with a docked tail.

Nothing can now be seen of the first Pewsey Horse, though its outline was dimly discernible when Morris Marples wrote his book *White Horses* in 1937. It too was the work of Mr Robert Pile, though at an earlier date, probably about 1785, so there may have been two Robert Piles, father and son. It was a small animal, only 43 feet long.

The second Pewsey Horse was cut, to a plan marked out by Mr George Marples, by the Pewsey Fire Brigade in 1937, to commemorate the coronation of King George VI. Thoughtfully, the date has been carved above it.

I am leaving the Pewsey Vale without giving due attention to the wealth of tall stories associated with Bishops Cannings. As one of them is the tale of the Wiltshire Moonrakers, I am reserving them for the final chapter. A sample concerns the church, which we have already noticed. Besides its fine spire it has some minor pinnacles, and it is said that the Cannings people determined to make one of them grow to match the spire, so they piled a great heap of farmyard manure around it. As the heap began to sink they exclaimed triumphantly, 'It be growin'! it be growin'!'

NINE

Marlborough and the Northern Downs

Over the hills to Marlborough! The mighty hills which seal off the Pewsey Vale on the north slope down gently on their far side to Marlborough and the valley of the Kennet. Beyond lies another great downland massif, the Marlborough Downs, which extend to the fringes of the Thames valley.

Visiting Marlborough on a festival day in the early nineteenth century, Sir Richard Colt Hoare, the antiquary, reports that there were '1333 partakers of conviviality seated at one long table from the market house to St Peter's Church, nearly half-a-mile'. As in so many African towns to this day, life in Marlborough was lived in its exceptionally broad High Street. The townsfolk used it for celebrations, for the great fairs which were held three times yearly (on 11 July, 22 August and 23 November) and for the busy weekly market, which in the time of John Aubrey was 'one of the greatest markets for cheese in the west of England. Here doe reside factors for the cheesemongers of London'. The pens for livestock and the market stalls were arranged along the centre of the broad street, just as parked cars are nowadays, leaving ample room for vehicles to pass on either side. Quite possibly they were there before the town, which may well have sprung up around a site of seasonal tribal gatherings in prehistoric times.

For Marlborough is a town of very ancient origin. Its motto, 'Tibi nunc sapientis ossa Merlini?' – 'Where now are the bones of wise Merlin?' – refers to the Merlin of the King Arthur legends, to the Merlin, too, who in one tradition is credited with having brought the stones of Stonehenge from Ireland. Conventional etymology admits that the name is derived from one Maerla, who evidently lived there at some unknown period. The inference is that the bones of this Maerla lie at Marlborough, doubtless in the barrow which supplies the second part of the name.

This barrow is now the 'Castle Mound', a not very conspicuous earthwork in the grounds of Marlborough College. A Norman castle once stood on it (coins of William I were minted here) but the mound itself is older than that, though it *is* man-made. During the civil war between King Stephen and the Empress Matilda, Marlborough Castle is said to have been the eyrie of Baron FitzGilbert, 'the worst robber-baron of them all', and Parliament held an important session in the castle in 1267, producing the Statues of Marlborough, which were a kind of codicil to Magna Carta.

The trade in wool and other agricultural commodities which developed during the Middle Ages proved of greater permanence than the castle, which fell into ruin in early Tudor times. The town was also of strategic importance because of its position on the London-Bath road and as such was the scene of fighting on several occasions between Royalists and Parliamentarians in the Civil War of the seventeenth century. One attack developed on a market day, when all the traders who had come to buy and sell goods were roped in to help defend the town against an assault by Royalist cavalry. They were none too successful and had to escape as best they could from a burning town. Town fires, as a matter of fact, were all too familiar to Marlborough. Besides the conflagration during the Civil War the town had three other disastrous fires in the seventeenth century, in 1653, 1679 and 1690, more than three hundred houses being destroyed in the first one. After the last one had occurred the town passed a bye-law prohibiting the use of thatch within its boundaries.

Meantime the dukes of Somerset had erected two mansions, one after the other, on the site of the old castle. In the middle of the eighteenth century the second one was converted into an inn, which did a good trade as a hostelry on the Bath road until the coming of the railways. It was then, in 1843, taken over as a school, which developed into Marlborough College, one of the great educational establishments of England.

The college was thus not one of Marlborough's earliest schools. King Edward VI Grammar School was founded nearly three hundred years earlier. There was also at the beginning of the nineteenth century a boys' school now chiefly remembered because in 1804 the boys cut the

Marlborough White Horse in the turf of Granham Hill, about a mile-and-a-half south of the town. Its annual scouring provided the boys with a popular holiday until the school was closed in about 1830. Thereafter it was scoured at irregular intervals at the expense of private individuals or, on one occasion, voluntarily by local Boy Scouts.

By approaching Marlborough from the south we have descended into the Kennet valley in the middle of its course through Wiltshire. Before following it downstream to the border with Berkshire we now travel upstream, westwards along the Bath road. Passing the villages of Preshute (to which the Marlborough White Horse properly belongs), Fyfield, Lockeridge, Manton, Overton and East and West Kennett, with the swelling downs rolling away on either hand, we find ourselves again, as at Stonehenge, in the evocative realm of prehistory.

Six miles beyond Marlborough the Kennet valley takes a right-angled turn to the north. It is accompanied, almost to the source of the river near Uffcot, by the main Devizes-Swindon road, and is parcelled out between the parishes of Avebury, Winterbourne Monkton, Berwick Bassett, Winterbourne Bassett and Broad Hinton. If we are making direct for Avebury from Marlborough we can take a short cut that avoids following the broad bend of the river, but if we do we shall miss Silbury Hill, which is situated close by the Bath road, due south of Avebury.

Our first encounter with the prehistoric Avebury complex is before even we reach the village of West Kennett. We become aware of numbers of round barrows on either side of the road, though particularly on the north. On the south side of the road Overton Hill is crowned by a site dubbed by eighteenth-century antiquaries 'The Sanctuary'. It was said by William Stukeley to consist of two concentric rings of stones, which were destroyed in 1724 to enable the land to be ploughed, for the sake of, as he puts it, 'a little dirty profit'. A hundred and fifty years later archaeologists were wondering whether Stukeley was mistaken, but excavations in 1930 confirmed his observations. The stones represented a late stage in the history of this neolithic monument, which had previously been marked by wooden posts. A current theory is that these supported a thatched roof, probably around an open courtyard.

Stukeley thought that the Sanctuary was an integral part of the Avebury complex. He visualised the whole being laid out as a temple to a Serpent God, Avebury itself representing a coiled body, like that of a cobra, the Sanctuary being the head, and an unmarked spot on Beckhampton Down being the tail. The Sanctuary is indeed linked with Avebury by the Kennet Avenue, which wriggles like a snake between the two and is marked by parallel lines of standing stones. Modern opinion, however, is that The Sanctuary is older than Avebury, though the creation of the Kennet Avenue perhaps coincides with the replacement of The Sanctuary's wooden posts by stone pillars.

The Avenue is about a mile long and gives access to the great circle of Avebury through a gap in the south-eastern corner. Many of the stones that marked its course have been demolished, but some authorities think they can detect that the stones were arranged alternately, first an erect pillar and then a lozenge-shaped stone, perhaps representing the male and female principles.

Avebury usually strikes transatlantic visitors as being somewhat incongruous. Here is a pleasant English village, with church, manor-house, thatched cottages and farmsteads, within the precincts of a mighty stone circle, with accompanying earth ramparts and ditches, coeval with Stonehenge. The perimeter trench is about 1250 feet across, originally steep-sided and flat-bottomed. The chalk excavated from the trench was piled up on the outside, leaving a ledge of about fifteen feet between the resultant formidable wall and the edge of the ditch. Just inside the ditch the sarsen stones of Avebury were hauled into position. There were originally about a hundred of them, the heaviest weighing more than 40 tons. Most have been demolished, but the survivors are sufficiently impressive to give some idea of the grandeur of the building in its glory.

Within the great circle were two smaller circles, each between 320 and 350 feet in diameter. One originally consisted of 30 stones, the other of 32, few of which are now standing. There were also huge stones in the centre of each of these circles, all of which have disappeared except two in the centre circle. There may have been a third circle, overlapping the northern edge of the earthwork, but if so it was never completed.

The inner circles antedated the great circle by about two hundred years, the probable dates of construction of the entire monument being between 1700 and 1500 B.C. The builders are thought to have been the Beaker people, who arrived in Britain about 1800 B.C., and who were probably responsible for the flint mines on Easton Down, Winterslow (see page 124).

19 (above left) *The Mompesson Monument, Lydiard Tregoze church.* 20 (above right) *The effigies of Elizabeth and Nicholas St John, Lydiard Tregoze. 21 (below) The Norman chancel of St John's church, Devizes*

Rather surprisingly, no notice is taken of Avebury in literature till John Aubrey 'discovered' it in 1648. He took King Charles II to see it in 1663 and made a plan which shows many more standing stones than now survive. Even in his time the pace of demolition was brisk, and he gives an account of how the great stones were split by toppling them into a trench, lighting a fire beneath them and then, when they were hot, drawing a line along the required fracture zone with cold water and cracking it with a heavy hammer. The stones broke easily under this treatment. Farmers of the eighteenth century, when pressure on land for enclosure became intense, were most active in the work, but it had begun at a much earlier date, for under one of the great stones was found the skeleton of a man, with coins of the fourteenth century and a pair of scissors in his pouch. It is assumed that he was either a barber-surgeon or a tailor who had been helping to destroy a stone when it toppled over and crushed him. An examination of the walls of some of the older buildings in Avebury will reveal what happened to many of the smashed stones.

Incidentally, none of the stones of Avebury, unlike those of Stonehenge, show any signs of having been dressed or tooled by man. Their source of origin is not far away. Giant sarsens still lie scattered in profusion over Fyfield Down, just to the east, and no doubt many more were available when Avebury was built. It has been suggested that some of the stones of Stonehenge may have been originally erected at Avebury, to be taken down and dragged to Stonehenge when that site assumed a greater importance, for reasons now unknown.

The guide-books call Silbury Hill 'the largest artificial mound in Europe'. It is, in effect, an earthen pyramid, 130 feet high and covering a base of $5\frac{1}{2}$ acres. On the north and west sides an enormous ditch, now largely filled with silt and rubble, is the source of the chalk and earth of which the mound is constructed. Professor Gerald S. Hawkins, the American author of *Stonehenge Decoded,* has calculated that more than a million cubic yards of chalk were excavated and manhandled to make the mound, requiring three million man-days of work.

Was it erected as a gigantic barrow, covering the remains of some mighty king? Successive excavations have failed to throw much light on the mystery. The first, in 1776, sank a shaft from top to bottom; later operations drove tunnels into the sides and probed the ditch and the approach causeway. Virtually nothing of interest was found. The latest

22 *Old houses and St Mary's church, Marlborough*

exercise, in incessant view of television cameras, in 1969 was as unrewarding as any. All the excavators found was an urn buried by a previous party in 1849; it contained contemporary coins, a newspaper and a poem written by one Emmeline Fisher of Salisbury.

Local tradition has supplied details which history and archaeology have failed to produce. It says that within the mound lies buried King Sil, or Zel, sitting upright on his horse and clad in a suit of golden armour. Sometimes at night he can be seen riding around the hill. The Devil is also said to have dumped the hill there, in a single night. Years ago the villagers of Avebury used to go in procession to the top of Silbury on Palm Sunday, 'to eat fig cakes and drink sugar and water'.

We have not yet finished with the prehistoric attractions of Avebury and its neighbourhood. On the downs about half-a-mile south-east of Silbury is West Kennett Long Barrow, which is even older than Avebury or The Sanctuary. Its probable date is about 2000 B.C., or perhaps earlier, but it was used for burials for about three hundred years. One of the largest long barrows in Europe, it is a chambered tomb or, in effect, a family vault. Its framework was a construction of sarsen boulders, over and around which a great mound of chalk rubble was piled. Within it was a long, central passage leading to a large chamber at one end and with two smaller chambers on either side. The whole construction is 350 feet long. In it interments were made over a long period of time, the corpses being buried on the floors of the chambers. Remains of about thirty skeletons, including ten of children, have been found, but there were probably more, some of the earlier having been removed to make room for later ones. Eventually the tumulus was firmly sealed, apparently by a different race of settlers — the probable builders of Avebury. As Professor Gerald Hawkins writes:

'For rituals concerned with death, one can hardly imagine a more impressive place than this vast earthwork, flanked by white trenches, stone-edged, with more great stones guarding the gateway to the tomb.'

The largest stones of the West Kennett barrow weigh about 20 tons.

There are four other long barrows in the immediate vicinity of Avebury, and a dolmen, known as The Devil's Den, on the downs near Preshute, is probably the remains of the chamber of a long barrow.

At Beckhampton, near where Stukeley thought the tail of his 'serpent' might be, are two huge standing stones, the larger about sixteen feet high

and weighing some 62 tons. They are known locally as the Devil's
Quoits, the Longstones and Adam and Eve. There are also known to
have been stone circles on the downs 'between West Kennett and
Avebury', another just east of the Kennet Avenue, and two apparently
concentric ones in a field between Winterbourne Bassett and Clyffe
Pypard. This last edifice was evidently quite a large one, the outer circle
being 234 feet in diameter.

A mile-and-a-half north-east of Avebury a rounded hill, Windmill Hill,
is crowned by three low concentric earthworks. The site was thoroughly
excavated in the 1920s and was shown to have been one of the earliest
settlements of Neolithic farmers known in Britain. It gave its name to a
culture, the Windmill Hill people, who found their way into England in
perhaps about 2400 B.C. In addition to keeping little long-horned cattle
and also sheep, pigs and dogs, they grew crops, including wheat, barley
and flax. The earthworks, probably crowned in those days by a hedge or
stockade, seem to have been intended chiefly as a cattle corral, where the
tribe would meet for the autumn slaughter of surplus animals. The
Windmill Hill people would have been responsible for some of the long
barrows in the district.

The farmers of two hundred years ago at Avebury could, of course,
have had no inkling of the value, not only to archaeologists but to their
own descendants, of the stones they were destroying. Nowadays between
100,000 and 200,000 visitors a year come to gaze and speculate, an
influx which is certainly to the advantage of the village inn, the Red Lion.
Many of them wander into the excellent little museum, which displays
most of the finds made during excavations at Avebury and Windmill
Hill.

Although overshadowed by its heritage from the remote past, the
village itself has a respectable antiquity. The church retains reminders,
including some windows and possibly the font, of its Saxon origins, and
the fine Elizabethan manor house is on the site of an early mediaeval
monastery. Broken stones from the ancient circle have provided much of
the material for both church and manor, as well as a number of other
houses and farm buildings. Just how much vandalism went into the
construction of Avebury and its neighbour villages is, however, difficult
to determine, for many of the sarsen stones which are undoubtedly used
may have come direct from the deposits which sprinkle the Marlborough

Downs. 'Grey wethers', Wiltshire people call them, for they resemble, from a distance, flocks of grazing sheep. There must once have been many more lying on the downs, for Canon Goddard, writing in *The Wiltshire Magazine* in the second half of last century, says;

'You will see them split up into gateposts in the fields, or into cubes for the pitching of every farmhouse or cottage pathway, and you will observe that the majority of the older cottages and houses, those at least which date from the seventeenth or eighteenth century . . . are built either of sarsen or of the hard chalk marl . . . In the parish church look carefully at the base of the tower, and the foundation of the buttresses, you will find that in church after church their sole foundations are large blocks of sarsen stone.'

This, he notes, holds good for the countryside from Bishopstone (on the Berkshire border) past Wroughton and Broad Hinton down to the Vale of Pewsey.

Geologically, the sarsens are the remnants of a very thin layer of early tertiary sandstone which once covered these downs.

The upper Kennet valley is dominated on the eastern side by the frowning heights of Hackpen Hill, in the name of which the element 'Hack' is probably a version of 'hag', a reminiscence of witches or of an ancient earth goddess. On its slopes is another of Wiltshire's White Horses. Tradition says that it was cut in 1838, on the occasion of Queen Victoria's coronation, by Henry Eatwell, the parish clerk of Broad Hinton. Around the corner of the great hill, on the crest of the scarp looking northwards to Swindon, is a magnificent Iron Age hill fort, Barbury Castle — a twelve-acre site encompassed by a formidable double rampart and ditch. It is thought that here was the site of 'Beranburh', recorded by *The Anglo-Saxon Chronicle* as the place where two West Saxon kings defeated a Roman-British army in 556. Those two distinguished Wiltshire naturalists, Richard Jefferies and Alfred Williams, who loved to wander over these austere hills, have their memorial on Barbury. Carved on an enormous sarsen from Overton Down are plaques epitomising their philosophies:

RICHARD JEFFERIES, 1848-1887.

It is Eternity now.
I am in the midst of it.

It is about me in the sunshine.

ALFRED WILLIAMS, 1877-1930

Still to find and still to follow
Joy in every hill and hollow,
Company in solitude.

Two churches in the upper Kennet valley are well worth a visit. Broad Hinton, though restored in 1880, retains a beautiful interior, with a fine hammerbeam roof of the seventeenth century and some splendid tombs. Winterbourne Bassett's fourteenth-century church also contains imposing memorials to a local landed family, the Baskervilles.

Away on the downs to the west the formerly isolated village of Yatesbury, the shocking state of whose lanes was once a byword, has in the present century achieved prominence, like so many other Wiltshire villages, by the establishment of a great aerodrome nearby. Also on the western downs the celebrated racehorse training stables of Beckhampton and, a little farther down the Kennet, of Manton House, have produced a number of Derby winners and provided horses for such well-known jockeys as Steve Donoghue and Sir Gordon Richards.

Two streams which follow roughly parallel courses to the infant Kennet are the Ogbourne and the Aldbourne. The former, which runs through the pleasant villages of Ogbourne St Andrew and Ogbourne St George, joins the main channel of the Kennet at Marlborough; the latter lies some six miles to the east. The Ogbourne valley, followed by the main Salisbury-Swindon road, offers a natural north-south highway and is thought by some authorities to be the key to the site of the battle of Mount Badon, the last of Arthur's twelve great battles against the invading Saxons in the sixth century. According to this theory, the whole northern escarpment of the chalk hills above the Thames valley was probably Mount Badon. The advancing Saxons, following the Ridgeway along the crest of the hill, were preparing to turn left along the Ogbourne valley when they were attacked by Arthur and his army at Liddington Camp, a hill fort that commands the gap in the downs, and overwhelmingly defeated.It seems as likely an explanation as any.

The valley was also the route of a secondary Roman road linking Cirencester with Cunetio, a Roman station on the site of the present village of Mildenhall.

The village of Aldbourne, in the second of the two shallow valleys, was in mediaeval times the centre of a waste of forest and scrub, extending over the Berkshire border. John of Gaunt, who had a hunting lodge at Upper Upham, is known to have been fond of hunting here. Aldbourne is rich in tradition and legend. In the seventeenth and eighteenth centuries its smiths developed into skilful bell-founders, specialising in bells for horses and other animals. The earliest known bells were cast there in the reign of James I, but most of the suriving ones (of which I have several fine specimens) were the work of the Wells family, who controlled the industry for several generations in the eighteenth century. The village had two other specialised industries, described by A. G. Bradley, writing in 1907, as 'willow-plaiting, for the decoration of fireplaces in summertime, the other, straw-plaiting in squares for exportation to the hat manufacturers'.

Aldbourne had a traditional feast, held on the feast-day of St Mary Magdalen and celebrated with the usual village enthusiasm. The feast was followed by robust sports and generally ended in a free-for-all with the villagers of neighbouring Ramsbury, with whom a perpetual feud simmered. The Aldbourne carrier used to pass through Ramsbury on his way to and from Marlborough and was the butt of jeers and insults by the Ramsbury boys, who used to run after him shouting, 'Yah! Aldbourne dabchick!' If they could procure a dead dabchick to tie to the tail of his cart, the insult was complete.

The story told to account for this behaviour was that a dabchick was once found on the old pond in the middle of Aldbourne, to the bewilderment of the Aldbourne people who had never seen anything like it. So they fetched the oldest inhabitant, an invalid so ancient that he had to be wheeled around the pond three times in a wheelbarrow, after which he identified the bird as a dabchick. And Aldbourne residents have been 'Aldbourne dabchicks' ever since. Some of the village's earliest bells bear the image of a little, long-necked bird which is said to be a dabchick.

In a downland valley above Aldbourne the little village of Snap, once a hamlet in Aldbourne parish, has been lost and obliterated within living memory. When the twentieth century began it consisted of about fifteen houses, with a school and a chapel, but soon afterwards the farms around were turned into a sheep ranch, and the villagers lost their means of livelihood. It was used by the War Ministry as a training ground in the

First World War and then endured the years of neglect between the wars. Here are some notes I made when I visited Snap in 1948:

'I found it difficult to know when I had reached the village. Only here and there were traces of the old walls visible. A stranger could pass by without suspecting its story, if it were not for the apple trees and a big walnut tree that still shade the long grass. I saw a thrush beating a snail against the foundation of a cottage wall, a thrush that no doubt was a lineal descendant of thrushes which sang to children playing there fifty years ago . . .'

From prosperity to oblivion within less than fifty years!

No such fate threatens the lively little town, or large village, of Ramsbury. Now a pleasant residential place of lovely gardens, it was in existence in early Saxon times and was, by the tenth century, of sufficient importance to be made the seat of a bishopric. Its first bishop, Athelstan, was appointed in the year 909, when the great unwieldy see of Sherborne was split and Ramsbury was made the centre of the eastern half of it, and it remained independent until 1058, when it was reunited with Sherborne for a time. During that period the diocese had ten bishops, of whom no fewer than three became archbishops of Canterbury. Some Saxon masonry, probably from the old cathedral, is to be seen in the parish church, which was restored in 1891.

Ramsbury church also contains a chapel, with marble tombs, of the Darell family, who once lived at Littlecote House nearby. The family achieved notoriety through the escapades of 'Wild Darell' who in the late sixteenth century culminated a reckless career by allegedly murdering his infant child. The story, told with much circumstantial detail, is that one stormy night a midwife, Mother Barnes of Shefford in Berkshire, was awakened and offered a lavish reward to come to an unspecified destination. She rode pillion and blindfolded to a well-furnished mansion, where she helped to deliver a baby. Her masked employer then entered and told her to throw the child on to a roaring fire on the hearth. When she refused and asked to be allowed to keep the baby he snatched it from her and himself threw it on the fire. She kept her wits sufficiently to snip off and smuggle away a fragment of the bedcover, and this was sufficient to bring the crime home to Darell. He was, however, apparently never punished. We can put what interpretation we choose on the fact that a relation of his was Attorney General, Sir John Popham, who later acquired the Littlecote estate.

It is said that Darell did not entirely escape retribution. He broke his neck when jumping a stile on his estate, and the site is still haunted by ghostly hounds, in full cry after his soul.

Littlecote House remains a splendid example of a Tudor manor and is a treasure-house of things Elizabethan and Stuart, including some excellent wall-paintings and a collection of early fire-arms.

At Chilton Foliat, just downstream from Littlecote, the Kennet, now a river of deep pools concealing many a splendid trout, passes into Berkshire. The county boundary swerves away over the downs to the north-west, past another hill fort, Membury Camp. At Baydon, in racehorse-training country between Aldbourne and Lambourn, we are in the highest village of Wiltshire, its altitude being 750 feet. Its name is reminiscent of that Mount Badon where Arthur won his renowned victory, and it sits astride the old Ermine Street, the Roman way from Cirencester to Silchester. Its church of St Nicholas has an unusual feature in internal piers of chalk blocks, over 700 years old, illustrating the fact known to generations of Wiltshire builders that chalk is durable enough provided it is kept dry.

TEN

Swindon
and the Thames Valley

In the census of 1801 no fewer than twenty eight Wiltshire towns had populations greater than that of Swindon, which had only 1,198 inhabitants. Places now regarded as villages, such as Downton, Ramsbury, Tisbury and Longbridge Deverill, were all larger. And Swindon's postal address was 'Swindon, near Highworth'.

Even three hundred years ago, however, Swindon was prospering at the expense of Highworth. Writing in the 1680s John Aubrey notes:

'At Highworth was the greatest market, on Wednesday, for the fatt cattle in our county, which was furnished by the rich vale; and the Oxford butchers furnished themselves here. In the late civill warres it being made a garrison for the King, the graziers, to avoid the rudeness of the souldiers, quitted that market and went to Swindon, four miles distant, where the market on Munday continues still, which before was a petty, inconsiderable one. Also, the plague was at Highworth before the late warres, which was very prejudiciall to the market there; by reason whereof all the countrey sent their cattle to Swindon market, as they did before to Highworth.'

Swindon's future was, of course, to depend not on agricultural markets but on the railway. Although it was not one of the considerations which influenced him, the Marquess of Ailesbury made a critical decision for Swindon in 1839, when he indignantly refused to allow a railway to be laid through his lovely estate of Savernake. Thus precluded from following the direct route from London to Bristol along the Kennet valley, the Great Western Railway had to look for one farther north. So Swindon came up for consideration and proved to have several advantages. It would be a convenient junction for a branch line which it was hoped to construct to Gloucester and Cheltenham, and it was served by the Wiltshire and Berkshire Canal, which had been constructed some thirty years earlier and which could bring coal and coke cheaply to the site.

Oddly, a legend very similar to that concerning Salisbury Cathedral sprung up about the selection of a site for the railway works at Swindon. It is said that when Daniel Gooch and Isambard Kingdom Brunel sat eating a sandwich lunch on a furzy slope near Swindon Brunel threw a sandwich and remarked, 'That's where we'll put up our first building.' It is reminiscent of the archer who, allegedly but improbably, shot an arrow from the ramparts of Old Sarum to fix the site of the new church.

However, local prejudice played its part. The Goddard family who had for centuries been lords of Swindon were less irrevocably antagonistic than the Marquess of Ailesbury to the new mode of transport, but they preferred to keep it at arm's length. So, for most of the rest of the nineteenth century, a distinction was drawn between Old Swindon, on its little hill, and New Swindon, hammering and clanking away down in the valley. It was not until 1900 that the two were combined to form a single municipal borough.

Conflicting reports exist as to what New Swindon was like in its initial decades. Post Office directories of the 1860s, determinedly maintaining that everything was for the best, stated,

'The town is neatly and regularly built . . . and is lighted by gas. The Mechanics Institution is a noble building, having a library containing upwards of 3,650 volumes, and is one of the finest institutions in the kingdom; lectures, concerts and dramatic performances are frequently given in it. A free recreation ground, with a permanent pavilion, has been established for the use of cricketers, of whom there are several clubs.'

At the same time, newly formed district councils found that 'sewers scarcely existed, the drainage was often into surface channels in the streets, the water supply was inadequate and often polluted. The death rate was high and was attributed directly to these causes.' And as late as 1907 the town's medical officer of health commented,

'The narrow thoroughfares and ill-adapted business premises of today are evidence of the haste with which the old order was made to change without due consideration of future requirements.'

An important element in the development of Swindon was that 'the persons who represented this rapid growth came not from the county but very largely from the industural areas of South Wales and northern England and were, accordingly, alien to Wiltshire.'

This feeling that Swindon is something apart from the rest of the county still prevails, especially in the agricultural districts of the south, though there must be few Wiltshiremen who do not take a pride in the achievements of Swindon's football team. Nowadays, of course, almost every town is cosmopolitan, so Swindon is not exceptional.

With typical Victorian pride in industrial prowess, an 1867 directory boasts;

'At the factory locomotives for the whole line are manufactured. Such is the perfection to which the building of engines has arrived here that one engine per week can be turned out. Also about 330 tons of rails per week are turned out at the rolling mill. The works cover about eighteen acres of ground . . .'

It adds, 'Every train stops here for ten minutes, as well for changing engines as for refreshment of passengers.'

Nowadays, although the great railway works have been phased out, Swindon is still well served by the railway. Fast trains deliver passengers in London in just over an hour. The new M4 motorway which passes close by offers an alternative mode of rapid transport to the metropolis for commuters.

Any fears that Swindon might decline with the passing of the railway age have been dispersed long ago. Far from being a one-industry town, it now has an almost bewildering wealth of industrial activities. Some of the largest engineering works in the country have grown up here, and the town has chemical, tobacco, clothing, building and many other factories. In recent years it has taken substantial overspills of population from London, and the newcomers may be partly responsible, together with the ease of access, for the transfer of commercial and business offices from the capital, which is proceeding rapidly.

Memories of the great days of the railway are perpetuated in Swindon's Railway Museum, which houses some of the splendid locomotives of the past as well as less imposing but equally fascinating small items such as old railway excursion advertisements, Brunel's drawing-board and plans, and some of the furnishings of Queen Victoria's special railway coach. Swindon also has a municipal museum and a fine Arts Centre and art gallery. Just after the war it was one of the first places in Britain to organise a scheme whereby the public could borrow pictures as well as books from the library, and now it is in the process of constructing a most ambitious Sport and Leisure Centre, with an indoor lake surrounded by palm trees and lapped by waves created by a specially-designed machine. It is, in fact, an exceedingly well-run town — in many respects a model of what a modern industrial town should be.

Since the arrival of motor transport any place within ten or twenty miles, by road, of a big town such as Swindon tends to become, if not suburban at least a residential dormitory for commuters. Stratton St Margaret has already been absorbed, and Lydiard Park, former home of the Bolingbroke family, was purchased by the Corporation in 1943 and the mansion turned into a conference centre. Not a moment too soon, either, for the house was falling into dereliction about the ears of the last private occupants, who, it is said, moved from room to room as the ceilings collapsed.

Lydiard Tregoze, the little village of which this was the great house, has virtually vanished, apart from its exquisite church, which must be almost unique among English village churches. It reminds me a little of the Borbach chantry at West Dean (see page 125) and, like it, is crammed full with magnificent family memorials. The structure is mainly thirteenth century and has several interesting interior features, including high, box-like pews, a fine barrel roof with the sky and heavenly bodies painted on it, and a splendid triptych. The memorials, heavily sculptured and canopied, are elaborate to the point of exuberance. Effigies abound, paint has been used profusely, and the whole interior is suffused with an almost twilight glow from the deep colours of the stained glass windows.

Curiously for an industrial town, two of Swindon's best-known sons were naturalists. Richard Jefferies was essentially a countryman, and so, at heart, was Alfred Williams, for all that much of his working life was spent as a furnace hand in the railway works at Swindon. Although, as we have seen (page 146), they share the same monument on Barbury Camp they hardly overlap in time, for Jefferies died in 1887, when Williams was only ten years old. Moreover, in the very year of Williams' birth Jefferies moved to London, and later to Sussex, never returning to his native county.

One of the inestimable assets of Swindon is the proximity of open country on all sides. Unlike many of the great industrial towns of the North and Midlands, it does not merge into a seemingly endless complex of other similar towns. Within half-an-hour one can leave the streets behind and be in the cuckoo-haunted, buttercup-carpeted meadows of the Thames valley or be striding over the thyme and milkwort of the unhedged downs. Jefferies and Williams both revelled in the escape route to rural serenity thus provided, Williams perhaps more than Jefferies, for he was more firmly enmeshed in factory life. Jefferies, belonging to an early phase of Swindon's expansion, was reared on a small farm, participating, though apparently with reluctance, in sowing and harvesting, dung-spurling and threshing and living on familiar terms with farm horses, spaniels and ferrets as well as with the wild creatures of downland and woodland. Williams, born in the village of South Marston, a little farther out from Swindon, belonged to a family slightly lower in the social scale, for his father was a carpenter, though the plain brick houses which were the respective birthplaces of the two seem much on a par. While Richard Jefferies was able to spend his youth in desultory idleness around the farm, to the despair of his harassed parents, the pressures of life weighed more heavily on young Alfred Williams, who later wrote,

'At the age of eight I half-timed from school and worked in a gang for the farmer, pulling weeds and thistles from the wheat. At other times we scared birds, tended pigs and worked in the hayfield or at corn harvest. To me it was a period of much happiness . . . '

He left school at the age of eleven, took a job on the farm for a time and then, to earn more money, went into the Great Western Railway factory at Swindon, where he endured the unpopularity of a man who is different from his fellows.

Both Jefferies and Williams were dogged by poverty and ill-health, and both came to early graves before their full potential had been realised. If there is a sense in which history repeats itself it is that each generation neglects and discourages the genius committed to it, while subsequent generations form appreciation societies and erect monuments to that same safely-buried genius but take no interest in the new genius struggling to emerge next door. Perhaps it is more satisfying to identify oneself, vicariously, with a tragedy than with a success story.

Swindon is, at any rate, now fully alive to the quality and merit of its two poets. Their houses still stand, the top floor of the farmhouse at Coate where Jefferies lived being now a museum. Coate Water, his favourite boyhood haunt, it now a lake in a public park, girdled by a concrete path but still a sanctuary for hordes of waterfowl.

Coate Water, which began life as a reservoir for the Wilts and Berks Canal, is on the right side of Swindon to allow easy access to the downs which here form a low, grey-green wall along the southern horizon. Richard Jefferies was often able to slip away from the uncongenial chores of the farm to stride for miles along their crest, doubtless following at times the old green Ridgeway trodden by men long before the Roman legions came to Britain. Anyone now trying to emulate him would find, though much of the downland remains intact, certain obstacles in the form of military establishments, an aerodrome and a hospital above the villages of Wroughton and Chiseldon.

As in other Wiltshire vales, a string of villages shelters beneath the downland scarp, each parish claiming its share of valley meadows and downland grazing. Liddington, which gives its name to the Iron Age earthwork on the hill behind it, has an Elizabethan manor-house in a most attractive setting, with part of an ancient moat forming a garden pond, and a thirteenth-century church believed to have been founded by an abbess of Shaftesbury who lies buried in the churchyard. Wanborough, or rather the hamlet of Nythe nearby, is thought to have been the Roman station of Nidum and was the scene of a battle in Saxon times. Its church has a tower at one end and a spire at the other. Both Little Hinton and Bishopstone churches contain good Norman work, including fine Norman doorways. Little Hinton has a lavishly decorated Saxon font, and Bishopstone an interesting home-made clock.

On the other side of Swindon, Purton is another of the few villages in England with both a tower and a spire. Local tradition says that the strange design was due to a quarrel between two sisters who endowed the church but could not agree as to whether it should have a tower or a spire, so the church had both. Unfortunately for the legend, a hundred and fifty years separate the building of the two. This village, too, is thought to have been the scene of a great battle in Saxon times — the battle of Ellandune between Wessex and Mercia in 823, when 'the brook of Ellandune ran red with gore, stood dammed with battle-wreck, grew foul with mouldering corpses'. Also within the orbit of Swindon, Stanton Fitzwarren, just off the road to Highworth, has a church of both Saxon and Norman workmanship and, in its furnishings, a wealth of modern wood-carving by Caldwall Masters who was rector here earlier this century. Nearby Hannington has an impressive Elizabethan mansion.

Highworth, a pleasant little town of broad streets, earns its name, for it stands on a ridge commanding a majestic view of the broad vale of the Thames, and of the little river Cole which reinforces it and here forms the boundary between Wiltshire and Berkshire. As befits a church with a tower on a hill, Highworth church is dedicated to St Michael, and it preserves a cannonball which struck the tower when Fairfax was besieging it during the Civil War. The town, now largely residential, has a number of attractive stone houses of the seventeenth and eighteenth centuries.

Down by the Thames, to the left of the main road just before it leaves Wiltshire for Lechlade, the tiny mediaeval church of Inglesham, hidden among trees down a narrow lane, is worth a visit. Here at last we reach the Thames, which is at this point joined by both the river Cole and the Thames and Severn Canal. The lovely young river is spanned by a high-arched bridge which permits only one line of traffic and is in summer gay with every kind of river craft.

Upstream from Inglesham the Thames serves intermittently as the county boundary, which however is here as intricate as the pieces of a jigsaw puzzle and makes frequent incursions north of the river. In one of these fingers of territory beyond the river the delightful little village of Marston Maisey, where my old friend and fellow-scribe, the late Reginald Arkell, used to live in a cottage in a flower garden, hides itself in the meadows. On that side of the river, too, lie Latton, with its Norman church among the riparian willows, and Ashton Keynes, where cottagers have footbridges to cross the Thames between their doors and the road. In the 1930s Ashton Keynes, gave temporary hospitality to a group of pacifists, the Cotswold Bruderhof, whose members were largely though not entirely refugees from the totalitarian regimes developing in Central Europe. I visited them several times on their 300-acre farm and found some of their ideals, though not all their practices, attractive. They had formed a peasant community, farming efficiently and using money only in transactions with the outside world, but they insisted on wearing a drab mediaeval peasant costume that was neither attractive nor practical. Just before the outbreak of war, foreseeing what was coming, they emigrated to Paraguay.

We have by-passed Cricklade, Wiltshire's only town on the banks of the Thames. This is an ancient place, important in Saxon times and probably even earlier, for it is on that important Roman road, Ermine Street. Some authorities think that a meeting between St Augustine and the Celtic bishops took place here early in the seventh century. There is some Saxon work in its parish church of St Sampson's, a splendid edifice embodying almost every style of mediaeval architecture and completed by a lofty and imposing Tudor tower. St Sampson was a Breton saint who was born in 465 and is said to have presided over a school at Cricklade. The town has another ancient church, St Mary's, which possesses a fine Norman arch and also a chained Bible. The remains of a mediaeval priory nearby have been incorporated into a residence, said to be connected with St Mary's by underground passages haunted by monks!

As is appropriate with such a venerable place, Cricklade has retained some of its old customs. For instance, it still holds its Court Leet, which administers the grazing rights, possessed by every Cricklade householder, in North Meadow. This 114-acre pasture by the Thames used to be the scene of a Lammas Fair, held on the first Sunday after 12 August. Formerly, like many other Wiltshire towns and villages, it had a mumming play, performed at Christmas, and a 'Village Wake'. Many Cricklade men were engaged in 'rining' oak in the neighbouring forest of Braydon for use in tanning. This was done in May, when the sap was rising, and at the beginning of June the Cricklade Bark Harvest Festival marked the end of the season. Miss Edith Olivier, collecting reminiscences from Women's Institute members in the 1920s and 1930s, said that old people remembered the feast as being similar to a Harvest Home, with plenty of food and drink, music and games, and she was able to write down the words of part of a play performed on that occasion.

Cricklade was once a 'rotten borough', sending two Members to Parliament, which doubtless prompted Cobbett's comment that it was 'a villainous hole, a more rascally-looking place I never set my eyes on'. Miss Olivier recorded some memories of election days at Cricklade. They lasted, she writes, for eight days 'which were spent by the householders in feasting and drinking. Canvassing went on for six months previously.

23 The staircase hall of Philipps House, Dinton

Candidates would visit the homes of the poor voters and attempt to buy something or other, offering a fabulous price for it, in order to secure the householder's vote. "I'll pay £5 for that canary", the candidate would say; and the bargain was made.'

A few miles farther up the Thames valley John Aubrey, who knew these parts well, found on Minety Common 'neer the rode which leadeth to Ashton Caynes, is a boggy place called the Gogges, where is a spring, or springs, rising up out of fuller's earth. This puddle in hot and dry weather is candid like a hoar frost; which to the taste seems nitrous ... After a shower this spring will smoake. The mudd or earth cleanses and scowres incomparably. A pike of eighteen foot long will not reach to the bottom.' Is there, one wonders, any connection between these curious surface deposits and the fact that, at the time of writing, exploratory borings for oil are proceeding nearby?

Minety was the family home of William Penn, founder of Pennsylvania. The Penns were in earlier times stewards to the Abbey of Malmesbury.

Just across the infant river, now only a tiny stream, the lovely village of Oaksey (by Wiltshire pronunciation 'Wuxy') was in the 1950s the home of Baron Oaksey who, as Lord Chief Justice Lawrence, presided at the Nuremburg trials at the end of the war. In earlier times it was a family estate of the great mediaeval family, the Bohuns, who had here a great fortified mansion which has now disappeared.

Officially the Thames rises just beyond the county boundary, in Gloucestershire, and enters Wiltshire between Oaksey and Ashton Keynes. The identification is, however, somewhat academic, for there is at least an equal volume of water in several of the little Wiltshire streams which, flowing past Crudwell, Hankerton and Minety, join forces with the Gloucestershire brook near Ashton Keynes. All rise in the meadows and foothills of the Cotswolds around the Fosse Way.

24 Beech trees in Savernake Forest

ELEVEN

The Populous Valley of the Bristol Avon

Sprinkled over a countryside of elm-fringed meadows almost as thickly as stars in the Milky Way, the villages of the valley of the Bristol Avon (so-called to distinguish it from the Salisbury Avon) conform to no pattern. Around the edges of the great vale is a margin of strip parishes, each with a section of valley meadows and then a ribbon of downland on the hills above, but in the vale itself they have sprung up higgledy-piggledy, comparatively few by the main river but many on its tributaries or on the little hills above them. Many of the parishes indeed are not well nucleated but consist largely of farms scattered about the meadows, each surrounded by its own fields.

Though the arrangement was probably fortuitous rather than intentional, it seems to have developed into a factor of some economic importance. At the beginning of this book we commented on the significance of the Wiltshire proverb, 'As difference as chalk from cheese' (see page 9). This is cheese country, and we have already noted that Marlborough was one of the great cheese markets of England, frequented by factors from London. In the eighteenth century the county was producing more than 5,000 tons of cheese a year, most of it from small farms supplying less than five or six tons. Aubrey remarked that eating too much cheese and butter made the North Wiltshireman 'melancholy, contemplative and malicious'!

Let us hear Aubrey on the subject of Wiltshire cheese:

'Sowre wood-sere grounds doe yield the best cheese, and such are Cheshire. Bromefield, in the parish of Yatton is so — sower and wette — and where I had better cheese than anywhere in all the neighbourhood . . .

'Now of late, about 1680, in North Wiltshire they have altered their
fashion from thinne cheeses about an inch thick, made so for the sake of
drying and quick sale, called at London Marleborough cheese, to thick
ones, as the Cheshire cheese.'

John Britton, who edited Aubrey's manuscript works in 1847,
comments:

'At the close of last century Reading was the principal seat of the
London cheese factors, who visited the different farms in Wiltshire once
in each year to purchase the cheese, which was sent in waggons to
Reading; often by circuitous routes in order to save the tolls payable on
turnpike roads.'

Thomas Davis, of Longleat, surveying the agriculture of the county for
the Board of Agriculture in 1811, says:

'These cheese of this district was many years sold in the London
market by the name of Gloucester cheese; but is now perfectly well
known by the name of "North Wiltshire cheese". It was at first,
doubtless, an imitation, and perhaps an humble one, of that made in the
Vale of Gloucester; but it is now allowed by many to be at least equal, if
not superior, to the cheese of the favourite district of Gloucestershire, the
hundred of Berkeley.'

Davis says that nine-tenths of the cattle kept in the dairies of North
Wiltshire in his time were Longhorns, now rare and regarded as almost
exclusively beef cattle. He claims, however, that the quantity of cheese
produced per cow is 'greater than is common in any other cheese-making
country; sometimes as high as $4\frac{1}{2}$cwt or near 5 cwt per cow; seldom
lower than 3 cwt. . . .'

Early writers also asserted that the arrangement of the fields of the
dairy farms of the Avon Vale, all fairly near the farm buildings, was an
advantage for cheese-making. Instead of having to be milked in the
pastures, the cows were brought home for milking twice a day. All the
milk could thus be transferred to the cheese-making process in one batch
and at an even temperature. Although the acreage of the Vale farms
tended to be small, the number of cows kept was often quite large. A
dairy of forty or fifty cows seems to have been quite common, and herds
of a hundred or more were not unheard of.

North-west Wiltshire's other great industry, weaving, was of course
based on the sheep that grazed the hills all around the Avon Vale. The

vast flocks that roamed over Salisbury Plain were matched by those of the Marlborough Downs and of the Cotswolds. All these were traditional sheep-breeding regions since Roman times, and it is likely that the Cotswold breed of sheep at least is directly descended from the flocks which grazed the Cotswold villa estates during the Roman era.

When, after the Dark Ages, the export trade in English wool began to be important is not known. We have already noted (page 95) that Tilshead was an important place at the time of the *Domesday Book* (1086). Professor W. G. Hoskins, in *Provincial England,* writes:

'Tilshead in 1086 had sixty-six burgesses. It was one of the largest boroughs in Wiltshire, and it has been suggested that the only possible reason for a borough in the middle of the Wiltshire Downs must have been the existence of sheep farming on a great scale all around it, to such an extent that trading in sheep and wool was already highly developed before the time of Domesday.'

By the thirteenth century wool had become England's No. 1 export commodity. Enormous flocks of sheep grazed the meadows and uplands, endless trains of packhorses carried bales of wool to the ports, and merchants in the trade accumulated huge fortunes, enabling them to build those glorious stone churches and mansions which draw innumerable twentieth-century tourists to the Cotswolds and other stone-blessed country. At first the bulk of the wool was exported for weaving in the looms of the Continent, particularly in the Low Countries. Even when the commerce was at its height, however, the wind of change was starting to blow. Home weaving was expanding. By the twelfth and thirteenth centuries Bristol was an important cloth-weaving centre, and in the next century Edward III brought over colonies of Flemings, who were skilled weavers, and settled them in, among other places, Bradford-on-Avon and Steeple Ashton. An essential process in the cloth-making business is fulling. In the Middle Ages simple machinery was invented whereby this could be done mechanically, in a mill driven by water power, instead of by human feet. The growth of the industry enhanced the value of streams that could be dammed and made to drive mill wheels. Such streams are abundant in Wiltshire, in both the chalk country and the broad vale of the Avon. Castle Combe, for example, now a placid and exceedingly picturesque village in a Cotswold valley, gave its name to a widely-distributed and popular type of cloth. Salisbury, from which the cloth industry has now fled, was once one of the greatest cloth-manufacturing cities in England, and wealthy to match. Salisbury's cloth trade had begun to decline by Tudor times, when the little manufacturing towns of west Wilts were rising to greater prominence.

Until Stuart times most of the export trade in cloth was in undyed material, dyeing being still carried on in the Netherlands and Italy. James I enacted a law compelling all broadcloths, the type of cloth mostly manufactured, to be dressed and dyed in London, and he gave the monopoly of the dyeing trade to a merchant, William Cockayne, to whom he was deeply in debt. The venture was a complete failure, but before this happened the West Country cloth trade had been ruined, much of it past revival.

Some of the Wiltshire weavers, however, proved resilient, notably those of Bradford-on-Avon and Trowbridge, which henceforth became the centres of a new trade, after James had rescinded his law, in coloured cloths. At one time Bradford had more than thirty cloth factories, and Trowbridge had fifteen only just over a hundred years ago. During the seventeenth and eighteenth centuries the cloth manufacturers of the district prospered greatly and sent consignments of cloth to the distant countries of the West and East with which England was now trading. What caused the decline of the industry is still a matter for controversy. Perhaps too much specialisation on one type of cloth was a factor; and machinery-smashing riots in the late 1780s certainly frightened some clothiers away. In general, however, it was one of the aspects of the Industrial Revolution, with the wholesale transference of industry to the Midlands and North, the cloth industry, of course, settling around that other Bradford in Yorkshire, where the easy availability of coal and iron was complemented by that ancient requirement of weaving — swiftly-flowing streams.

The great Abbey of Malmesbury undoubtedly played an important role in the survival of sheep farming and the revival of the wool trade in the early Middle Ages. Like most of the great monastic estates it farmed efficiently and experimented with new ideas that promised a profit. There was an abbey at Malmesbury before the year 941, when King Athelstan rebuilt it, and it endured, one of the architectural glories of mediaeval England, until suppressed by Henry VIII in 1549.

Malmesbury is said to owe its name to a combination of two

missionaries who laboured there, Maidulph and St Aldhelm. Maidulph was apparently an Irish priest who founded a school there in about 596; St Aldhelm, the first bishop of Sherborne, elevated it to the status of an abbey in about 680. Before Maidulph's time the place was known by the pleasant name of Ingelburne. St Aldhelm was a musician and the possessor of a powerful voice. In my book *Somerset* I describe how, when over seventy, he went on missionary tours in the forest of Selwood. When he came to a forest settlement he would sit on a bridge or on a wayside stone and sing popular songs until he had an audience, then switch to religion. He employed the same tactics at Malmesbury and is said also to have built in the abbey there England's first organ, 'a mighty instrument with innumerable tones, blown with bellows and enclosed in a gilded case'. The fern-hung Well of St Aldhelm, by which the saint used to sit and meditate, is still intact, though on private property.

Malmesbury was much favoured by King Athelstan, perhaps in gratitude for a great victory over the Danes in the vicinity. He not only rebuilt the abbey but gave the town five hundred acres of land. For hundreds of years rights on this fertile estate were handed down through generations of Malmesbury householders and still exist, though now commuted to a cash payment by farmers who rent the land.

The abbey and the town around it had grown up on a magnificent site, a rocky peninsula towering over the Avon, sixty or eighty feet below. During the Middle Ages successive additions and rebuildings transformed the abbey into one of the chief glories of English architecture. On that dominating height its Gothic spire, higher than that of Salisbury Cathedral, must have been truly impressive. One marvels at the intrepidity of an eleventh-century monk of Malmesbury, Elmer, who, according to the historian William of Malmesbury, 'had by some contrivance fastened wings to his hands and feet, in order that, looking upon the fable as true, he might fly like Daedalus, and collecting air on the summit of the tower had flown for more than the distance of a furlong; but, agitated by the violence of the wind and the current of air, as well as by the consciousness of his rash attempt, he fell and broke his legs, and was lame ever after. He used to relate as the cause of his failure, his forgetting to provide himself a tail.'

With true English perseverance, Elmer wanted to try again, but the abbot vetoed the idea.

William of Malmesbury himself was a twelfth-century monk who became librarian of the abbey and earned a reputation as a conscientious and shrewd historian. We owe much of our knowledge of early mediaevel times to his writings. As librarian he had at his disposal a superb collection of ancient books and manuscripts. As this was a literary treasure-house which we would give much to possess today, it is interesting to enquire what happened to it. John Aubrey throws some light on the subject. He says that when he attended the 'latin schoole at Yatton-Keynel' in 1633.

'the fashion then was to save the forules of their bookes with a false cover of parchment, sc. old manuscript, which I was too young to understand; but I was pleased with the elegancy of the writing and the coloured initial letters. I remember the rector here, Mr. Wm. Stump, great-grandson of Stump the cloathier of Malmesbury, had severall manuscripts of the abbey . . . When he brewed a barrell of speciall ale, his use was to stop the bung-hole under the clay, with a sheet of manuscript; he sayd nothing did it so well; which methought did grieve me then to see. Afterwards I went to schoole to Mr. Latimer at Leigh-delamer, the next parish, where was the like use of covering of bookes. In my grandfather's dayes the manuscripts flew about like butterflies. All musick bookes, account bookes, copie bookes etc. were covered with old manuscripts, as we cover them now with blew paper or marbled paper; and the glovers of Malmesbury made great havock of them; and gloves were wrapt up no doubt in many good pieces of antiquity . . . Anno 1647 I went to Parson Stump out of curiosity, to see his manuscripts, whereof I had seen some in my childhood; but by that time they were lost and disperst. His sons were gunners and souldiers, and scoured their gunnes with them.'

William Stumpe, the clothier, was a self-made man who, by methods that would stand comparison with those of nineteenth- and twentieth-century tycoons, amassed an immense fortune. When Henry VIII closed the abbey in 1539 Stumpe acquired it, at apparently a very considerable price. Leland, who visited Malmesbury after the Dissolution and within Stumpe's lifetime, found that every corner of the abbey buildings, though not the abbey itself, was full of weaving looms, and that Stumpe was planning to build two more streets of houses for the workers in his expanding business.

Much execration has been heaped on Stumpe for his vandalism at

Malmesbury and particularly for the destruction of the manuscripts. The temper of the times must be taken into account, however, and the fact that all over England monastic buildings and their contents were being demolished even more ruthlessly than at Malmesbury. To Stumpe's credit must be set the fact that he saved the great nave of the abbey and gave it to Malmesbury as a parish church. So, although much was lost, the majestic relic still not only survives but serves a living purpose, in contrast to the fate that befell Wilton, Glastonbury, Shaftesbury and a dozen other abbeys. The abbey offers so much to the visitor that it is invidious to select particular features, but the interior, with its magnificent Norman pillars and arches, is breathtaking, and there is fine and intricate carving on the Norman doorway.

Clustered closely around its abbey, the old town of Malmesbury has much to link it with the ecclesiastical past. The Old Bell Inn was probably once the abbey guest-house, and there are two other mediaeval inns. The market cross dates from the reign of Henry VII, and a group of almshouses started their career as a hospital of the knights of St John of Jerusalem. The suburb of Westport has an immense monastic barn, one of the finest in the county.

In later years Malmesbury developed several industries as alternatives to cloth-making. It had a silk mill, a gloving industry and a brewery, and a cottage lace-making industry survived until very recently, some of the lace-makers probably still living at the time of writing.

Malmesbury Abbey was only part of the booty acquired by William Stumpe at the Dissolution. With it went broad rural estates, including the manor of Charlton, two miles east of the town. Here his daughter, Lady Knevet (the Stumpe family used marriage as well as money to move up in the social world), and her husband built the first Charlton House, which is now incorporated in the much larger mansion designed by Matthew Brettingham in 1772-76. In the earlier house, in 1666, a group of young aristocrats took refuge from the Great Plague of London. Among them was John Dryden, son-in-law to the first Lord Suffolk who then owned the estate, and here he wrote his *Annus Mirabilis,* which describes the dramatic events of that year.

Garsdon, nearby, has a link with American history, for the Washington family lived here for several generations in the sixteenth and seventeenth centuries. A cousin of one of George Washington's direct ancestors lies buried in the church.

Downstream from Malmesbury we come to Great and Little Somerford, the latter of which has in its Early English church a lovely chancel screen said to have come from Malmesbury Abbey. Both are quiet farming villages, with many pleasing old houses and little history, until, of course, Great Somerford became the home of Captain Mark Phillips, who made Princess Anne his bride.

Here the valley of the upper Avon broadens, where a succession of streams, some of them after courses of six or seven miles through the meadows, flow into the main river on either side. Much of this part of the vale lies within the bounds of the old forest of Braydon. Braydon Pond, towards Minety, is said to be the largest lake in Wiltshire; Wootton Bassett is the 'wood-town' in the forest; and Bradenstoke would seem to commemorate a stone, apparently of some importance as a meeting-place, in the woods.

At Wootton Bassett we are back to within six miles of the centre of Swindon, into the orbit of which town it is being drawn, as a dormitory suburb. Before that happened it consisted almost entirely of one long street, in the middle of which sat its unusual little town hall, perched on stone pillars, or staddle-stones. Beneath its floor an accumulation of civic treasures was stored when last I was there, including the stocks, a ducking-stool (last used in 1787) and an ancient fire-engine. It once had two annual fairs and a weekly cattle market and was, until the Reform Act, a 'rotten borough', sending two Members to Parliament.

The white horse carved on the downs above Broadtown is sometimes known as the Wootton Bassett horse, it being only three-and-a-half miles away. It is supposed to have been cut by a local farmer in 1864.

Midway between Somerford and Wootton Bassett the village of Brinkworth has a fine fifteenth-century church, much restored but containing some interesting furniture. This is another manor with associations with William Penn, for his family once lived in Penn Lodge, still standing.

Bradenstoke, on a hill on the southern side of the Braydon river, was an important place in mediaeval times – the site of the Augustinian priory of Clack. Some of its ruins are still to be seen in the farmstead known as Bradenstoke Abbey, but its great barn and guest-house were taken down and carted away to South Wales as recently as 1930.

Nearby Lyneham, once an obscure village grouped around a green in the middle of a forest, is now internationally known for its great aerodrome, the base of R.A.F. Transport Command.

Several of the village churches in this neighbourhood have unusual treasures. Dauntsey, once an estate of Malmesbury Abbey, has a mediaeval doom painting and several other fine pictures and sculptures; Tockenham, a Roman statue of the god Aesculapius built into a niche in a wall. In Clyffe Pypard church are two statues to Tudor members of the Goddard family, unusual in that they are carved in chalk; it also has a fine wooden chancel screen. Both Tockenham and Clyffe Pypard have attractive Stuart manor-houses.

Clyffe Pypard and Broadtown are the northernmost of a thread of villages lying under the hills which form the eastern margin of the Avon valley. Highway, far from any highway, is a tiny place with a Norman door to its restored church. The church at Compton Bassett, which first rose in the twelfth century and has been embellished in every subsequent century, has in its nave an exquisitely carved stone screen of Tudor date.

Rounding a hill spur we come, on the northern side of the Bath road, to the village of Cherhill, with its elegant white horse ignoring the traffic below. The horse, 123 feet long by 131 feet high and said to be visible for more than thirty miles, occupies the slopes of a hill that is crowned by a formidable and well-preserved Iron Age fort, Oldbury Castle. Attempts have been made to establish a Saxon origin for this horse, but it seems fairly clear that it was cut by a Dr Christopher Alsop, of Calne, in 1780. Nearby is the Lansdowne Column, towering 125 feet above its hilltop site. It was erected by the third marquess of Lansdowne (1780-1863), apparently from mixed motives, for I have seen them described as a commemoration of the birth of the Prince of Wales, a memorial to a seventeenth-century ancestor who was a distinguished economist, and, simply, as a boundary mark. In the eighteenth century Cherhill was infested by a notorious band of highwaymen, known as 'The Cherhill Gang'. In the village is an immense tithe barn which quite dwarfs the tiny fifteenth century church which is its near neighbour.

A couple of miles along the Bath road we come to Calne, a town nowadays celebrated for and made prosperous by its bacon factory. The world-famous Wiltshire cure of bacon is said to have originated at Calne, and the great factory both dominates the town and provides a livelihood for most of its inhabitants.

Calne's bacon industry has, however, developed over only the past two hundred years. Before that Calne was yet another Wiltshire weaving town, with twenty busy mills a-working at one time. It was also a resting-place on the Bath road, not only for coaches, traders and wayfarers but also for drovers taking flocks and herds of livestock from the West Country to London. There was, in particular, a considerable traffic in Irish pigs, which were landed at Bristol and made to walk the rest of the way. A family of Calne butchers, the Harrises, took their pick of the grunting multitudes and eventually established the factory which still bears their name (though it now belongs to the Fatstock Marketing Corporation). This factory was the first to employ the principle of refrigeration in bacon-curing, taking out a patent for the process in 1864.

In 1645 the steeple of Calne parish church collapsed. John Aubrey, in whose time this happened, caustically remarks, 'One of the pillars was faulty, and the churchwardens were dilatory, as is usual in such cases.'

A public-spirited citizen had brought Inigo Jones to inspect the building, five years earlier, paying the fee out of his own pocket, and reported to the churchwardens that it could be made safe for £100. Nothing was done, and, after the collapse, the parish had to face a bill of over £1,000 for rebuilding. Aubrey adds the intriguing detail that the eventual disaster was 'occasioned by the throwing of a stone by a boy'. One lady was so frightened that she 'dyed in halfe an houre's time'.

Two miles from Calne is the great estate of Bowood, home of the marquesses of Lansdowne, who have been there since 1754. The first marquesses employed Robert Adam to improve, enlarge and beautify the house, on which assignment the great architect spent the best part of eight years. At the same time Capability Brown was at work on the gardens, park and 1000-acre estate. This same marquis filled his magnificent mansion with art treasures and lovely furniture from every available source, almost bankrupting himself in the process. Most of his collection had to be dispersed after his death, but his successors later resumed collecting, and Bowood now houses a fine gallery of pictures, including masterpieces by Reynolds, Raphael, Gainsborough, Turner and van Meulen.

Bowood estate was once part of the extensive mediaeval Forest of Chippenham, and Chippenham itself lies only five miles to the west and is almost a twin town to Calne. It is, however, a much larger place, with more diverse interests. In Saxon times English monarchs had a palace here, occupied presumably when the kings wished to go hunting in Chippenham Forest. It was here that Alfred was spending Christmas with his court in 877 when he was surprised by the Danes and chased away to temporary exile on the isle of Athelney, in the Somerset marshes.

Chippenham may owe its origin to the fact that here several roads from the west joined to form a main highway to London, but from very early times it developed as a market town. The name Chippenham seems to illustrate this, if it derives from 'cheaping', a market, though some authorities think that it comes from a personal name, Cyppa. The town used to have three market days, one for corn, one for cattle and one for cheese, its cheese market being considered, in the early part of the nineteenth century, the largest in the West of England. It was also, from the early Middle Ages, in the forefront of the wool trade, and Aubrey lists it as one of the great clothing towns of the West. At the Great Exhibition of 1851 a first prize for cloth was awarded to a Chippenham firm.

From mediaeval times Chippenham inherits one of its best-known possessions, Maud Heath's Causeway. Maud Heath was a market women who in the reign of Henry VII used to trudge to Chippenham every week from her home at Langley Burrell, carrying heavy baskets of eggs and butter. Many a time as she splashed through puddles and struggled over the muddy morasses that served as a track she must have wished for a more kindly path. So when she died in 1474 she left all her savings to make and endow a stone causeway linking the little villages of the Avon Valley with Chippenham. It is still there, offering a pleasant walk of four-and-a-half miles. The obvious starting-point is Chippenham church, near which, on a stone in a wall, is the inscription:

> *Hither extended Maud Heath's gift,*
> *For where you stand is Chippenham Clift.*

The path crosses the Avon over Kellaways Bridge, of sixty-four arches, and continues to Wick Hill, where we can see, high on a column a statue of the good lady, with her basket on her arm. The view she can enjoy from her perch is, incidentally, one of the finest in Wiltshire.

Chippenham today is a busy town, still a thriving market and shopping centre, though with also several factories, including a very large one making brakes and other equipment for locomotives. Its town hall is older than the date 1776, carved on one of its gables, suggests; and the centre of the town has a number of half-timbered houses and even more Georgian ones.

Between Chippenham and Calne, at Bremhill, a neglected poet, William Bowles, was for more than forty years to 1850 the incumbent of the fine thirteenth-century church. Though with claims to be the founder of the school of English poetry of which Wordsworth, Coleridge and Southey, all of whom had a high opinion of him, are the most distinguished stars, he is almost forgotten. A little further up the valley Hilmarton church possesses a chained Bible from the year 1611, the year in which the Authorised Version first appeared. The church itself has an imposing tower and a handsome barrel roof.

The chief distinction of the village of East Tytherton, just to the east of Chippenham, is that it was in the eighteenth century the home of John Cennick, one of the founders of the Moravian Church in England. In the 1740s Cennick became one of John Wesley's first lay preachers, but later he broke with the Methodists and established a Moravian church at Tytherton. The church and school he built still stand.

Hardenhuish, on the other side of Chippenham, also has an eighteenth-century church, an Anglican one, built by the two John Woods who were the chief architects of Bath. The building they erected, using the stones of the old Norman church, would fit perfectly into the setting of Bath.

Easton Piers, the birthplace of John Aubrey, Wiltshire's first great naturalist and antiquarian who is much quoted in this book, is a hamlet, once a fine estate with manor-house, chapel, graveyard and four farms, in the parish of Kington St Michael. Another Cotswold stone house has taken the place of the manor where Aubrey was born, and he himself did not occupy the estate for many years, for its was all swallowed up in legal expenses following the death of his father. His loss was our gain, for it sent Aubrey travelling around on visits to other estates, where he seems to have often stayed for long periods as a guest, thus greatly increasing his knowledge of the county. I think I would have got on well with Aubrey. He had a roving and probing mind, interested in too wide a range of subjects ever to become a specialist.

Less than a mile away, though 146 years later, another noted antiquarian, John Britton, was born. Much of his life was spent in doing detailed topographical work for London publishers, work at which he excelled but which, through lack of financial success, failed to bring him the recognition he deserved. He collected a mass of manuscripts by John Aubrey and had them published, with an introduction by himself, in 1847. He and Aubrey are jointly commemorated by a window in Kington's thirteenth-century church.

West Kington, six miles to the west, was Bishop Hugh Latimer's village, he being rector there for five years in the reign of Henry VIII. Its church still retains the pulpit from which he used to preach.

The Avon valley around Chippenham is rich in country mansions set in handsome parks, and quarries of Cotswold stone not many miles away ensure fine architecture in both houses and churches. Among the most impressive of the latter are those of Sutton Benger, the tower of which is surmounted by pinnacles with open tracery, the thirteenth-century church of St James at Draycot Cerne, and Stanton St Quinton church with its splendid Norman doorway. Yatton Keynell church has one of the finest towers in Wiltshire with a panelled belfry stage and battlements on which, says John Aubrey, young Tom Stump, daredevil son of the rector and a descendant of the William Stump who bought Malmesbury Abbey, used to climb and prance about. As we have noted earlier (see page 167) Aubrey attended the 'latine schoole' at Yatton Keynell. He mentions that in his day the village had a paper mill which manufactured brown paper for customers in Bristol.

Hullavington, approximately midway between Chippenham and Malmesbury, is another of Wiltshire's great R.A.F. air bases, with the packing of parachutes one of its specialities, though at the time of writing a decision has just been taken to close it.

Here, in the foothills of the Cotswolds, where craftsmen still practise the age-old skills of drystone walling, we encounter the Fosse Way, that ancient highway, metalled by the Romans, which transects England diagonally from Axmouth to Lincoln. Nearly fifty generations of human feet have trudged along the great road since the Roman legions marched along it, and still milk tankers and farm Land Rovers use the lanes that mark its course in Wiltshire. Several sectors of it coincide with the county boundary between Wiltshire and Gloucestershire, though Wiltshire has a series of salients on the far side.

In one of them the large village of Sherston is built partly inside an ancient earthwork which once fortified a peninsula between two streams.

Here in 1016 a hardly-contested battle was fought between the Danes under Canute and the English under Edmund Ironside, in the course of which a local knight, John Rattlebone, received a dreadful wound. But he fought on as valorously as ever, holding a tile against the wound to prevent his bowels spilling out. Evidently he recovered, for he received the manor of Sherston as a reward. Sherston people point out a small stone figure on a corner of the church, said to represent Rattlebone, while a strong timber chest, of at least early mediaeval date, is supposed to be the wardrobe where he kept his suit of armour.

Near Easton Grey, between Sherston and Malmesbury, is the probable site of Mutuantonis, a 'station' with mansion, or road-house, on the Fosse Way.

South of Sherston the county boundary runs along the edge of Badminton Park, of horse trials fame, and following it we arrive at Littleton Drew, at the head of the little river, By Brook. Like Stanton Drew, in Somerset, it has a surviving link with prehistoric times in its large tumulus, near Manor Farm, and some have suspected that the name Drew is connected with 'Druid'. Nettleton, on the other side of the brook, also has the remains of a tumulus, known as Lugbury, which long ago collapsed. The lintel stone, now fallen, lies as a table, twelve feet by six feet, and the whole tumulus was 180 feet long by 90 feet wide.

The recognised mecca for visitors to this corner of Wiltshire is Castle Combe, a village of such fairy-tale picturesqueness that it seems too good to be true. That it should be chosen as a fishing-port in the film of *Dr Doolittle* is entirely appropriate, for it might be on the coast of Queen Anne's Dorset, or in Disney-land, or in the pages of a Hans Andersen book. The cottages and houses of golden Cotswold stone, with their gables, thatch and stone tiles, are delightfully grouped around the church and market cross, with the little stream tying them together, and the old manor-house standing a little apart in its own grounds, in benevolent aloofness. Behind, the wooden hills, where once a castle stood, form an impressive green backcloth. Trying to live an ordinary life, with proper attention to such matters as drying the washing, packing the children off to school, gossiping with the neighbours at the Post Office and planting potatoes must be rather difficult in a village invaded every day during spring and summer by sightseeing visitors by car-load and coach-load.

It seems impossible that our ancestors were not influenced by the beauty of this place, but its history is much on a par with that of other west Wiltshire towns and villages. The Romans, who had an eye for the best sites, had a villa here; and later there was a castle. The Scrope family moved in as lords of the manor in the reign of Richard II and, appreciating their good fortune, stayed for nearly 500 years. Incidentally, it is claimed that a Tudor knight, Sir John Falstolf, who married into the Scrope family, was the original of Shakespeare's Falstaff. Castle Combe developed as a weaving town and an important market. Aubrey writes:

'The most celebrated faire in North Wiltshire for sheep is at Castle Combe, on St. George's Day, whither sheep-masters doe come as far as from Northamptonshire. Here is a good crosse and market-house; and heretofore was a staple of wooll . . . I have heard old men say long since that the market at Castle Combe was considerable in the time of the staple; the market days is Munday. Now only some eggs and butter, etc.'

The butter and eggs were no doubt sold around the old market cross.

Competing with Castle Combe in beauty and charm, Lacock, by the Avon four miles south of Chippenham, is a living reminder of Tudor England. Sir William Sharington, who bought the old abbey at the dissolution of monasteries, instead of demolishing it converted it into a manor-house for his own use. Almost everything was retained intact and remains so to this day. Visitors to the abbey, which is now National Trust property though still occupied by a member of the Talbot family who gave it to the nation, can see the mediaeval chapter house, cloisters, kitchen, sacristy and other features familiar to the nuns who once walked and worked there. The town itself, which also belongs to the National Trust, is a delightful place of neat streets of Cotswold stone cottages, many of them half-timbered and with casement windows and low stone doorways. The fourteenth-century church has a splendid lady chapel; there is a fifteenth-century house which is now an inn where excellent meals can be enjoyed; and the scene is completed by a fine old tithe barn facing a row of cottages across a narrow street.

Lacock has indeed been fortunate in its owners. The abbey was founded by one of Wiltshire's most distinguished ladies, Ela, Countess of Salisbury, in the reign of Henry III. Her husband was William Longespee, an illegitimate son of Henry II and one of the barons who led the revolt against King John; which explains how Lacock came to possess one of the three original copies of Magna Carta. Sir William Sharington, though of somewhat dubious character, was less of an iconoclast than most of the ruthless tycoons who acquired ecclesiastical property from Henry VIII. He not only preserved the abbey but such additions as he made were well executed and in harmony with the older buildings.

A romantic story attaches to the appearance of the Talbots on the Lacock scene. Olivia, daughter and heiress of Sir William Sharington's brother, was courted by young John Talbot, younger brother of the Earl of Shrewsbury, but her father strongly disapproved the match. So the lovers used to meet in secret, and one night were conducting a clandestine conversation, she from the battlements of the abbey church, he on the lawn below, when she laughingly offered to leap down. 'Come on, then', said John, not believing that she would. But she did. Her billowing skirts checked her fall a little, but when John attempted to catch her the wind was knocked out of him. Says Aubrey,

'She cried out for help, and he was with great difficulty brought to life again. Her father told her that since she had made such a leap she should e'en marry him.'

Two hundred years later Lacock Abbey was the home of another Talbot – William Fox Talbot, pioneer of photography. Pursuing work already begun into the principles of photography, he discovered how to make prints from negatives. Visitors to Lacock are shown the oriel window from which, in 1835, he took his first successful photograph.

Lackham House, on the banks of the Avon just north of Lacock, was purchased in 1945 by the Wiltshire County Council to be developed as the county Agricultural College. It has a well-run farm of some six hundred acres and under the wise guidance of its first principal, an old friend and fellow-worker of mine, J. O. Thomas, it has achieved an enviable reputation in the field of agricultural education. In recent years it has established an excellent and ever-growing museum of agricultural machinery and equipment.

Midway between Lacock and the county border with Gloucestershire Corsham has in our own time been largely taken over by the armed forces. Several Service establishments descended on it during the Second World War, and some have stayed. Before that it was a typical west Wiltshire weaving town, tastefully built of Bath stone, of which several quarries were worked in the parish from very early times. In 1801 it was the eighth most populous town in the county, jealously preserving a number of ancient rights, which include the right to hold a court leet and to have its own coroner. The parishioners were exempted from jury service, and the vicar was empowered to hold his own consistory court.

In and around Corsham is a group of handsome and distinguished country mansions – Hartham Park, Monks Park, Puckeredge House, seventeenth-century Pickwick Manor, Jaggards, of the same period, and Easton manor house, which is fifteenth century. Pickwick Manor has a delightful little village of stone grown golden with age and weathering and has given its name to one of the best-known characters in English literature, for Dickens is supposed to have taken it from the coaches of a Moses Pickwick of this place, who ran a service between Bath and London.

But the finest and most imposing of the great houses of the district is Corsham Court, home of the Methuen family. Built in 1582, it was purchased by a Paul Methuen, member of one of the great Wiltshire cloth-manufacturing families, in 1745 and has been their residence ever since. It houses a magnificent collection of pictures and is set in grounds once planned by Capability Brown, though he would hardly recognise the great yew hedges, the oaks and cedars and the gigantic plane tree, so increased in size since his day.

Another handsome little stone village in this neighbourhood is Biddestone, clustering around a village green with pond and stone cross and a splendid old barn in the background. The church has a good Norman doorway, and Sheldon manor, nearby, has a fine thirteenth-century porch attached to a house of later (Stuart) date.

Colerne, on the other side of the little By Brook, lies close to the Gloucestershire border and the Fosse Way. A Roman villa once stood here, and now the village has a superb church tower, crowning a largely twelfth-century building. In the present century a good slice of the parish has been taken for an R.A.F. station, at the time of writing threatened by an economy axe.

Aubrey has a curious little note about Colerne. Here, he said, the favourite game is 'Stobball'.

'They smite a ball, stuffed very hard with quills and covered with soale leather, with a staffe, commonly made of withy, about three feet and a halfe long. Colerne-downe is the place so famous and so frequented for stobball-playing. The turfe is very fine, and the rock is within an inch and

a halfe of the surface, which gives the ball so quick a rebound. A
stoball-ball is of about four inches diameter, and as hard as a stone. I doe
not heare that this game is used anywhere in England but in this part of
Wiltshire and Gloucestershire adjoining.'

Ditteridge, just south of Colerne, has restored, as a chapel, a
fifteenth-century hospice once used by pilgrims to Glastonbury. Its
pleasant little church retains much Norman work, including a fine
Norman porch.

Box, a hill-top village above a deep combe, is best known for its long
railway tunnel, the work of Brunel, and for its extensive stone quarries. It
used also to have tallow and brewing industries. A villa of the Roman
period, with tesselated pavement, has been found here, while another was
discovered at Atworth, nearby, as recently as 1938.

South Wraxhall has a handsome fifteenth-century manor, the home of
the Long family who owed their origins to the wool trade. It has been
claimed that here tobacco was first smoked in England, by Sir Walter
Raleigh and his friend Sir Walter Long. A rather similar mediaeval manor
at Great Chalfield, near Melksham, is, in my opinion, one of Wiltshire's
loveliest architectural gems – a mansion sitting on the edge of a moat in
rich meadow country. Whatever Great Chalfield may have been once, it
is no longer great in size. Its little church, with an attractive,
brightly-painted, home-built organ, is within the manor-house precincts.
Apart from its architecture, Chalfield's great treasures are the Tropenell
Cartulary and the Tropenell Portrait. The Cartulary is a kind of inventory
of all the property of Thomas Tropenell, a prosperous wool merchant
who acquired the estate in the fifteenth century and was responsible for
the house as it now stands. The portrait, discovered under the whitewash
of a wall, is thought to be of Thomas – and a grim character he appears to
be.

Yet another interesting manor-house stands at Monkton Farleigh, over
on the Somerset border towards Bath. It incorporates, in its commanding
position on the slopes of Bathford Hill, what little remains of a Cluniac
priory, which flourished here from the twelfth century till Henry VIII
disposed of it. A fine avenue of beeches links Monkton Farleigh with
South Wraxall. Broughton Gifford, a large village around a village green,
now almost a residential suburb of Melksham, was in mediaeval times a
manor attached to the priory at Monkton.

Melksham began life as a forest village, in the Forest of Melksham, but owes its name to the dairying which soon developed in the rich pastures of the neighbourhood. Like other towns of west Wiltshire it prospered as a wool town in mediaeval times, but the factories have been closed and taken over by other industries, notably Avon Rubber, which firm employs over 3000 people in the town. It is also the headquarters of a thriving farmers' co-operative trading society, Wiltshire Farmers. A busy but architecturally undistinguished town, Melksham at one time aspired to be a spa. Two promising mineral springs were discovered here in 1816, and all the necessary amenities, including a pump room, hot and cold baths, a handsome promenade and even crescents like Bath, were quickly provided, but for some reason the idea never caught on.

Bradford-on-Avon, in some respects a twin town of Melksham and only five miles away, is very different. Here we have a picturesque, compact, stone-built town of almost the quality of Castle Combe and Lacock. Unlike the relatively flat sites of Melksham and Trowbridge, Bradford is perched on the sides of a ravine through which the river forces its determined way westwards, undeterred by the barrier of the Cotswolds. Some of the tall houses have a front entrance three stories lower than the back door, which opens on to a street farther up the hill.

Bradford first appears in history in the year 652, when a West Saxon king, Kenwalch, fought a battle here against the Britons. St Aldhelm, on his missionary tours in and around the Forest of Selwood, founded a monastery at Bradford in 705. The town prospered exceedingly with the expansion of the wool trade in the Middle Ages and at one time had at least thirty woollen factories, not one of which is left. A new impetus to the industry was given as late as the seventeenth century when Paul Methuen, one of Bradford's great clothiers, brought over a colony of Flemish weavers to introduce improved techniques. In the census of 1801 Bradford was still the third most populous town in Wiltshire, with only a few hundred fewer inhabitants than Devizes and Salisbury. It is still a busy manufacturing town, though with a different set of industries. Avon Rubber has taken over some of the old wool factories towering over the banks of the Avon, and on the outskirts of the town a flourishing mushroom-growing enterprise has been established.

The town is a museum of virtually every period of its history. Its most ancient and priceless possession is the Saxon church of St Lawrence, probably standing on the site of the even earlier one founded by St Aldhelm. Built early in the eleventh century, the little church probably owes its survival to the fact that for centuries it was not recognised as a church at all. Families lived in it; a school was once housed in it; wool factories crowded against it; and at one time it was used as a kind of charnel house. The sharp eyes of a vicar of Bradford, Prebendary Jones, rediscovered it in 1858, and now the clutter of buildings which concealed it have been removed, to give a clear view of the venerable shrine in a setting of well-kept lawns. I find one feature of the little church puzzling. Its dimensions are, to say the least, unusual, for it is as high as it is long. About halfway up the interior walls are cavities in which beam-ends once rested but which are now filled with stone. Evidently it was a two-storied building, understandable if it was once used as a dwelling-house. Yet the upper parts seem to belong to the original construction; there is no evidence that they were added later. Why would a little Saxon church need an upper floor?

Another unusual feature is the very narrow chancel arch, only $3\frac{1}{2}$ feet wide. For the congregation in the nave looking towards the altar it is like peeping through a narrow doorway. There is also a proportionately large north porch, which may have been used as a separate chapel.

The Saxon church is just across the road from its successor, the oldest parts of which date from Norman times. It is a handsome building, with a fine stone-tiled roof and some interesting ornate tombs. Beyond lies Bradford's great tithe barn, one of the largest in England, being 55 yards long and consisting of fourteen great bays. Of this building, too, the roof is of stone tiles, estimated to weigh about a hundred tons. It was built early in the fourteenth century, to house the harvests of the Abbey of Shaftesbury, to which Bradford then belonged.

These three notable buildings by no means exhaust the architectural wealth of Bradford. Visitors can hardly escape passing over the main road bridge, once a pack-horse bridge but long ago widened, with the little stone cell surmounted by a weather vane in the form of a fish — the 'Bradford Gudgeon'. It was once a chapel 'for Masse' but later used as the town lock-up, among the distinguished prisoners who spent an uncomfortable night there being John Wesley. The many other attractive and historical buildings in the heart of the town include John Hall's hall (the home of a wealthy mediaeval wool merchant), some mediaeval almshouses, a group of Tudor houses in The Shambles, the Church House and Old Priory, which are fifteenth-century, and Chantry House, which is sixteenth. On a hill above the town the little chapel of St Mary, used as a hospice for travellers in the Middle Ages, then allowed to fall into ruin and restored in recent times, offers a magnificent view of the whole deep valley.

Three miles south-east of Bradford, the third of this trio of wool towns, Trowbridge, resembles Melksham much more nearly than Bradford. Trowbridge began life as a settlement on a ridge of stony subsoil by the little river Biss. Its growth to urban status started with the building of a castle by the de Bohuns early in the twelfth century, a castle which played a prominent role in the regrettable wars between Matilda and Stephen. An important market developed outside the castle gates and endured long after the castle had disappeared. The town was thus well established when the woollen industry brought a new prosperity to the west, and it shared in the general wealth associated with weaving mills for many centuries. Later, as the woollen industry declined, its place was taken by others, notably a factory for making steam engines (now departed), some breweries and a bed-making factory. Today the town has in addition a sausage factory and a number of light industries as well as two surviving cloth mills.

Trowbridge's chief distinction, however, is that it houses Wiltshire's county offices. For all practical purposes, it is the county town, or capital, of the county and has been since 1893. The arrangement strikes visitors, and many Wiltshiremen, as decidedly odd. Salisbury is Wiltshire's cathedral city, has a much more distinguished history and is much bigger; Swindon is nowadays easily the biggest town in the county; Devizes occupies a more central position. So why elevate this pleasant but undistinguished weaving town, within about three miles of the western border of the county, to such an important position? The conundrum is explained by a short study of the railway map. Communications between the north and south of the county, always hampered by the barrier of Salisbury Plain, were complicated by the coming of the railways. All the main lines ran through the county roughly from east to west, and none from north to south. County councillors from Swindon and Devizes would have had to change at Andover to get to Salisbury and possibly to make another change or two; and the same handicaps would have weighed against the choice of Swindon or Devizes as county town; whereas Trowbridge was easily accessible by rail from all of them. So Trowbridge it had to be, and still is.

The minor poet, George Crabbe, was rector of Trowbridge for eighteen years from 1814, but, made indolent by relative affluence, did little writing here.

In the great days of the woollen industry west Wiltshire had a fourth town, now sunk to the level of a large village, forming a quadrangle with Trowbridge, Melksham and Bradford. It was Steeple Ashton, whose very name is said to perpetuate the fact that it was once a 'staple' or important market. Set on a ridge in the heart of the Avon valley, it is an ancient place, being part of an estate granted to the nunnery at Romsey by King Edgar in 959. Leland, who visited it in the time of Elizabeth I, refers to it as

'a praty little market toune, and hath praty buildings. It standeth much by clothiers. There is in it a very faire chirche, buildid in the mind of men now lyvinge.'

That Steeple Ashton did not develop as a town like some of its neighbours was due to a succession of accidents. A series of disastrous fires in the fifteenth century resulted in Steeple Ashton's market being moved to Market Lavington, which, in due course, was superseded by Devizes.

So Steeple Ashton relapsed into the status of a mainly agricultural village, though retaining evidence of its past prosperity in its magnificent church, its market cross and a group of fine old houses, including one of the fourteenth century. The church itself has had more than its share of mishaps, as John Aubrey recounts:

'On the 25th July 1670 there was a rupture in the steeple of Steeple Ashton by lightning. The steeple was ninety-three feet high above the tower; which was much about that height. This being mending, and the last stone goeing to be putt in by two master workemen, on the 15th day of October following, a sudden storme with a clap of thunder tooke up the steeple from the tower and killed both the workmen *in nictu oculi*. The stones fell in and broke part of the church but never hurt the font.'

Two other interesting churches in the vicinity are those of Keevil and North Bradley. The latter has some particularly splendid roofs, and both contain rich interior decoration and monuments. Both villages, too, possess fine old stone and timbered houses. Talboys House, in Keevil, dates, though with some subsequent restoration, from the time of Edward IV, and Southwick Court, near North Bradley, preserves its ancient moat and the ruins of a chapel.

As we have seen, the Avon veers westwards between Melksham and Bradford and proceeds to break through the barrier of the Cotswolds and cut a gorge through to the Bristol Channel, instead of continuing its way southwards and linking up with either the Stour or the Wylye, as it might easily have done. Before it finally disappears into Somerset it claims several villages which, because of their hilly setting and the use they make of Bath stone, are inevitably picturesque. The last village of Wiltshire, on a salient thrust out westwards beyond the river, is lovely Limpley Stoke, a cliff-side village after the pattern of Bradford. Here a stone aqueduct carries the Kennet and Avon canal over the river and railway. The church has a Saxon arch which is now an interior feature of a later building.

Near Brokerswood is a mecca for all who love trees – the Woodland Park, which is run by trustees as an educational trust on a non-profit-making basis. The Centre, established for educational work in natural history and forestry, comprises a museum and exhibition hall, a lecture room and a library. There are marked nature trails, with guides to the trees and birds. Visitors may stroll, picnic and even, wonderful to relate though very sensibly, pick small quantities of wild flowers, though they are asked not to overdo it. It seems to me that the wholesale prohibition of the picking of wild flowers, so often enforced, has no logical basis, as almost all plants, except annuals which depend on each year's seeding, are helped by having their flowers picked, within reason.

Westwood has a fine old fifteenth-century manor-house and a church of approximately the same date. Iford, a charming manor by the river Frome, is noted for its extensive formal gardens.

On the southern edge of the vale of Avon, midway between Trowbridge and Warminster and under the shadow of the great chalk downs, is yet another wool town, Westbury. Like so many other Wiltshire towns, it began life as a Saxon borough, though there were settlements in the neighbourhood even earlier, in Roman times. Its fortunes fluctuated with those of the wool industry. As late as 1722, when Daniel Defoe visited it he wrote that Westbury was still the chief place in the whole world for the manufacture of Spanish cloth. One hundred years later the biased Cobbett found it 'a nasty odious rotten-borough, a really rotten place. It has cloth factories in it, and they seem to be ready to tumble down as well as many of the houses'. He has the grace to add, though, that 'Westbury is a place of great ancient grandeur; and it is easy to perceive that it was once ten or twenty times its present size' – another exaggeration.

As the cloth trade declined, so Westbury was fortunate in finding an alternative. Nearby is a ridge of higher ground, extending south-westwards from Seend, which is rich in iron. In the second half of the nineteenth century the ore was being worked energetically, and two blast furnaces were operating. Factories for agricultural machinery were established. Now only a few grass-grown mounds and pits remain as reminders of the old iron workings. Deep beneath Westbury there are also seams of coal, which have never been exploited.

For most people, however, Westbury is primarily associated with its White Horse. This, the oldest of all the white horses of Wiltshire, is carved on a chalk hillside which is the north-western scarp of Salisbury Plain. From its airy site it commands a magnificent panoramic view of the Vale of Avon and the Somerset hills beyond, and of the impressive advance of clouds like white galleons sailing in on the south-westerlies. It is a large horse, 166 feet long by 163 feet high, and when I was a boy in the 1920s a popular idea for a family outing in summer was to make an excursion to the White Horse and picnic on its eye, which was large enough to accommodate a family.

The horse in its present form was cut in 1778. Before that an earlier horse occupied the site, being incorporated into the body of the later one. This earlier horse, beside being smaller, was an animal of curious shape. It was a long, narrow figure, with very short legs, like a dachshund, an erect neck and an upward-curved tail, like that of a cat, with a crescent poised on the tip. It also had a saddle. It was, in fact, more reminiscent of the stylised, surrealistic animal that creeps up over Uffington Hill in the Vale of the White Horse (in Berkshire) than the more realistic attempts at depicting good horseflesh that are characteristic of the other Wiltshire horses. This strange appearance has tempted many conjectures about the antiquity of the Westbury Horse. However, Morris Marples, writer of a monograph on *White Horses,* dismisses such theories, and the claim that it was cut to celebrate Alfred's victory over the Danes, and attaches more importance to the statement by the Rev. F. Wise in 1742 that it had been 'wrought within the memory of persons now living or but lately dead.' It is perhaps significant that John Aubrey, who had an eye for such things, makes no mention at all of any white horses in Wiltshire in his day.

The White Horse is actually not in Westbury parish but in the next one, Bratton, and the earthwork which crowns the hill on which it stands is known as Bratton Castle. Here, according to one theory, is where the battle of Ethandune was fought between the Danes and the Saxons under Alfred in the year 878. In my book *Somerset* I have set out in some detail the reasons for supposing that the campaign was fought out on the Polden Hills of Somerset, not here. One of the secondary arguments is that a battle fought on this hill would hardly be called the battle of Ethandune, or Edington, Edington Hill being about two miles farther east.

Bratton itself, the village under the hill, had, like Westbury, flourishing ironworks, making agricultural implements, a century ago. Its thirteenth-century church is perched on a steep hillside, requiring a climb up and down over a hundred steps to reach it.

Before we follow the downland escarpment eastwards we should take note of two places on the other side of Westbury. Dilton has one of the most attractive small churches in the county, a pleasant place of late mediaeval date fitted with box pews and a three-decker pulpit. Westbury Leigh had a palace of the early Saxon kings, including Alfred. The census of 1801 shows this neighbourhood relatively densely populated; Westbury had a population of 1837, Westbury Leigh of 1475, Dilton of 1524, and Bratton of 1085. Most of the inhabitants are recorded as being engaged in trade of manufacture, which evidently means the cloth industry. This is the census in which Swindon is shown with a population of 1198, and Salisbury and Devizes, the two largest towns, have just over 7000.

Edington, the next village eastwards from Bratton, was another place of considerable importance in early times. It is mentioned in Alfred's will and was later given by King Edgar to the abbess of Romsey. In the reign of Edward III one of Edington's most distinguished sons, William of Edington, was bishop of Winchester and also the king's treasurer. When Edward's son, the Black Prince, showed interest in bringing over from France monks of an obscure Augustinian order known as the Bonshommes and establishing them in a foundation in England, William sugggested they should go to his native village, Edington. So it was arranged for the nuns to move out and the monks to take over, and the brothers rewarded their adopted country by building at Edington a church noble and splendid enough to be a cathedral. It has survived practically unaltered since its construction in 1352-1361 and is probably the best example of the Perpendicular style of architecture in Wiltshire. It was designed as a dual-purpose church, the chancel being the monastic section while the nave was reserved for the parishioners, with an altar under the western arch. Its battlemented exterior and decorated interior are equally impressive, and the golden-grey stone looks as though it had grown up from the daisies. Outside the church is guarded by an enormous yew which is probably its equal in age, and in the orchards around are fragments of masonry which are all that remain of the old priory. The church has ten bells and, on its flat roof, a mediaeval clock, without face and evidently blacksmith-made.

Here dramatic and tragic events took place in the year 1449. During the course of a peasant revolt, this one known as Jack Cade's Rebellion, the bishop of Salisbury, one William Ayscough, fled from Salisbury, which he held to be too hot to hold him, and took refuge at Edington. He was followed and seized by the mob when actually in the church. Their quarrel with him, they said, was that he spent too much time at Court, as confessor and secretary to King Henry VI, and neglected the affairs of his own diocese. So they dragged him out of the church and up the hill where they found a flint-heap and pelted him to death.

Two hundred years later George Herbert, the hymn writer and vicar of Bemerton, was married in this church. Today the church has a widely-known annual music festival, attracting entries from all over the country. It also houses the furnishings from the abandoned church of Imber, on the Plain.

Next door to Edington, Coulston has memories of two ladies of very different character. Mary Delany, after a long career as a society hostess in London in the reign of George III, settled down in her retirement at Coulston to make paper mosaics, which she did with such skill that ten volumes of them, exquisite works of art, are preserved in the Prints and Drawings Department of the British Museum. The other was a murderess, Constance Kent, who provided a baffling murder mystery for the Police and Press in the 1860s. She was never even suspected of killing her little half-brother, Francis, until, five years later, she confessed.

The next village under the hills, Erlestoke, is also noted for a lawbreaker, for here Thomas Boulter, the highwayman really responsible for many of the legends attached to Dick Turpin, stole his celebrated horse, whose name really was Black Bess!

My collection of agricultural bygones includes a number of sheep bells, some of which I have used on sheep within the past twenty years. At least some of them were made at Great Cheverell, near Erlestoke, by an old shepherd and craftsman, named Lancaster, towards the end of the nineteenth century. Either this village or the next one, West Lavington, was also the home of David Saunders, commemorated by Hannah More, the eighteenth-century moralist, in her tract *The Shepherd of Salisbury Plain.* This excessively meek and godly man, who reared sixteen children in a two-roomed hovel, was a popular character with contemporary philanthropists and their nineteenth-century successors, who thoroughly approved of his resignation in the face of adversity.

At West Lavington the south-north highway across Salisbury Plain descends into the vale, where the fertile greensand fields and abundance of merry little springs supply an exhilarating contrast with the austere downs. West Lavington is the home of that great school for boys, Dauntseys — named after a family which once owned the manor.

Earlier we saw that Market Lavington profited by a series of extensive fires at Steeple Ashton to become an important market and weaving town. Its Wednesday market has now long since been closed, for it was too near to Devizes for both to flourish. This, incidentally, was the home of the Smith family who, until the present century, were known far and wide as expert dew-pond makers.

At Urchfont, next village east from Lavington, we arrive at the scarcely discernible watershed between the Pewsey Vale and its streams which flow east and south to the Salisbury Avon and the westward-flowing streams which link with the Bristol Avon. Urchfont manor-house has become a rural university, run by the Wiltshire County Council and offering courses in a variety of subjects, chiefly rural.

Scores of little rivulets wander across the meadows between Devizes and the frontier of the Plain, uniting to form eventually streams large enough to bear names, such as the Lavington Brook, the Semington Brook and Summerham Brook. Several pleasant villages, chief being

Worton, Marston, Poulshot (birthplace of highwayman, Thomas Boulter), Bulkington and Keevil, nestle among trees in this flat countryside, while others look down on it from perches on the surrounding hills.

One of the latter, on the main road to Devizes from the south, is Potterne. Its church, poised high above the village street, is reputed to have had the same architect as Salisbury Cathedral, with which it is contemporary. On the roadside beneath it is a splendid half-timbered building known as the Porch House, which may have been the residence of the bishops of Salisbury when visiting this part of their diocese.

Potterne looks westwards across the valley to the ironstone ridge on which Seend is perched. This is another weaving village, almost a town, which enjoyed considerable prosperity in the great days of the wool industry. Aubrey offers a potted history of Seend, as follows:

'When King Henry VII lived in Flanders with his aunt the Dutchess of Burgundie, he considered that all or most of the wooll that was manufactured there into cloath was brought out of England; and observing what great profit did arise by it, when he came to the crown he sent into Flanders for clothing manufacturers, whom he placed in the west, and particularly at Send in Wiltshire, where they built severall good houses yet remaining; I know not any village so remote from London that can shew the like. The cloathing trade did flourish here till about 1580, when they removed to Troubridge, by reason of (I thinke) a plague; but I conjecture the main reason was that the water here was not proper for the fulling and washing of their cloath, for this water, being impregnated with iron, did give the white cloath a yellowish tincture.'

Aubrey was himself much interested in those iron deposits and experimented with them. His interest, however, lay entirely with the possibility of finding mineral springs that could be used medicinally, like those of Bath. He seems not to have considered their commercial exploitation as ore, though he met one 'George Newton, an ingeniose man, who from a blacksmith turned clock maker and fiddel maker, and he assured me that he has melted of this oare in his forge.' And the iron ores of Seend have never been exploited on any scale.

Another sandy plateau a few miles to the north, between Devizes and Calne, has fostered the development of a different industry. There, around Bromham and Sandy Lane, the soil has proved eminently suitable for the growing of market garden crops, and the district has become one of the main sources of supply of vegetables for Bristol, Bath and, to some extent, London as well as for Wiltshire towns. The industry is mainly in the hands of smallholders who are skilled at growing runner beans, leeks, cucumbers and suchlike crops.

Bromham, an important place in mediaeval times, has a fine old church with an octagonal spire 110 feet high. At Sloperton, near Chittoe, just to the west of the village, Thomas Moore, the Irish poet, lived for many years, writing many of his songs there. Heddington church, on the other side of Bromham, beneath Roundway Hill, has a chained copy of the rare Treacle Bible (a version which makes the prophet Jeremiah say, 'Is there no treacle in Gilead?').

Roundway Hill is the westward spur of that range of chalk downs which marks the northern boundary of the Vale of Pewsey and seals it off from the Kennet valley. It is crowned by an earthwork excavated in 1907 and found to be an Iron Age fort. Its popular name, Oliver's Camp, is doubtless due to association with Oliver Cromwell, whose troops under Waller were thoroughly beaten, in July 1643, by Royalist cavalry under Prince Maurice. Rowde, situated on a terrace beneath the hill, was the home of George Maundrell who, for maintaining the Protestant faith, was burned at the stake in Salisbury in the reign of Queen Mary.

We come, finally, to Devizes, where we might well have started our perambulation around Wiltshire, for it is at the very centre of the county and might easily have been its county town. As Wiltshire towns go, it is not remarkably old, for it had its beginnings in Norman times, when a castle was built at, it is said, the point where the parishes of Rowde, Potterne and All Cannings met. The place was thus named, Ad Divisas, and even in the early part of the present century old Wiltshiremen would refer to *The* Vizes, or *The* Vize.

As usual, a town quickly grew outside the castle and by 1135 was important enough to gain a charter, and by the early fourteenth century it was one of the most important cloth-manufacturing towns in the county, second only to Salisbury. A few mounds and earthworks are all that remain to mark the site of the old castle, but the church of St John, with its sturdy square Norman tower, like a castle keep, was almost certainly built by the same Bishop Roger of Salisbury, who was also responsible for the castle.

As might be expected from such an admirably situated town, Devizes developed a wide diversity of industries and interests. In mediaeval times and subsequently it became one of the greatest corn markets of the West, and it still has an important Thursday market for livestock and argicultural produce. Its present manufactures include beer, bricks, agricultural machinery and much light industry, and in the immediate post-war years it had for a time a thriving flax factory. It had an assize court until 1972, when this was changed to a crown court, and it houses the county museum, the county mental hospital and the county jail, as well as a splendid modern library.

Devizes has a second Norman church, that of St Mary, and a number of interesting houses and buildings, including the well-known Bear Inn, which used to be a coaching-house. The present 'Castle', though imposing, is nineteenth century and is now converted into flats. The Corn Exchange also dates from the middle of the nineteenth century, but an afternoon spent in exploring the town will reveal unexpected half-timbered houses almost shaking hands over cobbled alleys.

The central market place, once spacious enough for normal trade, is now, naturally inadequate as a car park, but the cars are chased away on market days. Visitors make a point of reading the admonitory inscription on Devizes market cross:

'On Thursday the 25th January, 1753, Ruth Pierce, of Pottern in this county, agreed with three other women to buy a sack of wheat in the market, each paying her due proportion towards the same. One of thse women, in collecting the several quota of money, discovered a deficiency and demanded of Ruth Pierce the sum which was wanting to make good the amount. Ruth Pierce protested that she had paid her share, and said that she wished she might drop down dead if she had not. She rashly repeated this wish; when, to the consternation and terror of the surrounding multitude, she instantly fell down and expired, having the money concealed in her hand.'

Devizes people evidently took to heart certain local happenings in the 1750s, for in the churchyard of St John's is another monument to five young people who were drowned in a pond on Sunday evening, 30 June 1751; and the addition of the words: 'Remember the Sabbath Day to keep it holy' implies that they ought to have been in church and not larking about on the pond.

TWELVE

Animals, Plants
and Humans

The geology of Wiltshire is simple, compared, for instance, with that of
Somerset. Two-thirds of the county consists of chalk, and most of the rest
of oolitic limestone measures. There is some lias, mainly in the Avon
valley – towards Bath, and the clays of the Hampshire basin invade the
south-eastern corner of the county along the Deanbrook valley.

In Chapter 2 I have indulged in some memories of the chalk country as
it used to be. A shepherd standing on the downs near Stonehenge would
have seen an ocean of close-cropped turf extending in undulations to every
horizon, with never a fence or hedge and with very few trees. Now the
plough has penetrated almost everywhere, except where hillsides are too
steep for it. Where for untold generations men could wander at will, with
sheep and skylarks for company, heavy-headed barley, effectively
protected by barbed-wire fences, yields crops of two tons to the acre.
Stonehenge itself is cordoned off by barriers equal to the demands of a
prisoner-of-war camp. There is indeed a decided dearth of open spaces
where legs can be stretched, lungs exercised and cars abandoned for an
hour. That the necessity for such safety-valves is sometimes deplored does
not alter the fact that it exists.

Meantime the threat to the ancient fauna and flora of Wiltshire and the
current interest in ecology have naturally led to the formation of
numerous organisations bent on preserving the county's heritage, as the
following list, which does not profess to be complete, illustrates:

Wiltshire Archaeological and Natural History Society;
Wiltshire Trust for Nature Conservation;
Wiltshire Folk Life Society;

Wiltshire Ornithological Society;
Wiltshire Association for Environmental Education;
Salisbury Natural History Society;
Westbury Naturalists' Society;
Corsham Young Bird-Watchers' Society;
Box Archaeological & Natural History Society;
The Army Bird-Watching Society;
The Woodland Trust.

In addition, there are local or county branches and/or offices of the British Trust for Ornithology, the Nature Conservancy Council, the National Trust, The Royal Society for the Protection of Birds, the Botanical Society of the British Isles and the British Deer Society.

Some of Wiltshire's rarest zoological treasures are protected in special reserves. For instance, one of the last strongholds in England of the snakes-head fritillary is in certain damp meadows in north Wiltshire, now the object of vigilant preservation, with the willing co-operation of the farmers concerned. South Wiltshire has, at Blackmoor Copse near Farley, one of the few nature reserves designed primarily for the protection of an insect, the uncommon and magnificent Purple Emperor butterfly. The great bustards have long ago disappeared from their downland haunts, but an attempt is being made to rehabilitate a few of them in an enclosure of several acres on the downs near Porton.

The great bustard, which appears on Wiltshire's coat of arms, is said at one time to have featured prominently at the inaugural feasts of the mayors of Salisbury. It was probably the first British bird to have its eggs protected by law, an enactment of Henry VIII providing that the fine for taking a bustard's egg should be 20 pence. It ought to have been quite an effective measure, for the sum was a large one for those days, and the informer got half of it! Even then, however, the species seems to have been on the decline, and by the end of the eighteenth century it was rare. William Chafin, who wrote a little book entitled *The Anecdotes and History of Cranbourn Chase* in 1818, mentions that in 1751 he saw twenty-five bustards together on the downs near Winterslow Hut (the Pheasant Inn). His comment is: 'I believe that such a number of Bustards will never be again seen together in England'. Now, as mentioned in Chapter 2, the bustard's smaller relation, the stone curlew, is being elbowed out in the same way. Salisbury Museum has, incidentally, a very fine collection of Wiltshire bustards, including a cock in full breeding display.

In the 1930s I used to find the nests of quails fairly regularly near Pitton, but their favourite haunts are now built over, and their summer call, once familiar, is seldom heard. Thirty years earlier the corncrake was even more plentiful, its croaking call being as much a feature of the spring as that of the cuckoo, but, although there is some mystery about it, its disappearance seems to have coincided with the introduction. of mechanical grasscutting on farms. Today only a few birds occur on migration, usually in late summer or early autumn. Red-backed shrikes were once sufficiently common in summer for the shepherds of Salisbury Plain to have a local name for them – 'high mountain sparrows' – but they are now very seldom seen.

Certain other birds which might have been expected to suffer from the extension of agriculture have taken the changes in their stride. Lapwings, for instance, – nearly always known as peewits in Wiltshire – are as abundant as ever. Gulls, which formerly came inland only in stormy weather, now forage in flocks wherever food is to be found, especially on newly-ploughed fields. Conservation exercises in the past few years have tended to write off the vast arable fields as near-deserts for wild life, but the conclusion is based on an erroneous method of assessment, namely, censuses of species during the breeding season. While these extensive acreages of barley, wheat or grasses hold only a few ground-nesting birds, they offer a rewarding foraging area in every season except late spring and summer. In autumn and early winter in particular they are alive with flocks of foraging birds, notably finches, larks and buntings, who feed on the shed seeds, while the opening up of the soil by the plough provides another generous bonus of food. Goldfinches and linnets in particular have greatly increased in numbers in the present century, probably due to the protection now afforded from bird-catchers.

One of the typical birds of the chalk downland is the corn bunting, which lives in colonies of considerable size, the presence of which may be detected by observing the plump, lethargic birds perched at intervals on telephone wires. The county is also one of the chief habitats of the now uncommon cirl bunting. One of the rarer birds of Britain, which has its headquarters on Salisbury Plain, is the hobby, a dashing little falcon similar to but smaller than the peregrine. Perhaps a dozen or so pairs nest in Wiltshire, mostly on military territory.

Around the fringes of the chalk country and on the wider rivers and lakes considerable numbers of waterfowl congregate in winter, and some, such as the tufted duck, now nest much more frequently than formerly. The area of open water has been considerably extended in recent years by the flooding of gravel workings after the extraction of the gravel. One such series of man-made lakes is at Steeple Langford, in the Wylye valley, but much more extensive are the lakes near Ashton Keynes, on the Wiltshire-Gloucestershire border, where they cover at present over 800 acres and are likely to spread over 2200 acres by the 1980s.

Among mammals, fallow deer and roe deer are plentiful. The former have now more than recovered their abundant pre-war status, after organised slaughter during the war years, and roe deer find a highly congenial habitat in the new conifer plantations of the Forestry Commission. There are, I think, still small numbers of red deer in Savernake and perhaps elsewhere, for these animals tend to wander. A few years ago a young stag appeared on the army land near Porton and hung around for a year or two, gradually making its way across country to the vicinity of West Dean, where it eventually had to be killed for injuring young heifers with which it was consorting. Reports also come in from time to time of muntjac, or barking deer, the latest I have seen being from the neighbourhood of Winterslow. Some of the Wiltshire woods also hold Sika, or Japanese deer.

Foxes are fairly common, and in some districts badgers seem to be on the increase. Grey squirrels have almost entirely replaced red squirrels, though apparently there are just a few of the latter left. Most of the smaller British mammals are found in Wiltshire, including the harvest mouse and the dormouse, both of which have become rather rare in the country as a while.

Chapter 2 gives some information on the butterflies of the chalk downs. They are still quite plentiful where suitable countryside exists, the over-all decrease in numbers being due to the destruction of so many old-established habitats.

The same chapter mentions some of the typical flowers of the downland, which have been similarly affected. The flowers of the chalk hills which many people find most interesting, however, are the orchids, of which Wiltshire has between twenty and thirty species. Spotted orchids, early purple orchids and green-winged meadow orchids are abundant in meadow-land, and I have found such comparative rarities as dwarf orchids, fragrant orchids and green man orchids growing in profusion in restricted localities. Some of the downland coppices harbour greater and lesser butterfly orchids, twayblades and two species of helleborine. Among the dead leaves under old hazel I have found the saprophytic bird's-nest orchis in spring, and a few downs where the bee orchis grows still survive.

A feature of the chalk downs is the existence of caps of glacial clay on the tops of some of them. These deposits are usually covered with scrub, resulting in two entirely different types of flora in close juxtaposition. Within a hill-top downland thicket one can step, from the porous chalk, into a wet, waterlogged jungle, choked with brambles, nettles and coarse grasses. Its flowers include pink campions, enchanters' nightshade and bluebells; ferns are abundant. and nesting birds may include garden warblers and blackcaps.

Beech trees are so much a feature of the downland landscape today that one wonders whether Aubrey might have been mistaken when he recorded that in the seventeenth century there were 'none in Wiltshire, except at Groveley'. He was, however, a reasonably accurate observer. Although churchyard yews have usually been planted, there are large groves of wild yews in many places on the chalk downs. Nothing at all grows under their dark, funereal canopy, and to walk far under them is to be tempted to credit fanciful stories of associations with esoteric rites of ancient religions. The commonest tree in the valleys, especially in the broad vales of the northern Avon and the Thames, is the elm, now devastated by Dutch elm disease, which has killed off thousands in the county.

The cattle which graze the valley meadows and indeed the downland pastures as well, for nowadays dairying is not confined to the vales, are mostly black-and-white Friesians. There are some Channel Island and Ayrshire herds and assorted beef cattle, but Wiltshire has no local breed of its own. As we have noted in Chapter 11, Thomas Davis stated that in the early nineteenth century nine-tenths of the cattle in north-west Wiltshire were Longhorns. This, however, may not mean the well-recognised Longhorn breed we know now but may simply signify that they were a mongrel lot though possessing the typical long, usually down-curved horns. Aubrey, writing a hundred and fifty years earlier, says that most of the cattle in north Wiltshire in his time were either pied or black, born or deep red.

Wiltshire does have its own breed of sheep, the Wiltshire Horn, though there is probably only one flock living in the county today. When Thomas Davis prepared his report for the Board of Agriculture around 1810 he estimated that there were 500,000 of this breed on Salisbury Plain alone. Forty years later only a few flocks were left, and by the start of the twentieth century the breed was entirely unknown in its county of origin. My father, who was born in south Wiltshire in 1874 and was brought up with sheep, saw the breed for the first time at an agricultural show in the late 1940s.

What happened was that early in the nineteenth century the Wiltshire Horns were deemed to offer considerable scope for the 'improvements' which were then fashionable. The opinion was justified, for the Wiltshire Horns were a scruffy, ungainly lot. Their horns were too big for their heads, and their heads were too big for their lean, scraggy bodies. They had little wool and poor carcases. When the improvers had done with them, they had been improved out of recognition, but with the snag that they were no longer able to exist on the poor pickings available on the high downs! So they retreated from their homeland and were saved from oblivion only by the foresight of certain Midland flock-masters, who established them on lusher and more congenial meadows in Northamptonshire and Buckinghamshire.

In another branch of agriculture, the Guinness Barley Research Station at Warminster, presided over by Mr Tom Davis, carries on the important work of breeding new and better varieties of barley, begun by Dr E. S. Beaven in the 1890s. South Wiltshire was also the scene of much of the pioneering work of Professor Sir R. G. Stapledon, the prophet of lay farming and alternate husbandry, who was the genius behind the ploughing-up campaign before and during the Second World War. He lived for years at Teffont Evias and was associated with Dunns Farms Seeds, of Salisbury. Today Salisbury Plain around Druids Lodge is the scene of other large-scale experiments in cropping by another leading seed firm, Nickersons.

Although it is possible to define a positive *Wessex* character, to try to make general differentiations between *Wiltshire* folk and their neighbours in the other counties that comprised Old Wessex would be to attempt too great a degree of precision. One could speak of the Wessex speech (with its 'v's', 'z's', thick 'dh's' and broad vowels and its Anglo-Saxon verbs), of the Wessex slowness of movement, of the Wessex sense of humour, of Wessex customs; but to say wherein Wiltshire differed from, say, Dorset in these matters would involve going into a great deal of detail.

Certain dialect words, for instance, are used in one county and not in the others. 'Panshard', meaning an unbaptised infant, is a Dorset word, not known in Wiltshire; so is 'rafferty', meaning someone who has spent a term in a mental asylum. Somerset has 'tunigar', meaning a funnel; 'eddish', meaning the aftermath of grass; and 'gladdigloasters', meaning woodlice; none of which I have ever heard in Wiltshire. Some of the more intriguing Wiltshire words (which I have not heard in other counties, though I would hesitate to say they are exclusive to Wiltshire) are:

> to *pussyvanter*, meaning to dither, or waste time;
> to *bivver*, to quiver or tremble;
> to *snark*, to snore;
> *gallybagger*, a scare-crow;
> *bruckle*, brittle (with especial reference to straw);
> *diggles*, an abundance;
> *dumbledore*, a bumble-bee;
> *succour*, shelter, the leeward side;
> *nammit*, a lunch in the fields;
> to *shrip*, to shred or whittle;
> *suent*, soft, even, smooth (a favourite word with A. G. Street!);
> to *lollop*, to lounge;
> to *wim*, to winnow;
> *twoadstabber*, a large pocket-knife;
> *caddlen*, the familiar type of weather which the forecasters term 'unsettled'.

When, just before the First World War, a group of farmers from north Wiltshire took farms in and near the south Wiltshire village where my family lived, the local people noticed certain differences in their speech. Notably, the newcomers used 'Us' instead of 'We', and 'Her' instead of 'She'.

'Us must git on an' empt thik waggon avore the rain comes.'

'Her didn't take nar mossel of notice of we.'

This is typical Devonshire usage, and it is difficult now to determine whether it was ever widespread in north Wilts.

Aubrey thought he could detect definite differences between the inhabitant of the two divisions of Wiltshire, and one would not think from the character he gives his fellow-countrymen, that he himself was born in the north of the county. He writes:

'In Indigenae, or Aborigines, speake drawling; they are phlematique, skins pale and livid, slow and dull, heavy of spirit; hereabout is but little tillage or hard labour, they only milk the cowes and make cheese; they feed chiefly on milke meates, which cooles their braines too much, and hurts their inventions. These circumstances make them melancholy, contemplative and malicious; by consequence whereof come more law suites out of North Wilts, at least double to the Southern parts. And by the same reason they are generally more apt to be fanatiques; their persons are generally plump and feggy; gallipot eies, and some black; but they are generally handsome enough. It is a woodsere country, abounding much with sowre and austere plants, as sorrel, etc., which makes their humoures sowre, and fixes their spirits. In Malmesbury Hundred, etc (ye wett clayy parts) there have ever been reputed witches.

'On the downes, the south part, where 'tis all upon tillage, and where the shepherds labour hard, their flesh is hard, their bodies strong; being weary after hard labour, they have not leisure to read and contemplate of religion, but goe to bed to their rest, to rise betime the next morning to their labour.'

One gathers that Aubrey, writing soon after the Restoration, had had a bellyful of Puritanism, which was strong in the north-west. My own experience of farming in more leisurely days than the present would not have led me to claim that downland shepherds worked harder than vale dairymen; rather the reverse.

Nowadays, of course, cosmopolis has triumphed. What happened at Swindon when the railways came and brought in workers from Wales, the Midlands and other distant parts, has now spread to the entire county. During the past thirty years the invasion has penetrated even the remotest villages, which tend more and more to become residential, or even suburban. To take an example with which I am fairly familiar, a village which before the war had about sixty houses has lost twenty-four of them (many of them pleasant old cottages demolished by red tape) but has gained nearly a hundred more. Of the sixty families which were reckoned as 'natives' in the 1920s and 1930s, only fourteen remain. Such a wholesale mingling of populations obliterates the minor differences that once distinguished the inhabitants of our various counties, districts and even parishes. It is difficult to realise that it was only one hundred and fifty years ago William Cobbett met a married woman of about thirty, living near the village of Tangley (which is a mile or two over the border, in north Hampshire), who had never been more than two-and-a-half miles from the place where she was born.

Yet the tradition of being Wiltshire folk is still treasured by those who belong to the county by birth or by adoption. They still take a proprietary interest in the sarsens of Stonehenge and the daffodils of Stourhead, in the Saxon church of Bradford-on-Avon and the latest exploits of Swindon Town Football Club. They are still proud to be Moonrakers.

The tale of the Wiltshire Moonrakers is one of a group of stories relating to the village of Bishop's Cannings, near Devizes. In several earlier chapters we have referred to rivalry and feuds between neighbouring villages. For reasons unknown, Bishop's Cannings seems to have aroused more antagonism than most, but rivalry of a gentler type, finding an outlet in the ridicule of tall stories. The type of humour that they illustrate is typical in its appeal to at least the older generations of Wiltshire people. Here are a few of them.

A carter from Bishop's Cannings heard when visiting Devizes market that there was to be an eclipse of the moon that night. So in the evening he turned up in the market place with his family, all arriving to see the eclipse. He also brought a rick ladder to set up against the waggon, so that they could climb on it and get a better view.

A new band was once formed at Bishop's Cannings. Someone remembered that the village had had a band once before, so a search was made for any old instruments that had survived. Several, including the big drum, were found in the church vestry, which prompted the decision to use the vestry for band practice. In due course, the band felt sufficiently expert to parade around the village on the occasion of the summer fête. The bandsmen assembled at the vestry and then found, to their consternation, that the doorway had been rebuilt since the time of the previous band and was now too narrow to allow the drum to pass. So the band marched around the village, while the drummer sat, beating the time, in the vestry.

A dog ran into a garden at Bishop's Cannings and bit the handle of a wheelbarrow. Whereupon the gardener sawed off the handle, for fear he should catch rabies.

A Bishop's Cannings man who was notorious for his grumbling went to a farm to buy a hundredweight of potatoes. The farmer, knowing his reputation, allowed him to pick them out for himself, so naturally he selected the biggest ones. Next time he saw the farmer he complained,

'They there big taties were holler in the middle. Thee dost owe I some more. They holes don't weigh nothing, sno.'

A Bishop's Cannings man tried to mend a barrel. It is a difficult job, so he got his small son to sit inside and hold the staves while he hammered. When he had finished he was admiring his handiwork when a small voice from inside said,

'Vayther, how be I gwaine to get out?'

And he had to knock out the other end of the barrel to release the boy.

Said another Bishop's Cannings man,

'Thesem yer electricity cuts baint run fair. Missus were just cookin' me tea when the tricity all went off. But whiles we were sittin' there in the dark, the bus went by wi' all his lights on.'

It could be that this plethora of yarns originated in jealousy, for Bishop's Cannings achieved some fame three hundred and fifty years ago. We will allow John Aubrey his say for the last time:

'Mr. Ferraby, the minister of Bishop's Cannings, was an ingenious man, and an excellent musician, and made severall of his parishioners good musicians, both for vocall and instrumentall musick; they sung the Psalms in consort to the organ, which Mr. Ferraby procured to be erected.

'When King James the First was in these parts he lay at Sir Edw. Baynton's at Bromham. Mr. Ferraby then entertained his Majesty at the Bush, in Cotefield, with bucoliques of his own making and composing, of four parts; which were sung by his parishioners, who wore frocks and whippes like carters. Whilst his majesty was thus diverted, the eight bells (of which he was the cause) did ring, and the organ was played on for state; and after this musical entertainment he entertained his Majesty with a foot-ball match of his own parishioners. This parish in those days would have challenged all England for musique, foot-ball and ringing. For this entertainment his Majesty made him one of his chaplains in ordinary.'

A little later Mr Ferraby and his parishioners, this time dressed in 'shepherds' weeds', were entertaining Queen Anne (King James' queen) with a 'pastorall'. 'A copie of his song was printed with a compartment excellently well engraved and designed, with goates, pipes, sheep hooks, cornucopias, etc.'

One can understand than any proper Wiltshire neighbour, on hearing of this lot, would feel the urge to take the Bishop's Cannings parishioners down a peg or two, lest all the glory should go to their heads.

Bishop's Cannings' crowning claim to immortality, however, is in the story of the Moonrakers. Two Bishop's Cannings men were one moonlit night found raking the surface of a local pond with hay rakes. On being challenged they pointed to the reflection of the moon in the pond and said they were trying to retrieve 'thik gurt yaller cheese.'

The men who had challenged them rode away laughing and quickly spread the tale about these 'dunner-haided coons, a-rakin' atter the shadder of the moon.' Verses were made up about it, and the story has circulated merrily ever since. Any Wiltshireman is a Moonraker.

There is a twist to the tale, The challengers were excisemen, searching for smugglers, which is just what the Bishop's Cannings men were. At the bottom of the pond were kegs of brandy, deposited there earlier for safety. The mime of drunken half-wits raking for the reflection of the moon was the best the pair could think of on the spur of the moment, but it worked.

Like good Wiltshiremen in general, they had the last laugh. No doubt when later they told their version they would exclaim, with true Wiltshire modesty,

'Ah, we were too vly var they! There bain't no vlies on we!'

And that sentiment, too, all good Wiltshiremen will echo.

Index

Adam, Robert, 171
Addison, Joseph, 76
Ailesbury, Marquess of, 128, 180, 151, 152
Aldbourne, 10, 147, 148, 150
Alderbury, 19, 20, 60, 61, 122, 132
Aldhelm St, 87, 166, 180, 181
Alfred, King, 21, 22, 23, 44, 92, 93, 130, 132, 172, 185, 186
Alfred's Tower, 92, 93
All Cannings, 10, 133, 134, 135, 190
Allington, 118
Alton, Barnes, 133, 135
Alton Priors, 133, 135
Alvediston, 101, 103, 111
Amesbury, 16, 19, 43, 58, 63, 65, 66, 67, 74, 75, 119
Anglo-Saxon Chronicle, 19, 22, 24, 44, 58, 92, 146
Anne, Princess, 169
Ansty, 109
Antrobus family, 67
Army, The, 27, 28, 31, 32, 76, 80, 85, 95, 96, 116, 117, 119, 193
Arnold, Dr, 88
Arthur, 14, 16, 17, 65, 147, 150
Arundell, Lady Blanche, 27, 98
Arundell family, 98, 99, 100, 101
Ashton Keynes, 157, 161, 195
Astley, Francis, 116
Athelstan, Bishop, 149
Athelstan, King, 23, 165, 166
Atkinson, Prof. R. J. C., 73
Atworth, 179
Aubrey, John, 30, 32, 34, 38, 47, 69, 81, 83, 87, 112, 122, 137, 143, 151, 161, 162, 163, 167, 171, 173, 174, 177, 178, 183, 186, 189, 196, 197, 199, 201
Augustine, St, 158
Avebury, 11, 12, 41, 73, 139, 140, 143, 144, 145
Avon (Bristol), R., 10, 132, 162-191, 192, 196
Avon (Salisbury), R., 19, 38, 39, 40, 44, 46, 47, 58-77, 78, 120, 188
Ayscough, Bishop, 26, 187

Badminton Park, 175
Badon, Mount, 147, 150
Barbury Castle, 146, 154
Barford St Martin, 43, 84, 97, 109
Barnes, William, 105

Barrington, Bishop, 50, 51
Barrows, 11, 68, 69, 139, 144
Baskerville family, 147
Bath, Marquess of, 88, 91
Battlesbury, 13, 87
Baverstock, Squire, 38
Baydon, 150
Beach, Hicks, 76
Beacon Hill, 76, 117
Beaker people, 70, 140
Beavan, Dr E. S., 197
a'Becket, Thomas, 25, 120, 121
Beckford, William, 104
Beckhampton, 140, 144, 147
Bedwyn, Great, 127, 128, 130, 131
Bedwyn, Little, 130
Belgae, 13, 103
Bemerton, 80, 81, 187
Berwick Bassett, 139
Berwick St James, 39, 93
Berwick St John, 40, 106, 110, 111
Biddestone, 178
Bilbury Rings, 84
Bingham, Bishop, 58
Birinus, St, 22
Bishop Cannings, 133, 136, 200, 201, 202
Bishopsdown, 38
Bishopstone (north), 146, 156
Bishopstone (south), 111
Bishopstrow, 86, 87
Biss, River, 182
Black Death, 26
Blackmoor Copse, 193
Blackmore Vale, 40, 105
Blandford, 10
Bodenham, 40
Bohun family, 161, 182
Bolingbroke family, 154
Bonham, Sir Thomas, 82, 83
Borbach family, 125, 154
Borenius, Dr Tancred, 121
Boscombe, 118, 119
Boulter, Thomas, 188, 189
Bourne, River, 19, 37, 40, 59, 115-122
Bowerchalke, 103, 111
Bowles, William, 173

Bowood, 171
Box, 179, 193
Boyton, 85
Braden, Forest of, 25, 158, 169
Bradenstoke, 25, 169
Bradford-on-Avon, 55, 85, 164, 165, 180, 181, 182, 183, 184, 200
Bradley, A. G., 94, 148
Bradley, North, 183, 184
Bratton, 186
Bray, C, H., 119
Bremhill, 173
Brinkworth, 169
Britford, 12, 58, 59, 60
Britons, 12, 14, 16, 58, 59, 116
Britton, John, 163, 173
Brixton Deverill, 88, 92
Broadchalke, 81, 111, 112
Broad Hinton, 139, 146, 147
Broadtown, 169, 170
Brokerswood, 184
Bromham, 189, 190, 201
Bronze Age, 69, 73
Broughton Gifford, 179
Brown, 'Capability', 91, 128, 130, 171, 178
Brown, Eric, 29
Brunel, Isambard Kingdom, 152, 153, 179
Bryant, Sir Arthur, 109
Bulford, 27, 31, 74, 76, 117
Bulkington, 189
Burbage, 115
Burcombe, 109
Bustard, Great, 31, 57, 193, 194

Cade, Jack, 187
Calne, 23, 170, 171, 172, 173, 189
Canute, King, 24, 175
Casterley Camp, 77
Castle Combe, 24, 164, 175, 176, 180
Celts, The, 12, 15, 16
Cennick, John, 173
Cerdic, 14, 16, 58
Chafin, William, 102, 193
Chalfield, Great, 179
Chalk, 9, 10, 11, 15, 28, 32, 34, 37, 40, 41, 42, 43, 150, 192, 195, 196
Chalke Valley, 30, 38, 40, 97-114
Charford, 16, 58
Charles I, 79, 92, 123, 126
Charles II, 27, 63, 92, 109, 110, 123, 143
Charlton (north), 168
Charlton St Peter, 134
Cheese, 9, 10, 15, 28, 162, 163, 172
Cherhill, 135, 170
Cheverell, Great, 188
Chilmark, 40, 49, 85, 110
Chilton Foliat, 150
Chippendale, Thomas, 106
Chippenham, 10, 21, 171-174
Chirton, 133
Chisbury, 128, 130
Chisenbury, 76
Chisledon, 156
Chitterne, 34, 40, 93, 96
Chittoe, 190
Cholderton, 118
Christie-Miller, Mrs, 121
Chute, 127

Chute Forest, 25, 115, 127
Cirencester, 13, 14, 147, 150
Civil War, 27, 98, 138, 157
Clack, 169
Clarendon, 19, 20, 25, 60, 120, 121, 122, 123, 124, 125
Clearbury Camp, 62, 63
Cley Hill, 22, 92
Cloth, 27, 163, 164, 165, 182, 184, 185
Clyffe Pypard, 145, 170
Coate, 156
Cobbett, William, 64, 76, 85, 87, 117, 132, 158, 185, 200
Codford, 84, 85, 86
Cole, River, 157
Coleridge, S. T., 134, 173
Colerne, 178, 179
Collingbourne Ducis, 115, 116, 117, 131
Collingbourne Kingston, 115, 116, 117
Compton Bassett, 170
Compton Chamberlayne, 109
Conholt, 127
Constable, 56
Coombe Bissett, 111, 112
Corsham, 177, 178, 193
Corsley, 88
Cotswolds, 15, 161, 164, 173, 174, 175, 176, 180, 184
Coulston, 187
Crabbe, George, 183
Cranborne Chase, 25, 97-114
Cricklade, 158
Crofton, 131
Crudwell, 161
Cunetio, 13, 14, 147
Cunnington, Mrs. M. E., 13, 68, 77
Cursus, The, 74
Cynegils, King, 22
Cynric, King, 44

Danes, The, 21, 23, 45, 166, 172, 175, 185, 186
Darell, 'Wild', 149, 150
Dauntsey, 170
Dauntsey's School, 188
Davis, Thomas, 33, 38, 95, 163, 196, 197
Davis, Tom, 197
Dean family, 96
Dean Hill, 125
Deanbrook, 40, 125, 192
Defoe, Daniel, 184
Dereham, Elias de, 49
Deverill Valley, 88
Devizes, 10, 24, 25, 27, 31, 45, 63, 95, 96, 131, 139, 180, 182, 183, 186, 188, 189, 190, 191, 200
Dickens, Charles, 60, 178
Dilton, 186
Dinton, 109, 110
Ditchampton, 82
Ditteridge, 179
Domesday Book, 24, 95, 115, 125, 164
Donhead, 43, 106, 109
Downton, 16, 58, 61, 62, 126, 151
Draycot Cerne, 174
Drowners, 38, 39
Druids, 73, 74, 118, 175
Druids Lodge, 197
Dryden, John, 168
Duck, Stephen, 134
Dunstan, St, 23
Durnford, 63, 64

Durrington, 75, 76, 117
Dyrham, 14, 19

Easton Grey, 175
Easton Piers, 173
Eatwell, Henry, 146
Ebbesbourne Wake, 111
Ebble, River, 19, 40, 81, 97-114
'Ecbryghtstone', 22, 92
Edgar, King, 23, 44, 78, 183, 186
Edington, 22, 186, 187
Edith, St, 78
Edmund Ironside, 23, 175
Edmund, St, of Abingdon, 49, 55
Edward III, 55, 60, 121, 164, 186
Edward IV, 56, 184
Edward VI, 26, 49, 115, 129, 138
Egbert, King, 78
Ela, Countess of Salisbury, 176
Elizabeth I, 26, 59, 79, 82, 91, 122, 129
Ellandune, Battle of, 156
Elmer, 166
Ely, Nicholas of, 49
Enford, 76
Erlestoke, 188
Ermine Street, 13, 150, 158
Esturmey family, 128
Etchilhampton, 132
'Ethandune', 22, 186
Ethelfrida, Queen, 66
Ethelred I, 21
Ethelred II, 23
Evelyn, Sir John, 63, 125
Everley, 116, 117
Eyre, Sir Giles, 126

Fairfax, General, 157
Farleigh Abbey, 25
Farleigh, Richard of, 49, 50
Farley, 15, 19, 20, 40, 123, 125, 193
Ferraby, Mr, 201, 202
Ferndirch, 102
Fifield Bavant, 111
Figheldean, 75, 76
Fisherton, 51, 52
Fittleton, 76
FitzGilbert, Baron, 24, 138
Fonthill Bishop, 104
Fonthill Gifford, 104
Ford, 119
Forestry Commission, 130, 195
Fort, Alexander, 123
Fosse Way, 13, 161, 174, 175, 178
Fovant, 19, 43, 79, 109
Fox, Sir Stephen, 27, 123
Frome, 56
Frome, River, 184
Froxfield, 131
Fugglestone, 80
Fyfield, 139, 143

Gainsborough, 60, 171
Garsdon, 168
Gawen family, 103, 111
Gay, John, 67
George II, 102
George III, 81, 128, 187
Gifford family, 85

Gloucester, Earls of, 100
Goddard, Canon, 146
Goddard family, 152, 170
Gomeldon, 119
Gooch, Daniel, 152
Gorges, Sir Thomas, 59, 60, 82
Grafton, 131
Granham Hill, 139
Great Ridge Wood, 97
Grey, Lady Jane, 129, 130
Grimstead, East, 15, 19, 40, 123, 125
Grimstead, West, 19, 40, 122, 125
Grimsdyke, 113
Grobham, Sir Richard, 82
Grovely Wood, 25, 32, 83, 84, 97, 196
Guinness Research Station, 197

Hackpen Hill, 146
Hamptworth, 126
Hanging Langford, 84
Hankerton, 161
Hannington, 157
Hardenhuish, 173
Harewood, 25
Harnham, 43, 51, 56, 81, 100
Harris's of Calne, 171
Hartham Park, 178
Hawkins, Professor G., 12, 67, 69, 70, 144
Hazlitt, 124
Headington, 93
Heath, Maud, 172
Heaven's Gate, 88
Heale House, 63
Heddington, 190
Henry I, 24, 45
Henry II, 25, 66, 121, 176
Henry III, 176
Henry VI, 121, 187
Henry VII, 110, 122, 168, 172, 189
Henry VIII, 26, 66, 128, 129, 130, 165, 168, 174, 177,
    179, 193
Herbert, Lord of Lea, 80, 82
Herbert, George, 80, 81, 187
Herbert, Sir William, 79
Herman, Bishop, 45
Hewitt, Morley, 62
Heytesbury, 85, 86
Highworth, 151, 157
Hilmarton, 173
Hindon, 93, 98, 104, 105
Hippenscombe, 127
Hoare, Henry, 92, 106
Hoare, Sir Richard Colt, 99, 100, 106, 137
Holland, Earls of, 123, 124
Homington, 111
Hooker, Rev R., 118
Horningsham, 91
Hosier, A. J., 131
Hudson, W. H., 62
Huish Hill, 132
Hullavington, 174
Hungerford, 38, 95, 130, 131
Hurdcott, 119
Hyde family, 63, 110

'Icglea', 22
Idmiston, 115, 118
Iford, 184

Ilchester, Earl of, 123
Imber, 31, 34, 40, 93, 95, 96, 187
Ina, King, 44, 116
Inglesham, 157
Inkpen, 14, 128
Ivychurch, 122, 132

James I, 79, 101, 129, 148, 165, 201
James II, 27, 131
Jefferies, Richard, 146, 154, 155, 156
Jocelyn, Bishop, 45
John, King, 46, 106, 176
John of Gaunt, 148
Jones, Inigo, 67, 69, 171
Jones, Prebendary, 181

Keevil, 183, 184, 189
Kellaways Bridge, 172
Ken, Bishop, 91
Kennet, River, 127, 137, 139, 146, 147, 150, 151, 190
Kennet & Avon Canal, 131, 184
Kennett, East, 149
Kennett, West, 139, 140, 144, 145
Kenwalch, King, 61, 180
Kilmington, 40
Kington St Michael, 173, 174
Kington, West, 26, 174
Kingston Deverill, 88, 93
Kiwi, Bulford, 76
Knap Hill, 132
Knoyle, East, 105
Knoyle, West, 105

Lackham, 177
Lacock, 176, 177, 180
Lancaster, Shepherd, 188
Landford, 10, 126
Langley Burrell, 172
Langford, Little, 84
Lansdowne, Marquess of, 170, 171
Larkhill, 27, 31, 76, 117
Latimer, Bishop Hugh, 26, 174
Latton, 157
Laverstock, 120
Lavington, West, 96, 117, 188
Lawes, Henry, 110
Lechlade, 157
Leland, 167, 183
Liddington Camp, 147, 156
Limpley Stoke, 10, 131, 184
Littlecote House, 149, 150
Little Bedwyn, 130
Little Hinton, 156
Littleton Drew, 175
Little Woodbury, 12
Lockeridge, 139
Lodge, Sir Oliver, 64
Longbridge Deverill, 88, 93, 151
Longespee, William, 176
Long family, 179
Longford, 58, 59, 60, 82, 126
Longhorn cattle, 163, 196
Long Knoll, 92
Longleat, 27, 88, 91, 92, 93, 95, 129, 163
Lovell family, 85
Ludgershall, 24, 29, 117, 118
Ludlow, General, 92
Lugbury, 175

Lydiard Park, 154
Lydiard Tregoze, 154
Lyneham, 170

Maddington, 94
Maiden Bradley, 92
Maidulph, St, 166
Malmesbury, 10, 23, 24, 26, 45, 161, 165-168, 169, 170, 174, 175, 199
Manningford Bruce, 133
Manton, 139, 147
Marden, 21
Margadale, Lord, 104
Market Lavington, 135, 183, 188
Marlborough, 24, 27, 38, 43, 63, 69, 70, 74, 76, 115, 116, 128, 137-150, 162, 163, 164
Marples, Morris, 136, 185
Marston, 189
Marston Maisey, 157
Marten, 131
Martin, 62
Martinsell Hill, 132, 135
Mary, Queen, 26, 129, 190
Masters, Caldwell, 157
Matilda, 24, 117, 138, 182
Maundrell, George, 26, 190
Maurice, Prince, 190
Melchet, Forest of, 125
Melksham, 10, 25, 179, 180, 182, 183, 184
Membury Camp, 150
Mendips, 13, 84
Mere, 29, 97, 105, 109
Methuen family, 178, 180
Methuen, Rev. Anthony, 134
Midsummer Tithes, 84
Milford, 40, 55, 120
Milk Hill, 132
Mildenhall, 13, 147
Milston, 76
Milton Lilbourne, 132
Minety, 161, 169
Mompesson family, 85
Monkton Deverill, 88
Monkton Farleigh, 179
Moonrakers, 136, 200, 202
Moore, Thomas, 190
Moravians, 173
More, Hannah, 188
Mozley, Rev. Thomas, 118

Nadder, River, 19, 39, 40, 43, 47, 59, 78, 81, 84, 85, 97-114
Nelson, Admiral, 61
Neolithic, 68, 145
Netheravon, 76
Netherhampton, 81
Nettleton, 175
Netton, 64
Newton Tony, 118
Nomansland, 126
Normanton Down, 68
Normans, 10, 24, 25, 61, 100, 103, 117, 120, 133, 138, 190
Nunton, 111
Nythe, 156

Oaksey, 161
Odstock, 111, 112, 113, 114

Odo, Bishop, 23
Ogbourne, River, 147
Ogbourne, St Andrew, 147
Ogbourne, St George, 147
Oldbury Castle, 170
Old Sarum, 13, 23, 24, 44, 45, 46, 47, 48, 49, 51, 55, 56, 58, 63, 65, 78, 119, 122, 152
Oliver's Camp, 190
Olivier, Miss Edith, 64, 103, 133, 158
Orcheston, 93, 94, 95
Orchids, 196
Osmund, St, 45
Overton, 139, 146
Oxenmere, 135

Padua, John of, 129
Paine, James, 99
Palmerston, Lord, 134
Parr, Catherine, 129
Patney, 133
Pembroke, Earls of, 32, 79, 80, 81, 83, 111
Penn, William, 161, 169
Penruddocke family, 109
Pepperbox Hill, 125
Pewsey, 132, 133, 134, 135, 136
Pewsey Vale, 21, 39, 58, 64, 76, 116, 131, 132, 133, 134, 135, 136, 137, 146, 188, 190
Pewsham, 25
Phillips, Capt. M., 169
Pickwick Manor, 178
Pierce, Ruth, 191
Pile, Robert, 135, 136
Pitt, William, 65, 104
Pitton, 15, 19, 20, 31, 37, 40, 123, 124, 194
Pitt-Rivers, General Augustus, 103, 106
Plaitford, 10
Pleydell-Bouverie, Hon. B., 132
Poore, Bishop, 47, 56
Poore family, 124
Popham, Sir John, 149
Port Way, 13
Portishead, 14, 127
Porton, 31, 119, 124, 193, 195
Potterne, 10, 189, 190, 191
Poulshot, 189
Prescelly Hills, 12, 70
Preshute, 139, 144
Purton, 156

Queensberry family, 67
Quidhampton, 47, 81

Radnor, Earl of, 59, 60, 133
Radstock, 87
Raleigh, Sir Walter, 88
Ramsbury, 10, 23, 45, 148, 149, 151
Rattlebone, John, 175
Reading, 163
Redlynch, 126
Reformation, 50, 66, 85, 118
Rich, Edmund, 49
Richard I, 81, 121
Richard II, 176
Rivers, Lord, 101
Robin Hood's Ball, 75
Rockbourne, 62
Roger, Bishop, 45, 190
Rollestone, 94

Romans, 12, 13, 14, 15, 16, 44, 60, 62, 103, 110, 124, 125, 164, 176, 178, 179
Roman Roads, 13, 14, 16, 19, 40, 42, 58, 84, 119, 122, 124, 127, 147, 150, 158, 174
Roundheads, 98
Roundway Down, 27, 190
Rowde, 190
Royalists, 27, 109, 138, 190
Rushmore, 102

Salisbury, 10, 19, 26, 27, 29, 38, 39, 40, 42, 43, 44-57, 58, 59, 60, 61, 62, 63, 64, 73, 74, 78, 79, 80, 81, 83, 84, 85, 86, 95, 102, 109, 110, 111, 112, 114, 115, 116, 119, 120, 122, 125, 126, 132, 147, 164, 165, 180, 182, 186, 187, 189, 190, 193, 197
Salisbury Plain, 10, 11, 13, 27, 29-43, 55, 57, 61, 65, 67, 68, 80, 85, 86, 93, 97, 105, 109, 115, 116, 117, 124, 125, 132, 164, 182, 185, 188, 194, 197
Sandy Lane, 189
Sarsens, 69, 143, 145, 146, 200
Saunders, David, 188
Savernake Forest, 25, 26, 43, 115, 127, 128, 129, 130, 151, 195
Saxons, 14, 15, 16, 19, 21, 22, 32, 44, 61, 65, 78, 117, 120, 132, 135, 146, 147, 149, 156, 172, 180, 181, 184, 186
Scratchbury, 13, 87
Scrope family, 176
Seend, 185, 189
Selwood, Forest of, 12, 23, 25, 92, 166, 180
Semington Brook, 188
Serrington, 24
Severn, River, 00
Seymour family, 26, 66, 92, 115, 128, 129, 130
Shaftesbury, 43, 97, 98, 101, 106, 109, 168
Shakespeare, 79
Sharington, Sir William, 176, 177
Shears, Lyddie, 124
Sheep, 9, 26, 33, 37, 38, 80, 163, 164, 165, 188, 197
Shefford, 149
Sheldon Manor, 178
Sherborne, 23, 45, 149, 166
Sherrington, 24, 85
Sherston, 24, 174
Shrewton, 39, 75, 93, 94, 95
Sidbury Hill, 116
Sidney, Sir Philip, 79
Silbury Hill, 12, 139, 143, 144
Silchester, 13, 150
Sloperton, 190
Smith family, 135, 188
Smith, Assheton, 116
Smith, Dr John, 118
Smith, Sydney, 76
Snap. 148, 149
Somerford, Great, 169
Somerford, Little, 169
Somerset, Dukes of, 66, 129, 131, 138
Sorbiodunum, 13, 19, 44, 84
South Marston, 155
South Newton, 82, 112
Southwick, 184
Spratt, Jack, 133, 134
Stanton Fitzwarren, 157
Stanton St. Quinton, 174
Stapleford, 39, 93
Steeple Ashton, 164, 183, 188
Steeple Langford, 85, 195

Stephen, King, 24, 25, 45, 117, 138, 182
Stockton, 38, 84, 86
Stockton Earthwork, 84
Stoford, 82
Stone Curlew, 28, 31, 193
Stonehenge, 11, 12, 29, 41, 43, 63, 65, 67-75, 99, 100, 119, 137, 140, 143, 192, 200
Stour, River, 40, 105, 184
Stourhead, 92, 105, 106, 200
Stourton, 40, 105
Stratford-sub-Castle, 58, 59, 63, 65
Stratford Tony, 111
Stratton St. Margaret, 154
Street, A. G., 82
Stuart, Lady Arabella, 129
Stukeley, William, 139, 144
Stumpe, William, 167, 168, 174
Sutton Benger, 174
Sutton Mandeville, 109
Swallowcliffe, 109
Sweyn, King, 44
Swindon, 10, 27, 132, 139, 146, 147, 151-161, 169, 182, 183, 186, 199, 200

Talbot family, 176, 177
Taliesin, 62
Tan Hill, 132, 135
Teffont Evias, 110, 197
Teffont Magna, 19, 93, 110
Test, River, 40, 125
Thames, River, 14, 15, 16, 137, 151-161, 196
Thynne, Sir J., 88, 91, 129
Tidcombe, 127
Tidworth, 31, 76, 116, 117, 118
Till, River, 19, 39, 93
Tilshead, 34, 39, 40, 68, 93, 94, 95, 164
Tisbury, 97-98, 99, 100, 103, 104, 151
Tockenham, 170
Tollard Royal, 10, 40, 106
Tottenham House, 128, 129, 130
Trafalgar House, 61
Tropenell Cartulary, 179
Trowbridge, 10, 24, 165, 180, 182, 183, 184, 189
Tryon family, 64
Tudor period, 25, 26, 138, 150, 165
Tytherton, East, 173

Uffcot, 139
Upavon, 39, 58, 76, 77
Upham, Upper, 148
Upton Lovell, 85
Upton Scudamore, 83, 88
Urchfont, 188

Vespasian's Camp, 75

Waleran, 85, 125
Waller, 190
Wanborough, 13, 156
Wanda, William de, 49
Wansdyke, 14, 15, 16, 127
Wardour, 24, 27, 98-100, 103, 109
Warminster, 13, 27, 31, 39, 82, 85-88, 184
Washington family, 168
Water-meadows, 37, 38, 39
Webb, John, 79
Wedmore, 22
Wells family, 148

Wesley, John, 173, 181
Wessex, 21, 22, 23, 45, 78, 156, 197, 198
Westbury, 31, 184, 185, 186, 193
Westbury Leigh, 22, 186
Westbury White Horse, 22, 185, 186
West Dean, 16, 24, 40, 125, 154
West Kennett Long Barrow, 144, 145
Westport, 168
Westwood, 184
Wexcombe, 131
Weymouth, Viscount, 91
Whaddon, 19, 60, 122
White Horse Vale, 185
Whiteparish, 125, 126
Whitesheet Hill, 81, 110
Whitsbury, 42, 62
William I, 24, 45, 85, 111, 120, 128, 130, 138
William of Edington, 186, 187
William of Malmesbury, 166, 167
Williams, Alfred, 146, 147, 154, 155
Wilsford, 63, 64
Wilton, 21, 24, 25, 26, 30, 39, 47, 49, 51, 52, 58, 78-81, 82, 84, 168
Wilton (near Bedwyn), 131
Wilton, Abbess of, 47, 78, 79, 111
Wiltshire & Berkshire Canal, 152, 156
Wiltshire Horn Sheep, 197
Wincombe Park, 109
Windmill Hill, 145
Wingreen, 106
Winklebury Hill, 106
Winterbourne Bassett, 139, 145, 147
Winterbourne Cherborough, 37, 119
Winterbourne Dauntsey, 37, 119
Winterbourne Earls, 19, 119, 120, 121
Winterbourne Gunner, 37, 119
Winterbourne Monachorum, 37, 119
Winterbourne Monkton, 139
Winterbourne Stoke, 39, 68, 84, 93
Winterslow, 19, 20, 40, 123, 124, 125, 140, 193, 195
Wishford, 82, 83, 84
Woodford, 63, 64
Woodhenge, 74, 75
Woodborough, 132
Woodbury, Little, 12
Wool Trade, 55, 56, 57, 80, 138, 163, 164, 165, 172, 180, 182
Wootton Bassett, 169
Wootton Rivers, 133, 135
Worton, 189
Wraxhall, South, 179
Wren, Sir Christopher, 27, 105, 123
Wroughton, 146, 156
Wulfhall, 26, 128, 130
Wulfhere, 86
Wyatt, James, 50, 51, 79
Wylye, River, 19, 24, 39, 40, 43, 47, 59, 78-96, 184, 195
Wylye, 38, 84
Wyvil, Bishop, 49

Yarnbury Castle, 84, 85
Yatesbury, 147
Yatton Keynell, 162, 167, 174
Yeatman-Biggs, 86

Zeals, 105, 106